IMAGES
of America

Miller Beach

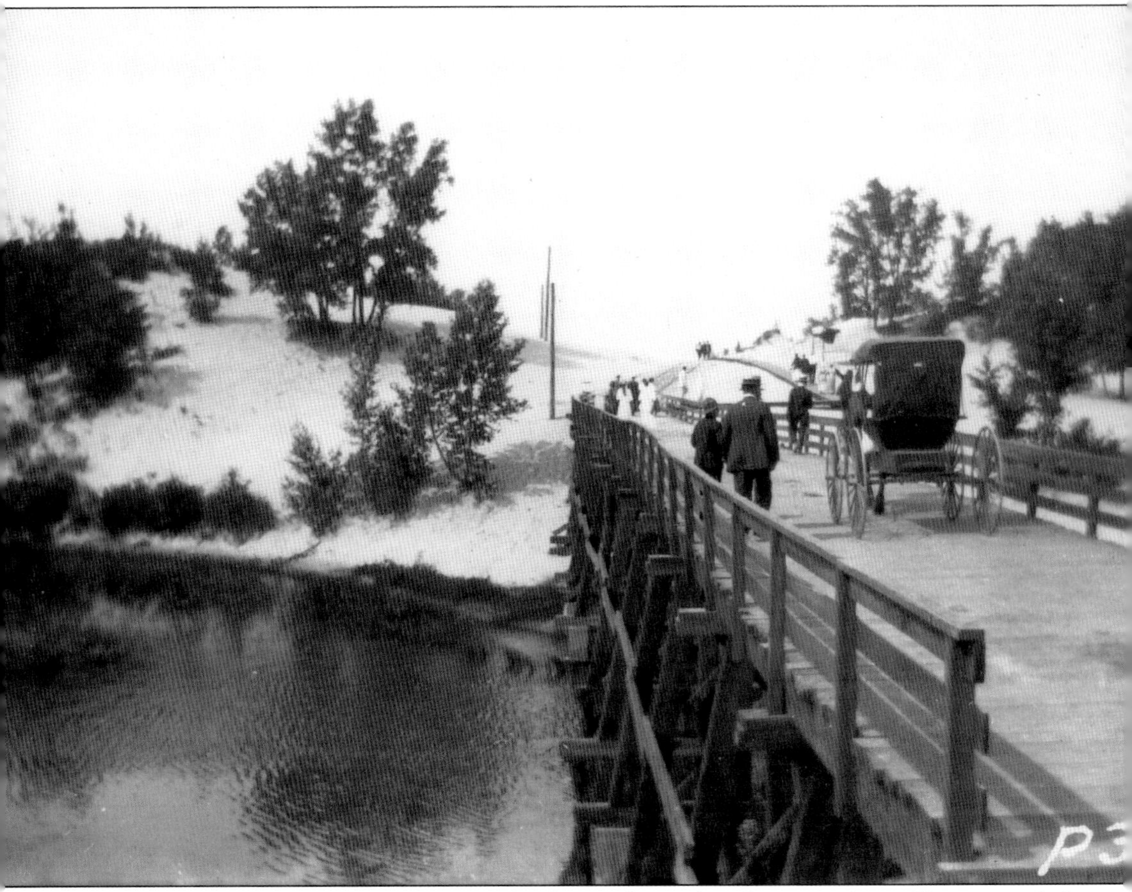

The magic of the dunes and waters of Lake Michigan lured visitors from Chicago and the surrounding areas starting in the late 1800s. At one time, getting to the beach meant crossing the wooden bridge that crossed the Grand Calumet River. (Courtesy of the Calumet Regional Archives, IU Northwest.)

On the Cover: Originally the long stretch of sand and water now known as Miller Beach was for squatters, people who settled here and built unheated shacks often without even a floor and definitely not indoor plumbing. Robert and Drusilla Carr were one such couple, marrying in 1874 and building a two room cabin in the isolated dunes where Robert made his living fishing. Robert died in 1903 and thereafter Drusilla helped develop the lakefront, as mill workers and visitors from Chicago discovered the beach as a place not to work but to have fun. The Carr family eventually had as many as 100 lakefront cabins for rent, but their ownership was threatened, first by rival claimants and then by the steel mill. While Drusilla fought to establish her rights to her family's lakefront parcel in court, her son Fred helped manage the family's large amusement business, which included a dance hall, bathhouse, miniature railroad, lakefront cabins, shooting gallery, and roller rink on what was known as Carr's Beach. A series of storms in the 1920s destroyed the Carr homestead and dance hall but Drusilla continued to fight for her land. When she died in 1930, her family took over the battle. Although they prevailed in court, they lost the land under burden of back taxes and legal bills. By that time, however, the mill no longer wanted the property for expansion and it eventually became Marquette Park. Drusilla's efforts succeeded in preserving the beachfront after all. This photograph was taken July 4, 1917. (Courtesy of the Calumet Regional Archives, IU Northwest.)

IMAGES
of America

MILLER BEACH

Linda Simon and Jane Ammeson

ARCADIA
PUBLISHING

ISBN 978-0-7385-9364-7

Published by Arcadia Publishing
Charleston, South Carolina

Printed in the United States of America

Library of Congress Control Number: 2012937411

For all general information, please contact Arcadia Publishing:
Telephone 843-853-2070
Fax 843-853-0044
E-mail sales@arcadiapublishing.com
For customer service and orders:
Toll-Free 1-888-313-2665

Visit us on the Internet at www.arcadiapublishing.com

*Dedicated to our children, Benjamin, Daniel,
and Nicholas; and Evan and Nia*

Contents

ACKNOWLEDGMENTS

One of the wonderful things about writing a book like this is getting to meet people who also treasure their town and work hard to preserve its history. This seems particularly true in Miller, where we met so many people who shared their photographs, their memories, and their time. We would like to thank these wonderful past and present Miller residents: Gene and Judy Ayers, Holly Breese, Sylvia Collins, Betty Davin, Jim Doyne, Clara Harmening (a descendant of Drusilla and Robert Carr), the Jancarich family, Laura Valentine Jones, Marilyn Leech, Carol McQueary at Bethel Lutheran Church, Dody Nabhan, John and Peggy Newton, Alice Pickford, Len Pryweller, Eric Reaves, Greg Reising, Chris Papineau Rogers, and Donna Simon, who shared memories and photographs with us.

The authors would like to thank Steve McShane at the Calumet Regional Archives, Indiana University Northwest for friendly help on many occasions; James Lane, PhD, author of *Gary's First Hundred Years*, for generously giving us a copy of his book *City of the Century: A History of Gary, Indiana*; and Ron Cohen, PhD, one of the founders of the archives, without whom so much of the region's rich history would have disappeared. Cohen and Lane also coauthored *Gary: A Pictorial History*, and Cohen and McShane edited *Moonlight in Duneland*, which has wonderful posters of the dunes, the South Shore Line, and Miller Beach.

The Calumet Regional Archives are an amazing place for anyone exploring local history, and *Steel Shavings*, edited by James Lane, is a great source for the cultural and social history of our area.

Other great sources of photographs and information were Verlaine Wright, who writes the *Epitaph*, the newsletter of Bethel Lutheran Cemetery, and wrote *Sand in My Shoes*, a book preserving the memories and writings of her grandmother Ruth Lindstrom; Steve Spicer, with his invaluable Chanute Pages that describe Octave Chanute's experiments along the south end of Lake Michigan, his online Miller history site, and his knowledge and insight; Joyce Davis, who has maintained and collected pictures and stories of old Miller at her Lake Street Gallery for almost 20 years; and Simine Short, author of *From Locomotive to Aeromotive: Octave Chanute and the Transportation Revolution*, for tirelessly answering our questions about Chanute and his time in Miller. Also, the Westchester Township History Museum in Chesterton allowed us access to their photographs and museum curator Serena Sutliff was very helpful in answering questions. The Miller memory books prepared by Don O. Carlson and Wally McCormack were also helpful.

Finally, a word of deep appreciation goes to our families for their patience and understanding while we worked to put this book together. Thank you, Greg, Benjamin, Daniel, Nicholas, Evan, and Nia. We could not have done this without you.

Introduction

This is the story, in vintage photographs, of some of the early immigrants, beach settlers, visitors, industries, and places that helped shape Miller. By necessity, it is only a snapshot. Some images have been lost to time, memories are imperfect, and we have only included photographs through the 1930s. The story of the dune area we call Miller starts with the first people who were here, the Illinois, the Miami, and later the Potawatomie Indians. We glimpse the paths of these earliest people in roads we still travel and names we still hear, but their history is lost to a photographic book. And, of course, the history of Miller is now a part of the history of Gary, the city of which it is a part.

Miller owes its development to the resources of Lake Michigan and the fact that east-west travelers were forced to pass through at its southern end. A few early developers thought the lakefront would be a source of rapid development. Fur-trader Joseph Bailly purchased 2,000 acres of land from the government in the 1820s, including a large tract on the Grand Calumet River in what is now Miller. Bailly envisioned a village on the site, which he named Bailly's Harbor, but it did not materialize. In 1837, Indiana City was planned at the old eastern mouth of the Grand Calumet. Plans for a subdivision of 25 blocks between the lake and Old Indian Boundary Line were drawn up, but Indiana City never developed beyond that.

Many sources also show that Miller was the site of the first family dwelling in Lake County. It was a stage house built by a man named Bennett and his family in 1833. It served as a stopping place for travelers on the stagecoach path between Detroit and Chicago, a portion of which ran along the beach.

The modern settlement of Miller started shortly before the arrival of the Michigan Southern & Northern Indiana Railroad (later the Lake Shore & Michigan Southern Railroad) in 1851. Miller's name can be traced to Samuel and Susan Miller and their family, who lived for a short time in Miller before moving to Illinois, and later California after the death of their young son, John, who is buried in what became the Miller Cemetery. The 1850 census for North Township lists Samuel Miller as an innkeeper. The family left milk for pickup near the railroad. The railroaders called it Miller's Milk Station and shortened the name to Miller's Station after the Baltimore & Ohio Railroad established a stop here in 1874. Over time it became Millers, or Miller.

Settlement began around 1840, and early names, which represented many nationalities, included Ansbro, Carr, O'Connor, Zelibor, Sabinske, Johnson, and MacIntosh. An 1882 history of Lake and Porter Counties shows Magnus and Anna Anderson of Sweden arriving in Miller's Station in 1864, purchasing 80 acres and making their living by farming and gathering moss. James Ansbro of Ireland and his wife, Catherine, moved from Porter County to Miller's Station in 1863. As there was no Catholic church in Miller at the time, the Ansbro family attended St. Patrick's in Chesterton. William Cook came to Indiana with his parents in 1848. Around 1869, he was appointed agent for the Lake Shore & Michigan Southern and Baltimore & Ohio railroads, at Miller Station, and then postmaster in 1871. In 1872, he married Christina Nelson of Miller's

Station. Nils and Anna Blank arrived with their family from Lake Station in the early 1870s. Their son started the first general store in Miller.

In 1850, the census listed 97 inhabitants of North Township, and 10 in the area that is now Miller. In 1870, Miller still only contained about 12 families. Immigration grew after the Great Chicago Fire in 1871, when many Swedes moved to Miller from Chicago. The town of Miller was incorporated in 1907 in an effort to maintain independence after the founding of Gary in 1906. Independence did not last long, however, as Miller was annexed by Gary in 1918.

Early Miller residents were connected to neighboring areas. Charles Blank, in his diary from the early 1900s, recounts a trip to a Chellberg wedding in Porter County and frequent visits to Chicago on the train, for both work and fun. The Miller School was part of Hobart Township Public Schools for a time. Many Miller residents worked at Aetna Powder Works. After the steel industry was established in Gary in 1906, Miller's population grew more rapidly. Many of these new citizens worked at the mill.

Drusilla Benn moved to Miller in the 1870s to work as a housekeeper for her brother, a fisherman. A short time later, she married Robert Carr, who had come to Miller in the 1860s. Carr was a fisherman and Drusilla helped him with his trade while raising their four children. She also harvested cranberries to sell in downtown Miller. Robert died in 1903. In 1907, only seven cottages existed on the Miller lakeshore, but by 1911, when Drusilla Carr opened a bathhouse, beach visitors began to come in larger numbers. Carr's Beach eventually included a boardwalk, a dance hall, and 100 cottages for rent. The Carr family lost the property under the burden of legal fees and back taxes, even after winning their legal battles, and the land eventually became Marquette Park.

Many natural features of Miller have changed. The Grand Calumet no longer flows into Lake Michigan at Miller. In addition, a drainage ditch built in 1910 by resident Gus Strom eliminated wetlands that had fed Long Lake, reducing the lake's footprint substantially. The blueberries, cranberries, and sand cherries that once provided food and a livelihood to settlers are mostly a memory. The loss of the cranberries can be attributed to Magnus Anderson, who moved to Miller's Station in 1864 to "take up the timber for the Lake Shore railroad." After Anderson noticed the long white moss growing on the marsh near the railroad, he decided to stay. For the next 14 years, Magnus raked up the moss with potato hooks and shipped it to Ohio, Illinois, and Florida for use in wrapping trees for shipping. The moss was loaded into 175-pound crates, for which he was paid $3 each. Without the protection of the moss, the cranberries did not survive.

The Prairie Club was established by Henry Chandler Cowles, who did ecology research in the Miller woods, along with Jens Jensen and others in 1908. It was the first group to propose protection of the Indiana dunes. The Prairie Club held a town hall meeting at the Art Institute of Chicago in support of the creation of a national park along Lake Michigan in 1917. One speaker at the event was Alice Gray, "Diana of the Dunes," who referred to the Indiana dunes as a gift that the wind has given from the lake: "As a dower for her sons and her daughters; The heedless young city shall take; This gift of the wind and the waters; From her mother, her lake." (From *Diana of the Dunes: The True Story of Alice Gray*, by Janet Zenke Edwards.)

Much of Miller's early character remains, and its most important feature, the Lake Michigan shore, is still a gift to its citizens and to the broader community.

One

Early Settlers
Carr Family and Downtown Swedes

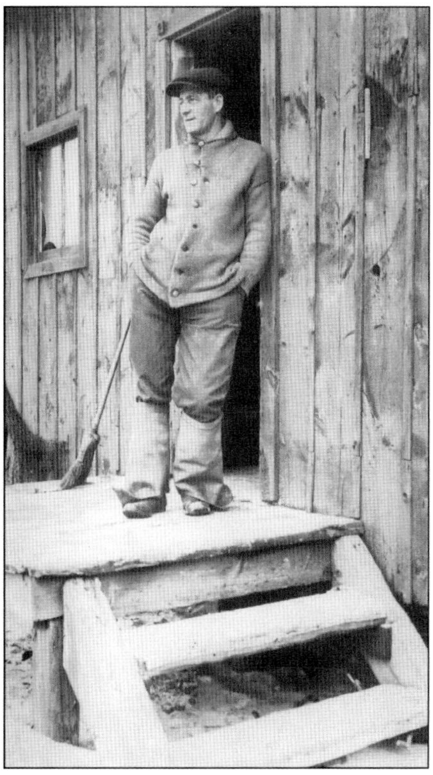

By most accounts, Miller is named for Samuel W. Miller, an innkeeper who likely lived along one of the stagecoach routes that passed through the area. Miller's three-year-old son John was the first to be buried in the old Miller Cemetery. Other early settlers included the Carr family, who were ultimately responsible for the development of Miller as a vacation destination in the early 1910s. Drusilla Benn came to Miller in March 1872 to keep house for her brother, who worked at a fish house owned by John and Hank Granger. Drusilla cooked for them until she married Robert Carr and began working for his mother, Carolina Carr, who had settled in Miller in 1862. Robert Carr and his sons made their living fishing. Robert and Drusilla's son, Fred, is seen here in the 1910s. (Courtesy of the Calumet Regional Archives, IU Northwest.)

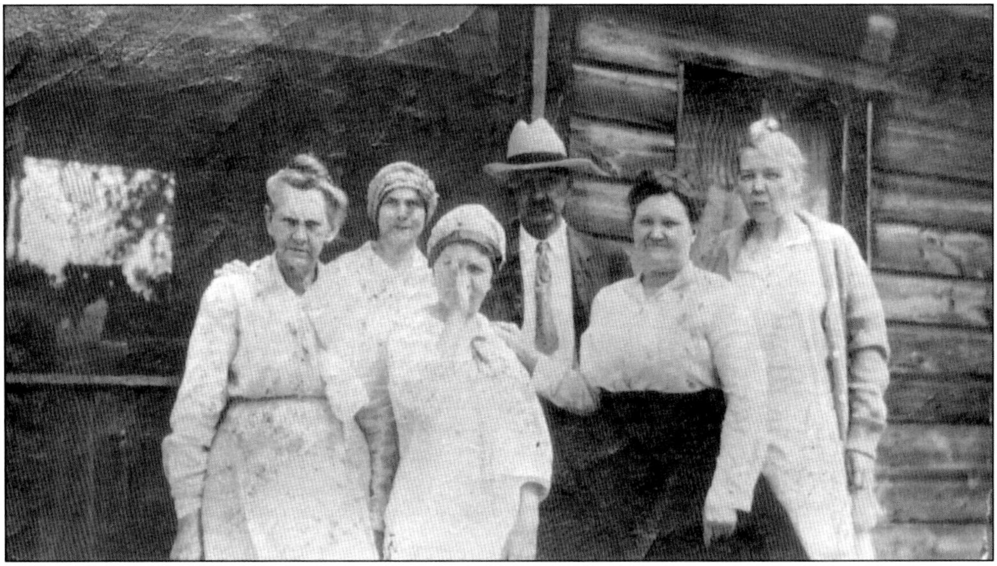

Drusilla Carr, who is better known than her husband because of her lifelong fight to retain her family's rights to their lakefront property, helped her husband with the fishing business and also picked cranberries to sell in town. Until some of the Swedish settlers started moving to the area, she was the only woman on the lakefront during those early years. She is shown here on the far left with other early members of the Carr family. (Courtesy of Joyce Davis, Lake Street Gallery.)

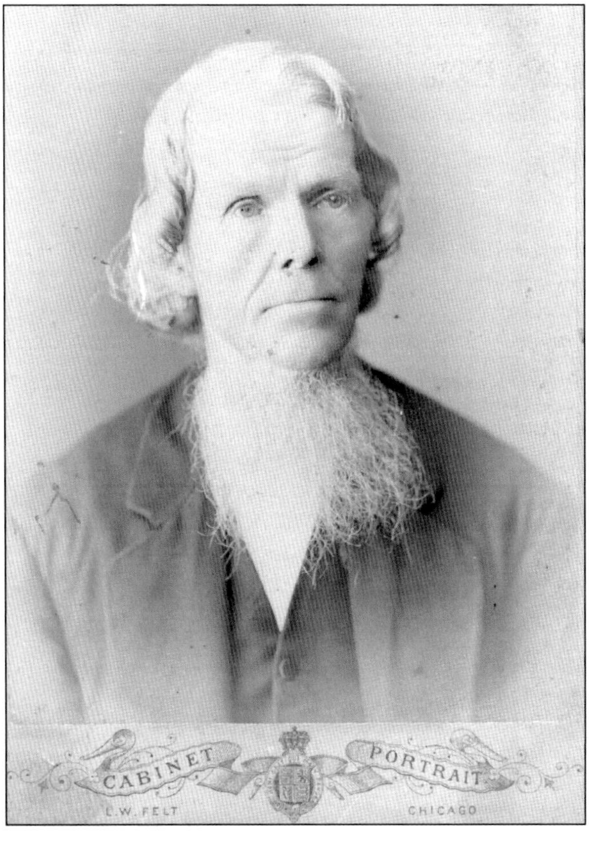

Svanti Nordstrom was born in Sweden and moved to Miller after hearing of the area from friends in La Porte and Baillytown. He was a preacher and was instrumental in the founding of the Swedish Evangelical Lutheran Church of Miller (now Bethel Lutheran Church). Nordstrom was known by children in the congregation for composing verses for them on their birthdays. (Courtesy of Verlaine Wright.)

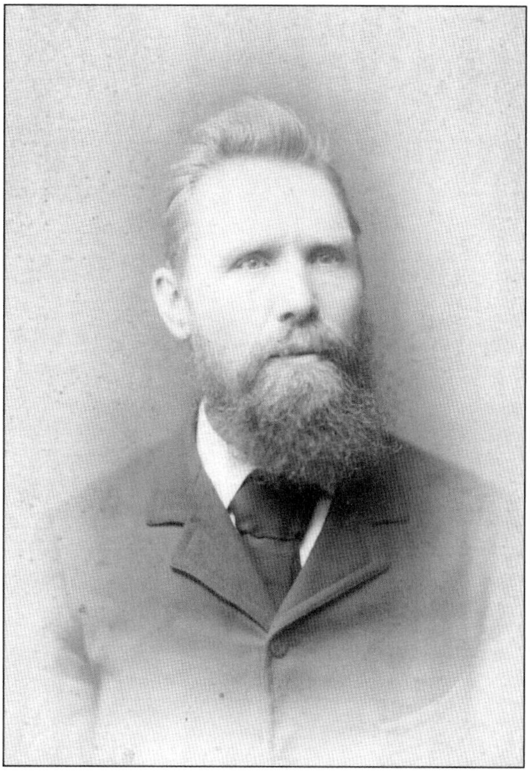

Hokan Hasselgren (right) was born in Sweden in 1846 in a town on the Baltic Sea. He was a member of the Swedish Navy. In 1869, he married Caroline, who was born in Ronneby, Sweden, in 1844. They came to Miller with their daughter, Hannah, in 1880, after hearing from friend and Miller pioneer Svanti Nordstrom about the opportunities available in America. The Hasselgrens both worked at the Aetna Powder Company packing dynamite. Caroline (seated below, with Hannah) was also a midwife in Miller. (Courtesy of Verlaine Wright.)

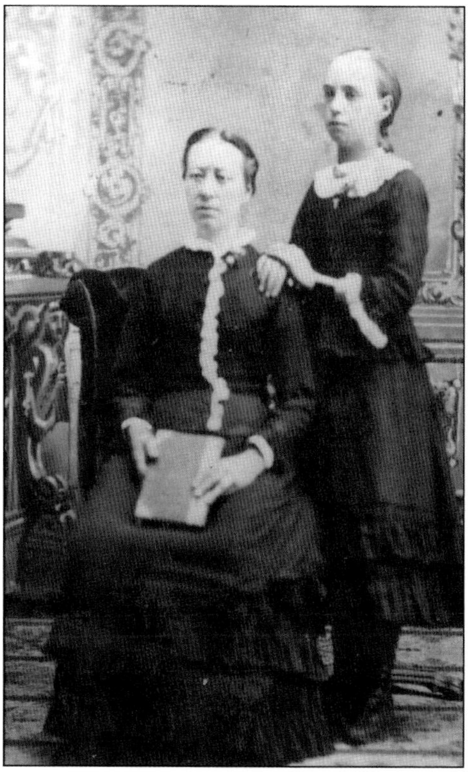

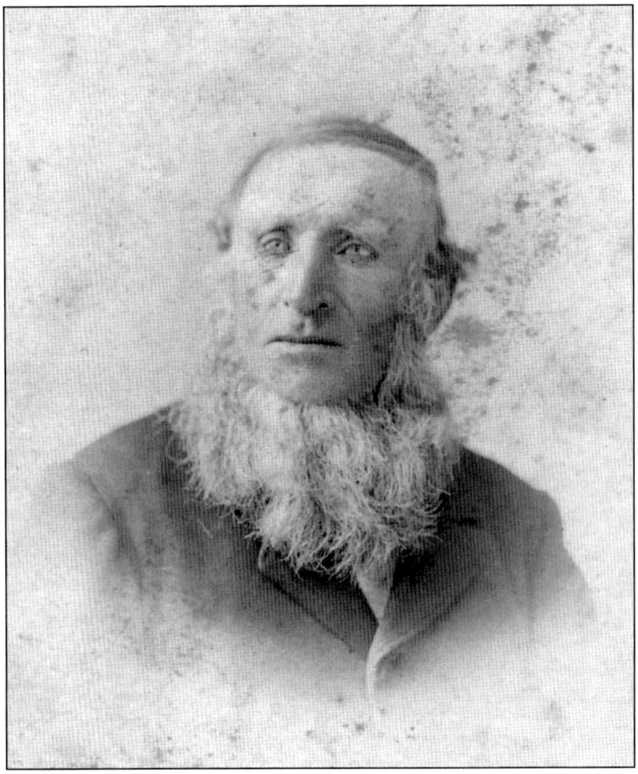

Nicklas (left) and Anna (below) Christiansdotter Nicklasson immigrated to America with their children in 1868 and settled in Chicago. Their home was destroyed in 1871 during the Great Chicago Fire. When the Red Cross supplied them with lumber to rebuild, they asked an uncle who lived in Miller to haul it there instead, where they built a house and raised cattle. Nicklasson worked on the railroad, working 10 to 12 hour days for $1–$1.25 a day. Nicklasson (later Americanized to Nicholson) descendant Verlaine Wright recounts a family story wherein Nicklas once strapped a 200-pound barrel of salt onto his back and carried it home from the train station. (Courtesy of Verlaine Wright.)

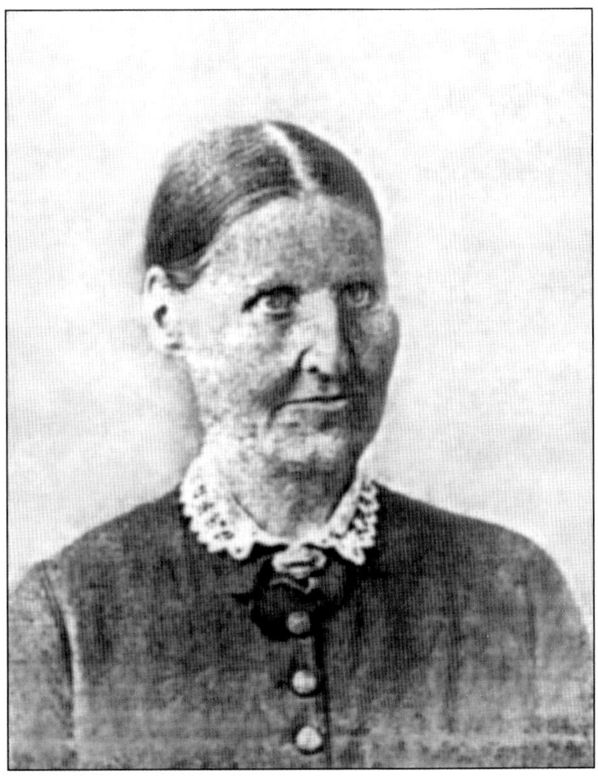

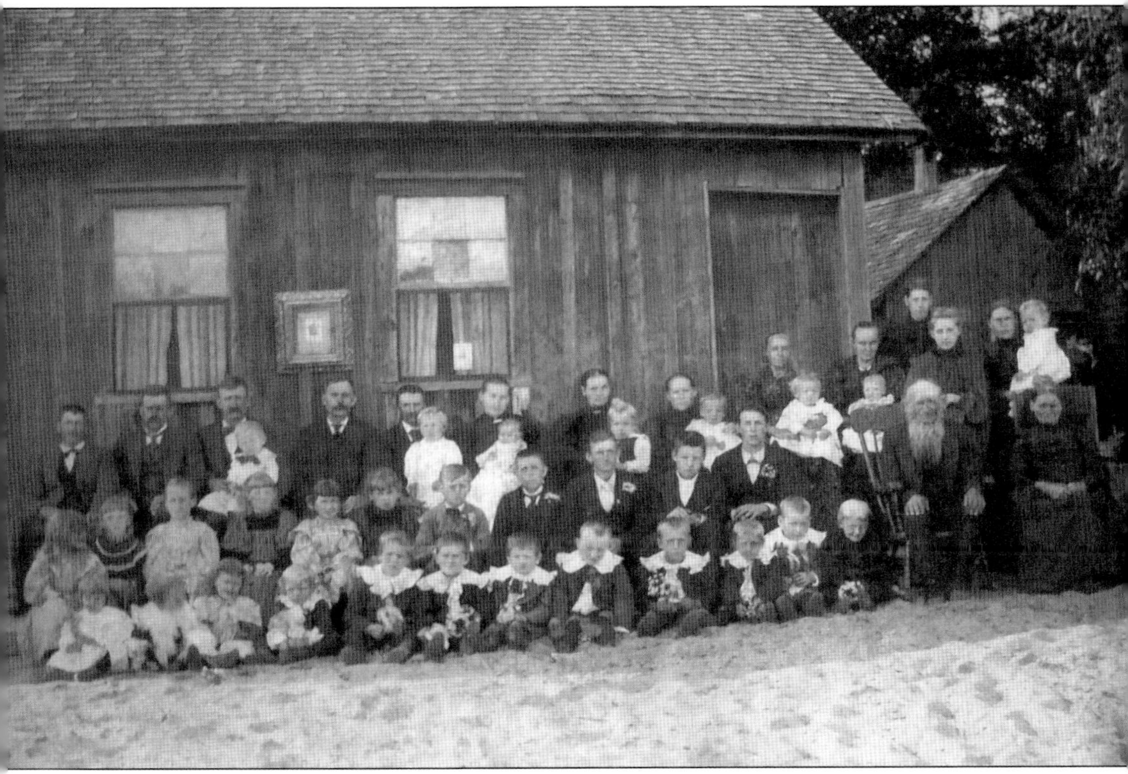

Nicklas and Anna Nicklasson (both seated, far right) posed with their extended family in front of their house in 1895. They had a busy homestead, raising cattle and chickens, growing food and making homemade wine, with Nicklas also working on the railroad and Anna weaving carpets for her and her children's homes. Anna had a fenced-in garden full of vegetables and lovely, fragrant flowers, including petunias and sweet william. The house had a barn, a fruit and wine cellar, and a summer kitchen. Anna made wine out of her own grapes, wild grapes, and sometimes from the plentiful sand cherries that grew along the beach. According to her granddaughter Ruth, Anna Nicklasson gave each firstborn grandchild a cow and a quilt. (Courtesy of Verlaine Wright.)

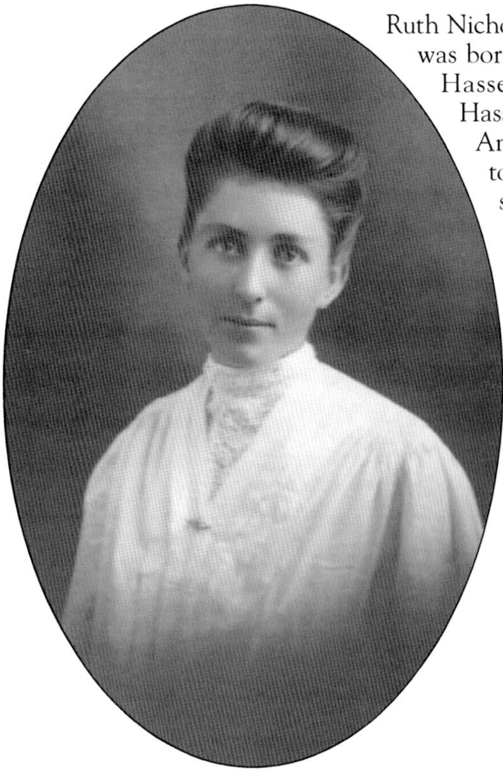

Ruth Nicholson Lindstrom, pictured on her wedding day, was born to Peter Nicklasson and his wife, Hannah Hasselgren—daughter of Hokan and Caroline Hasselgren—in 1888 in Miller. She later married Andrew Lindstrom of Sweden, who had immigrated to America in 1902. After the death of their first son, the two moved to a Minnesota farm for 12 years. They later moved back to Miller, where they raised their eight remaining children in a two-story Sears craftsman-style home on Old Hobart Road. Ruth Lindstrom was an active member of the Bethel Lutheran Church, as well as an amateur historian and writer. In her writings, Ruth reflects on a Miller filled with natural bounty, blueberries, blackberries, cranberries, wild strawberries, raspberries, and grapes, as well as hunting geese and ducks and plentiful fishing on Long Lake. (Courtesy of Verlaine Wright.)

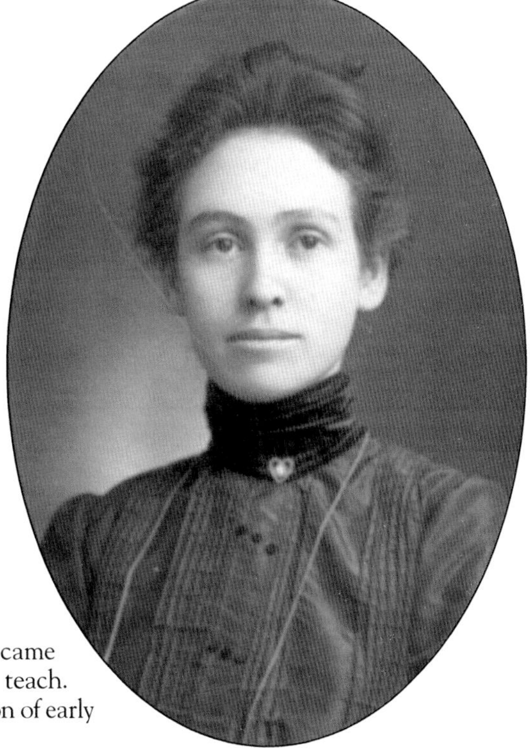

Lena Triebess, shown here in the early 1900s, came to Miller from Hobart as a young woman to teach. She later married George Frederic Peterson, son of early Miller settlers. (Courtesy of Donna Simon.)

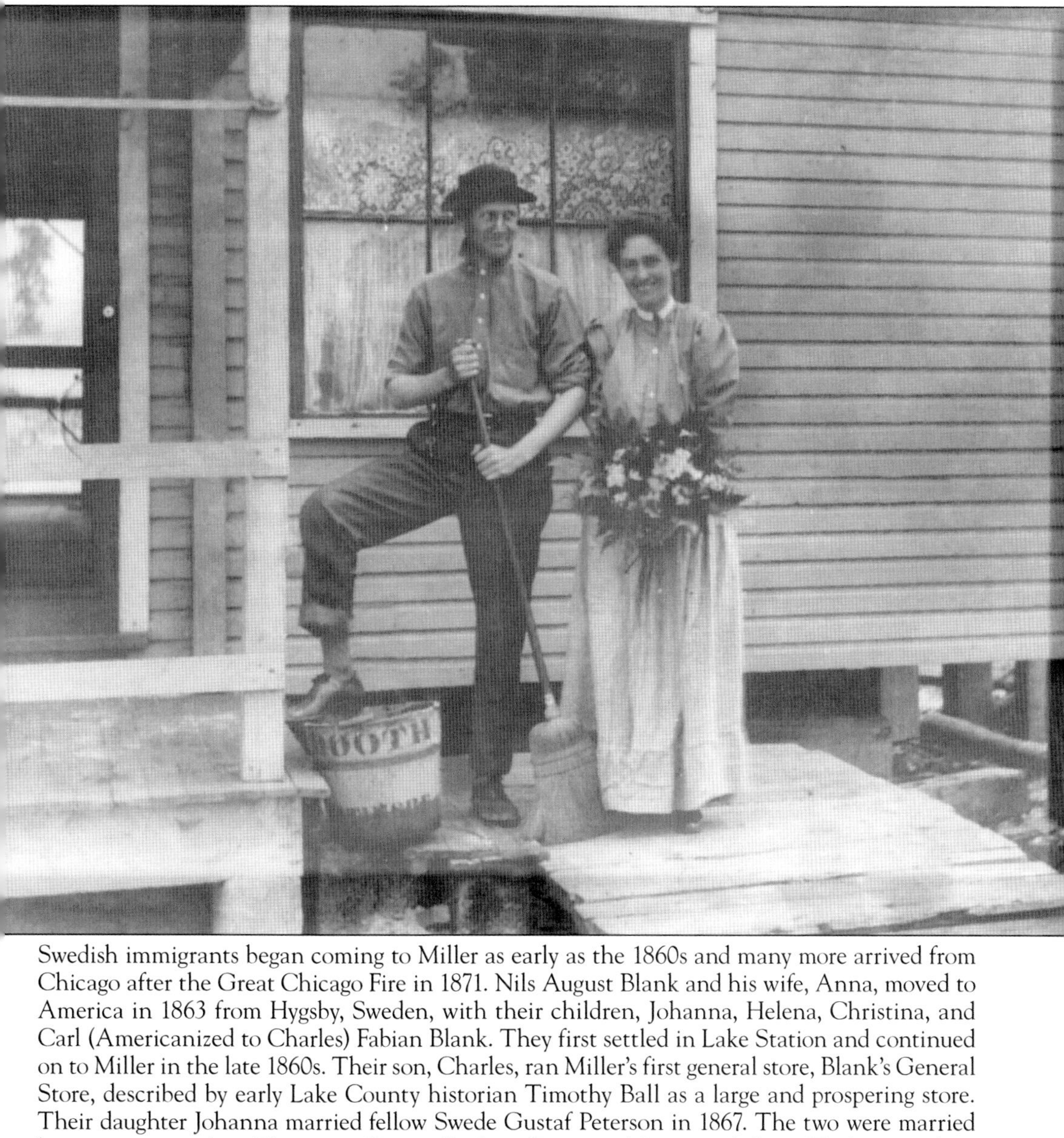

Swedish immigrants began coming to Miller as early as the 1860s and many more arrived from Chicago after the Great Chicago Fire in 1871. Nils August Blank and his wife, Anna, moved to America in 1863 from Hygsby, Sweden, with their children, Johanna, Helena, Christina, and Carl (Americanized to Charles) Fabian Blank. They first settled in Lake Station and continued on to Miller in the late 1860s. Their son, Charles, ran Miller's first general store, Blank's General Store, described by early Lake County historian Timothy Ball as a large and prospering store. Their daughter Johanna married fellow Swede Gustaf Peterson in 1867. The two were married by a circuit preacher. Their son, George Frederic Peterson (above, with Lena Triebess on their wedding day), was born in Miller in 1875. George Peterson, who had electrical engineering degrees from Purdue, worked as a superintendent of electrical construction in the coke plant department of the Indiana Steel Company, starting in 1907. He wrote "Electrical Installation of a Steel Mill" for the *Purdue Engineering Review* in 1910. (Courtesy of Donna Simon.)

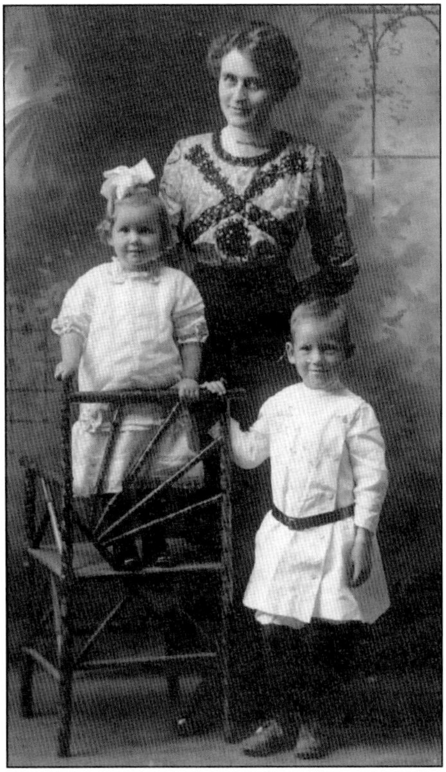

Gustaf and Johanna Blank Peterson's daughter Clara Olivia Peterson was one of the earliest members of the first English-language church in Miller, the First Congregational Church of Miller. She served as primary superintendent of the church's Sunday School until she fell ill in 1925. She also organized the Get-Together Club, taking teenage girls hiking and sponsoring parties for them. Somewhat unusual for the day, Clara also attended college. After her death in 1926, the Get-Together Club was renamed the COP Club, using her initials. Clara Olivia Peterson posed with her niece and nephew, Anna and Roger, for the portrait at left in 1912. Below, Anna Jeanette Peterson, daughter of George and Lena Peterson, plays with her doll in the woods outside her house in 1912. (Courtesy of Donna Simon.)

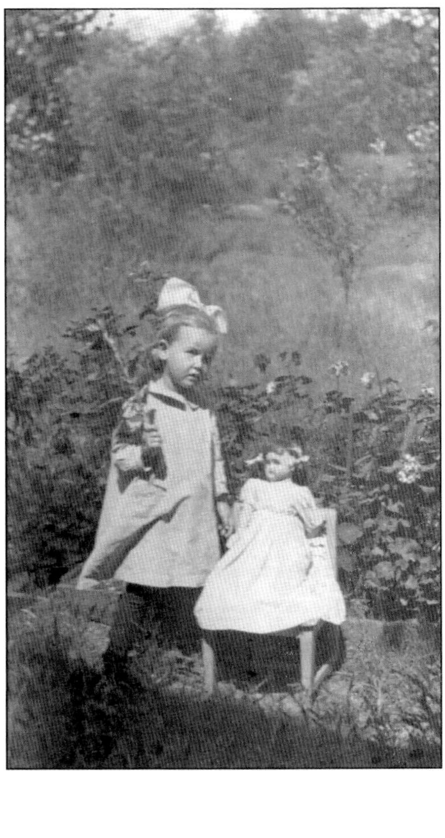

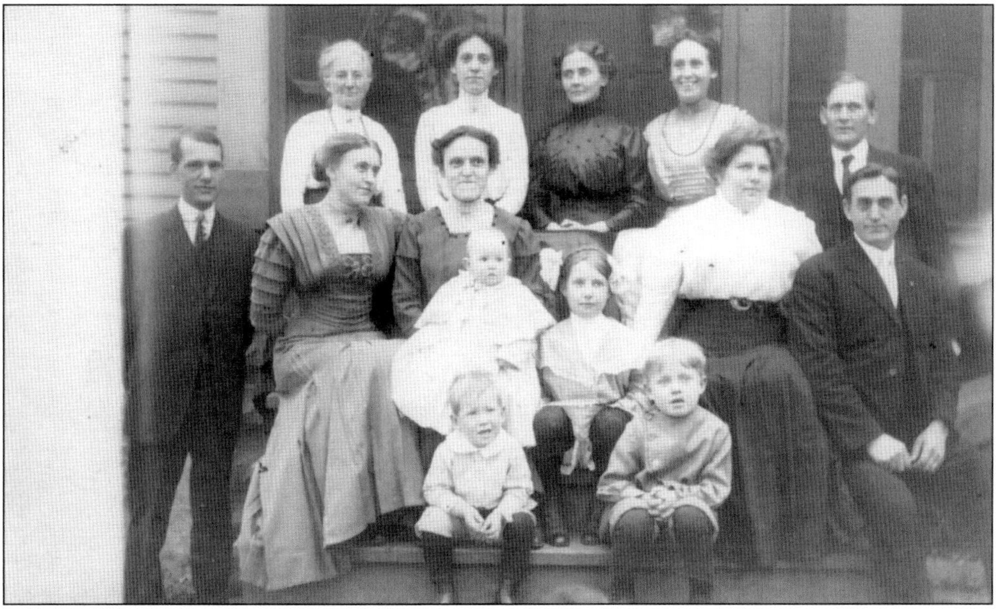

George and Lena Peterson were teachers in Miller in the late 1890s and early 1900s and in 1911, George was a member of the board of education, along with his cousin Charles A. Blank and Howard E. Carlson. The Petersons were instrumental in the founding of Chapel of the Dunes and George was known there for bringing fresh flowers to decorate the altar every Sunday. Here, a group of Miller residents congregate at the Peterson house on Hancock Street in October 1911. (Courtesy of Laura Valentine Jones.)

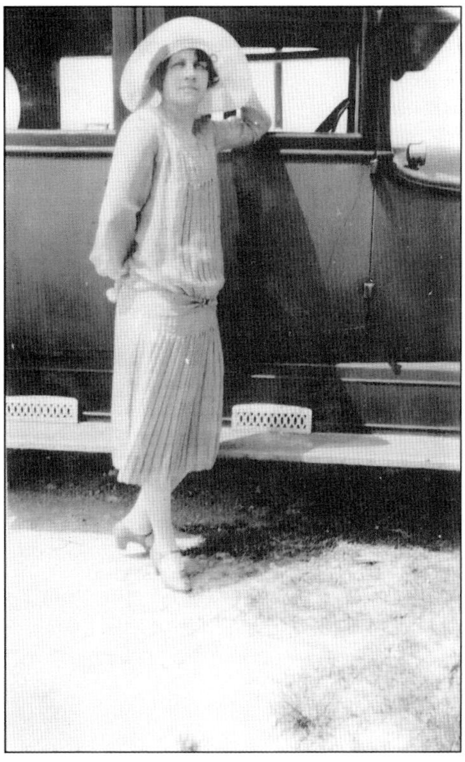

Charles F. Blank, owner of the first store in Miller, married Johanna Erlandson in 1875. Their children were all born in Miller: Lillie and her unnamed twin in 1876, both of whom died shortly after birth; Nella Charlotta in 1877; Charles August in 1879; Lilly Augusta in 1881; Ester Charlotta in 1882; and Arthur M. in 1886. They lived in a fine two-story house completed in the fall of 1882. Charles and Johanna Blank's daughter, Ester Charlotta Blank Meyers (pictured in the 1920s), lived for a time with her husband above Blank's General Store after it was taken over by her brother. (Courtesy of Laura Valentine Jones.)

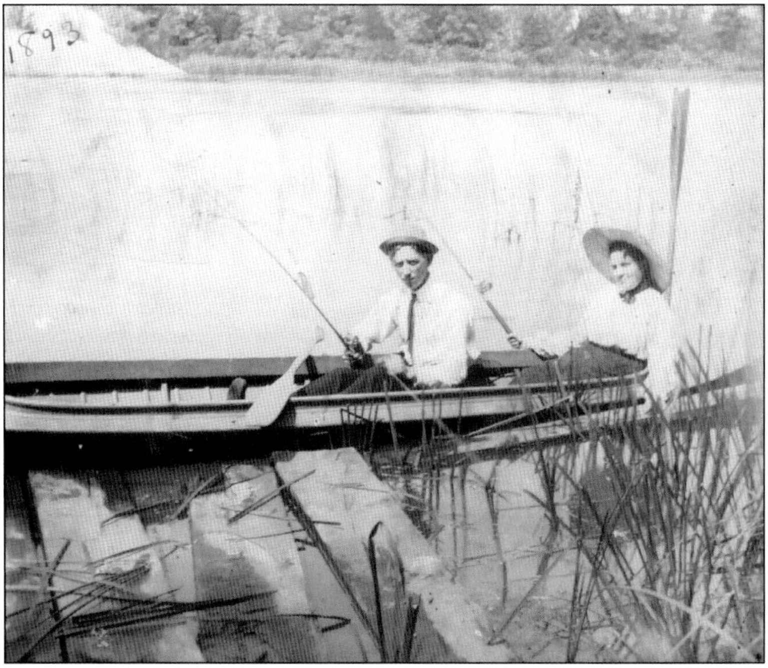

William Westergren was born in 1868 in Sweden, a year before his parents brought him to America. The family first lived in Chicago and then moved to Miller Station in the 1880s, purchasing 17 acres. William married Nellie Nelson in Chicago in 1893, and together they had five children. He was a policeman, justice of the peace, and a small store owner, as well as an avid hunter and fisherman. After his retirement, he worked as a crossing guard for students at the old Miller School. In addition to their house on Hamilton Street, the couple had a fishing and hunting cabin in an area they called "Dock Siding." In Arthur Blank's 1900 diary, he noted, "The girls went to Dock Siding. Willie Westergren will bring them home." Above, William and Nellie Westergren take a rowboat out in 1893, most likely on the lagoon in what is now Marquette Park. Below, children pose at Dock Siding in 1910 or 1911. (Courtesy of the Calumet Regional Archives, IU Northwest.)

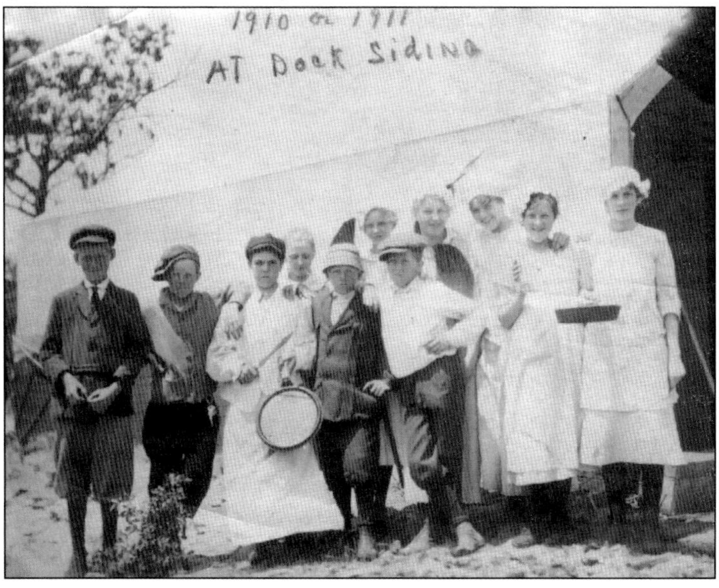

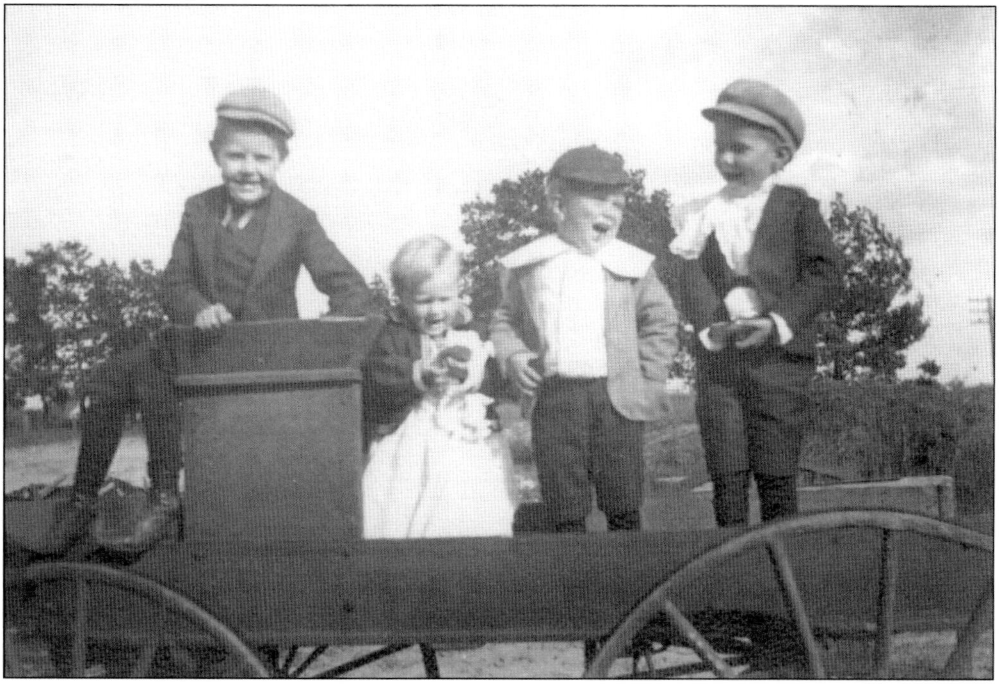

William and Nellie Westergren had five children: Rudolph, William, Clarence, Martin, and Lillian. Rudolph married Sylvia Leech, whose parents, Isaac and Mamie Leech, built several buildings on Lake Street in the 1910s and 1920s, including one that housed Leech's Tavern. Martin married Gertrude Stillson, and their daughter Peggy recalls her father's stories of the swamps surrounding the family's home on Hamilton Street. Martin told how his father, William, would have Martin and his brothers take turns collecting tolls from travelers who wanted to use the family's property, which was elevated in an otherwise wet area, to cross from Lake Street. Above, from left to right, are Rudolph, William, Clarence, and Martin Westergren around 1898. In the below image, they are joined by their younger sister, Lillian. (Courtesy of Peggy Westergren Newton.)

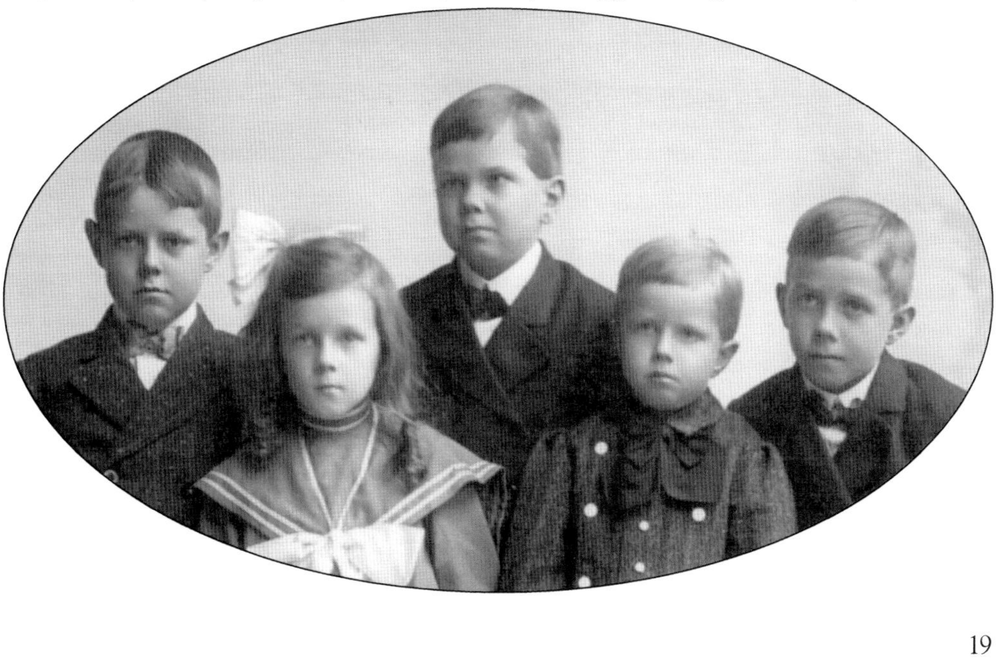

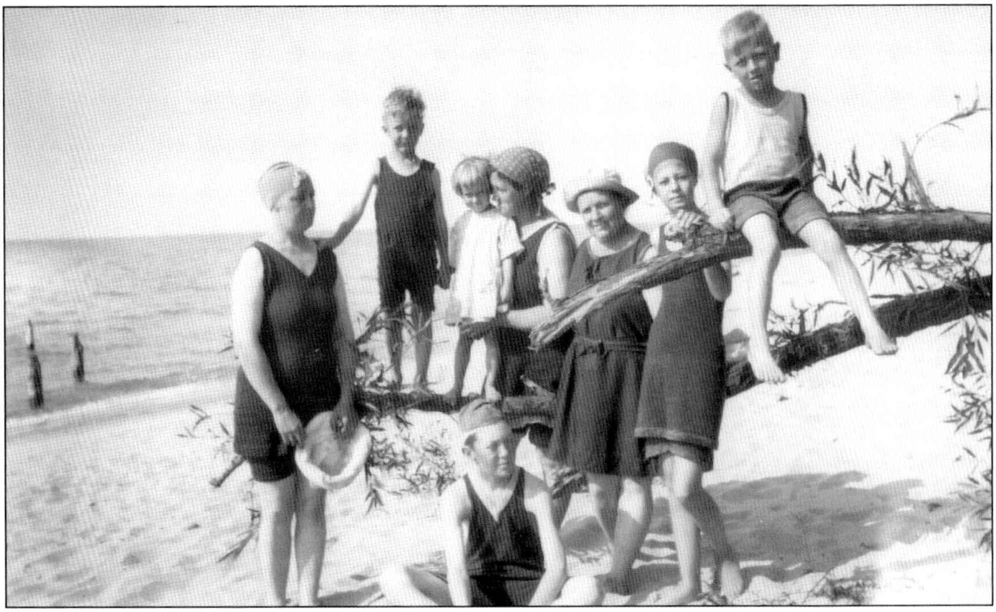

Lillian Pearl Westergren was born in 1898 to William and Nellie Westergren and married Arthur B. Weiger in 1926. Her parents rented out rooms in their home to workers building the city of Gary in 1906. The area around the home was wild and Lillian recalls her family keeping a pet wolf and skunk. In the winter, the children's father would flood an area in the backyard for ice skating, and in the summer, Lillian and her friends would spend whole days hiking in the woods. In the 1920s, Lillian worked as a hostess at the Gay Mill. Above, the Westergren family poses at the beach in the 1910s. Below, a group of girls, including Lillian, clutch their dolls at Christmastime in Miller in the early 1900s. (Above, courtesy of the Calumet Regional Archives, IU Northwest; below, courtesy of Peggy Westergren Newton.)

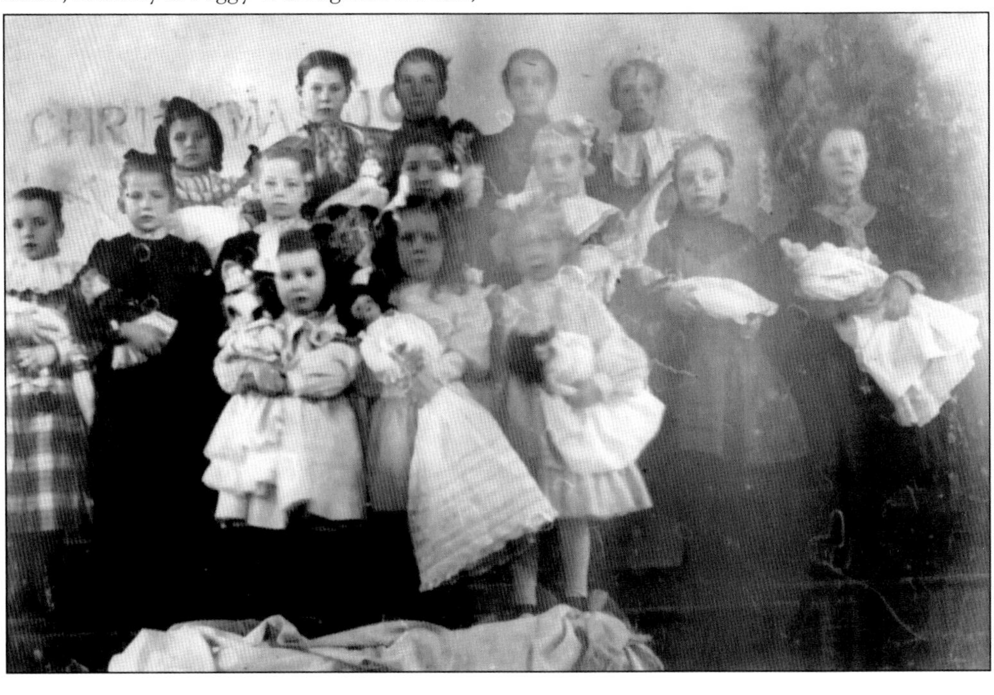

Warren and Anna Stillson were early Wisconsin settlers who moved to Chesterton, Indiana, and eventually to Miller in the early 1910s. Warren Stillson ran bars in Wisconsin and Chesterton. When they moved to Miller, they settled in Blankville, an area of houses off Miller Avenue and west of Lake Street that was named for the Blank families who had come to Miller a few decades before. They also ran an early store on Lake Street called Stillson's. Here, the Stillsons pose against a tree early in their marriage. (Courtesy of Peggy Westergren Newton.)

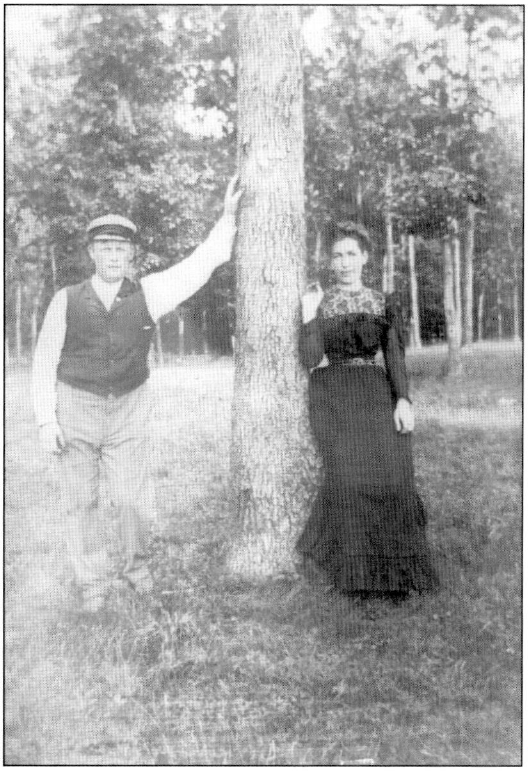

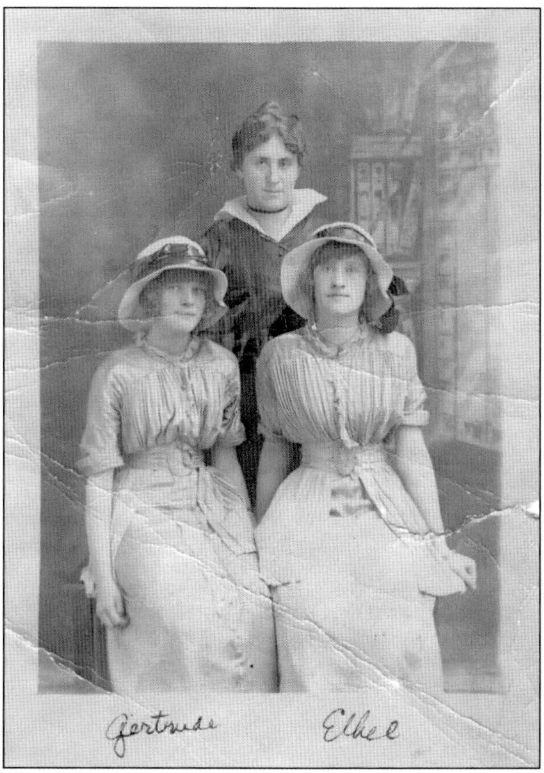

Anna Stillson is seen in this portrait with her daughters, Gertrude and Ethel. A third daughter, Gladys, died at a young age. According to Gertrude's daughter, Peggy Westergren Newton, Gertrude's parents were upset when she started dating Martin Westergren, whom she eventually married, because they thought the four Westergren boys were a bit on the wild side. (Courtesy of Peggy Westergren Newton.)

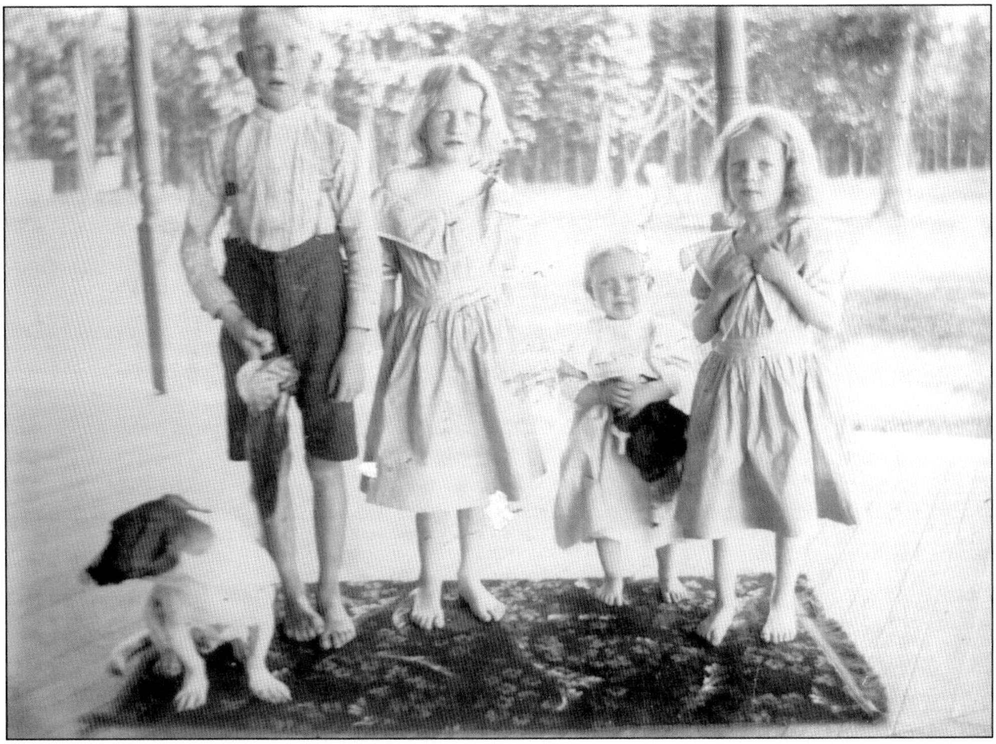

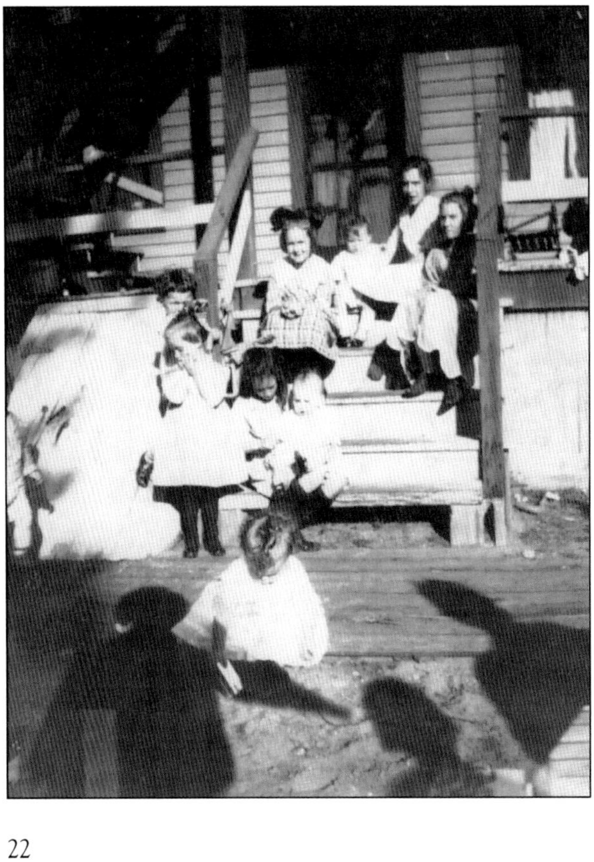

Warren and Anna Stillson had five children: Floyd in 1893, Ethel in 1895, Gertrude in 1898, Gladys in 1901, and Thomas in 1907. Floyd and his three younger sisters posed for this photograph with the dog in the early 1900s. Floyd Stillson took over the family grocery store on Lake Street in the 1920s. His sister Gertrude was named postmaster in 1919 and operated a post office out of the store. (Courtesy of Peggy Westergren Newton.)

A group of neighborhood children played at the George and Lena Peterson house on Hancock Street around 1920. Anna Peterson is on the steps at far left and Laura Valentine Jones, with a large bow in her hair, is at front left. (Courtesy of Laura Valentine Jones.)

Herbert Leech, shown here in 1905, was born to Isaac and Mamie Leech in 1902 and raised in Miller. The Leech family built several buildings on Lake Street and operated Leech's Tavern. (Courtesy of Marilyn Leech and Holly Rodino Breese.)

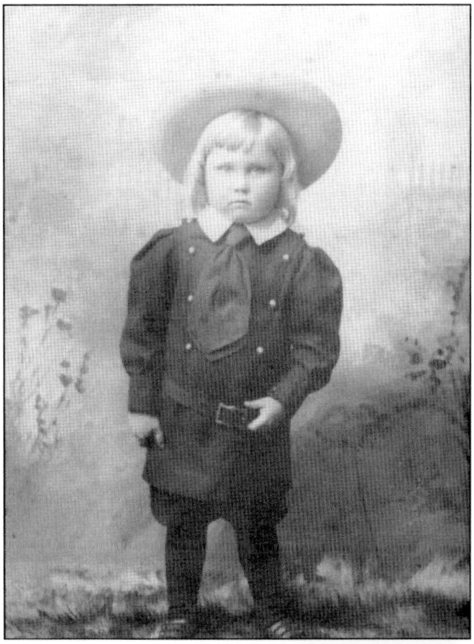

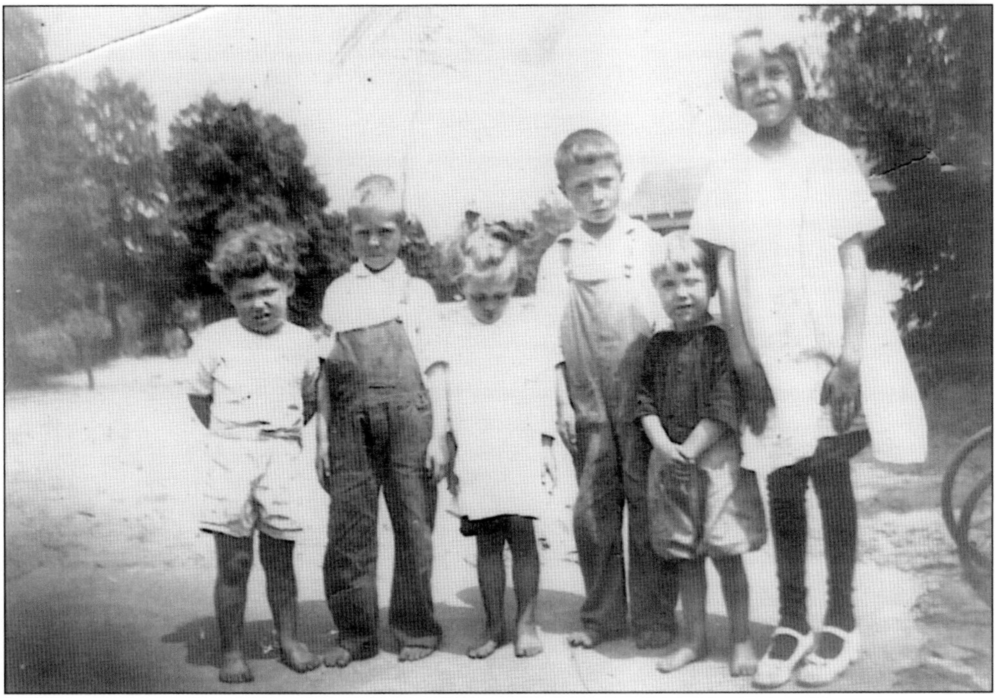

Laura Valentine Jones recalls that as a youngster in Miller in the late 1910s and early 1920s, she and other kids in the neighborhood enjoyed a lot of freedom to play outside together. The boys outnumbered the girls, which was fine for tomboys like her. Jones also recalls her mother dressing her in dark-colored socks, as she never kept the white ones clean. From the looks of many of the pictures, the kids played barefoot as well. This early 1920s photograph includes, from left to right, Bobby Brandon, Leonard Bowgren, Laura Valentine, Everet Honsard, Otto Dumont, and Ethel Bowgren. (Courtesy of Laura Valentine Jones.)

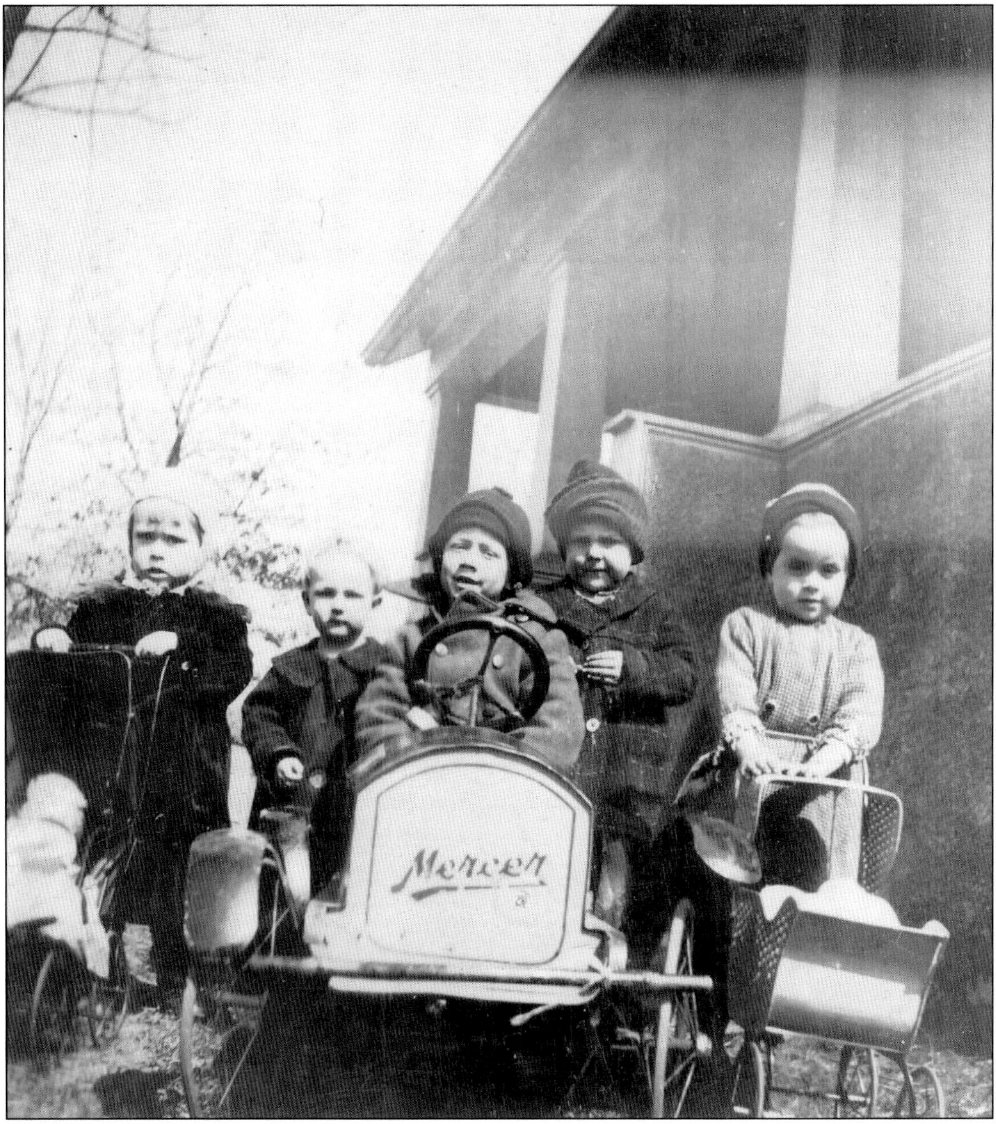

From left to right, little kids Naomi Kietzman, Otto Dumont, Leroy Kietzman, Gilbert Carr, and Laura Valentine played around with a toy car in 1920. Gilbert Carr was the son of Fred and Amanda (Bullock) Carr, and the grandson of Robert and Drusilla Carr. Leroy and Naomi Kietzman's father had a real estate office on Lake Street. (Courtesy of Laura Valentine Jones.)

Two

ON THE GO

TRAINS, HORSES, AND AUTOMOBILES

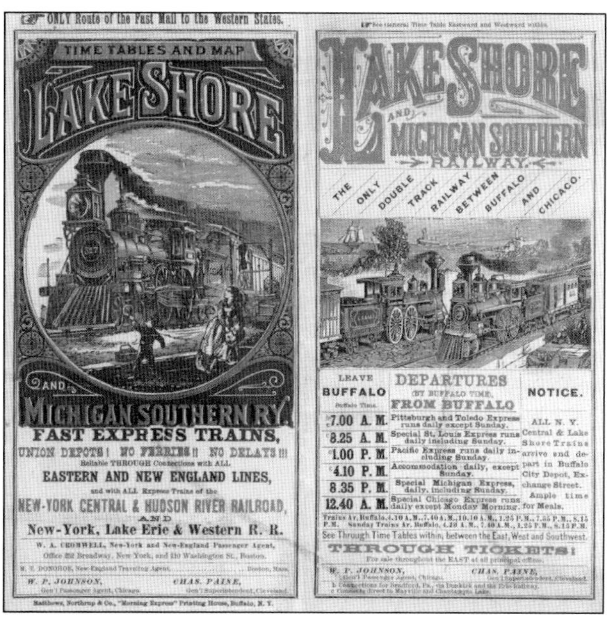

The Lake Shore & Michigan Southern Railroad laid the first tracks through the Calumet region of northwest Indiana in 1851, passing through a small spot which had many names over the years, including Miller's Station and Miller's Junction. The terrain, made up of marshes, wetlands, and sand, was the most difficult part of the entire line to build, but once it was, it helped create Miller Beach. Pres. Abraham Lincoln's funeral train made its way down these tracks towards Illinois in 1865. Years later, the most glamorous of trains—the *20th Century Limited*—ran first on these tracks. (Courtesy of Simine Short.)

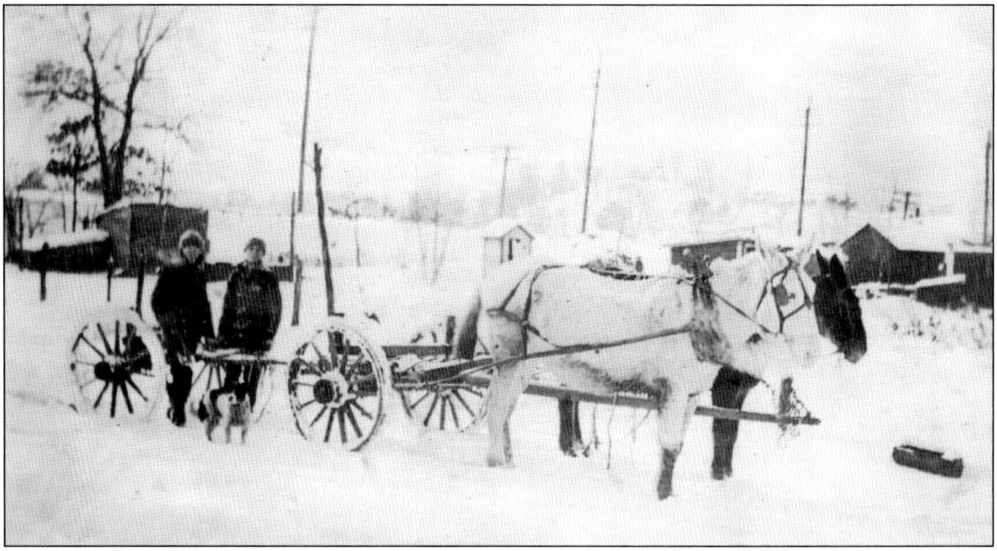

When eight-year-old Alfred Anderson arrived in Miller in the fall of 1864 on an ox-pulled wagon loaded with his family's possessions, it took more than half a day to make the trip from Hobart, just a few miles away. The only buildings in Miller were a boardinghouse under construction by the Lake Shore Railroad and a tiny frame cottage. Anderson's father was a contractor and came to work for the new railroad. (Courtesy of the Calumet Regional Archives, IU Northwest.)

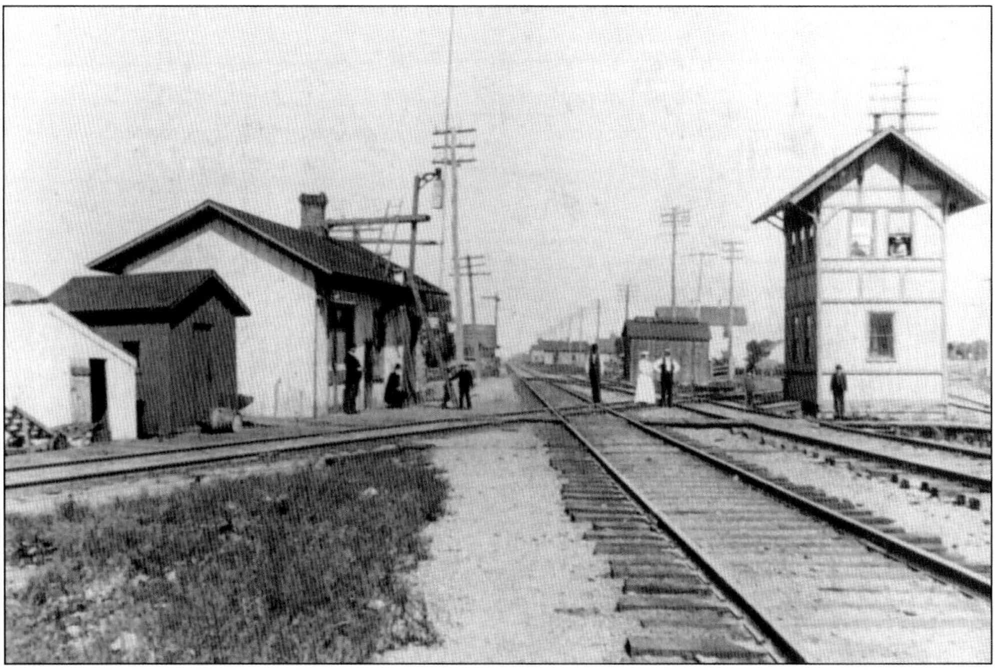

This 1889 photograph shows the intersection of the Baltimore & Ohio (B&O) and Lake Shore & Michigan Southern (LSMS) tracks in Miller. The B&O tracks run down the center of this photograph and the LSMS tracks intersected them in front of the passenger station—the big white building on the left—and the water tower on the right. Note the watchman leaning out the window. In the distance, beyond the passenger station, is the Point Tavern, which still stands in Miller's downtown. (Courtesy of the Calumet Regional Archives, IU Northwest.)

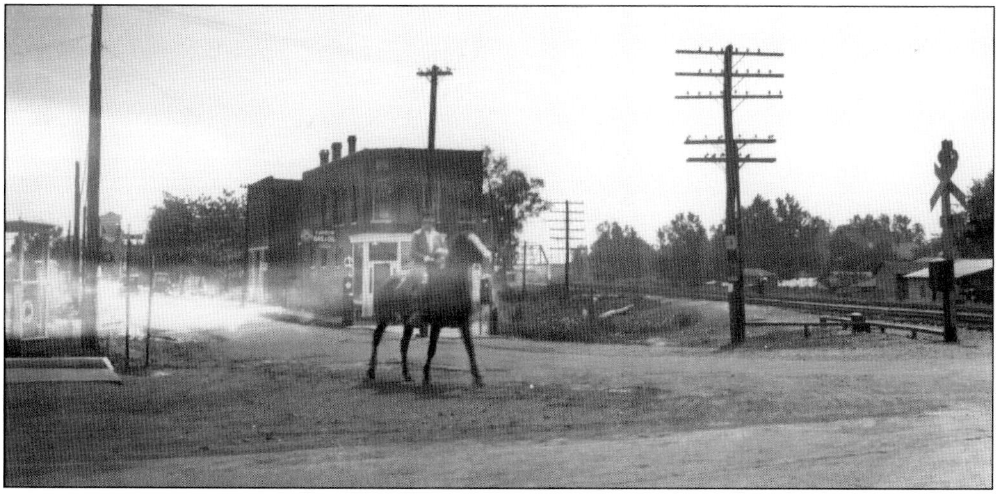

Before automobiles, the train was the easiest way to get to Miller from Chicago, a trip that took all day by wagon. There was quicksand along the Grand Calumet River and one night when Miller resident Doc Foster was coming home from Chicago, his horse got mired in the quicksand that lined parts of the riverbank and drowned. But horses remained the primary form of in-town transportation as this photograph of downtown Miller shows. (Courtesy of the Calumet Regional Archives, IU Northwest.)

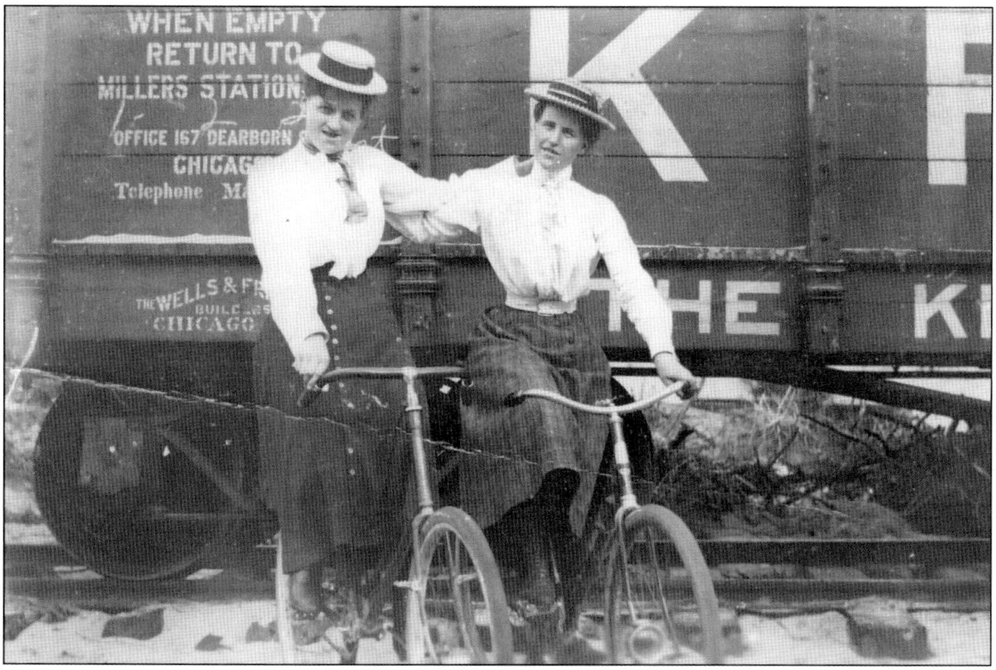

In 1869, the Lake Shore & Michigan Southern Railway was formed by the consolidation of four smaller railroads, including the Michigan Southern & Northern Indiana Railroad, into one complete line between Chicago and Buffalo, New York. A few years later, the Baltimore & Ohio Railroad was built in Miller. It did not take long for hucksters to try to make a buck, and soon a Chicago real estate company sent excursion trains in an attempt to sell lots or acreage in the sandy marshland north of the B&O train tracks. They named the stop "Humbolt," but Miller realtors instead called it "Humbug." (Courtesy of the Calumet Regional Archives, IU Northwest.)

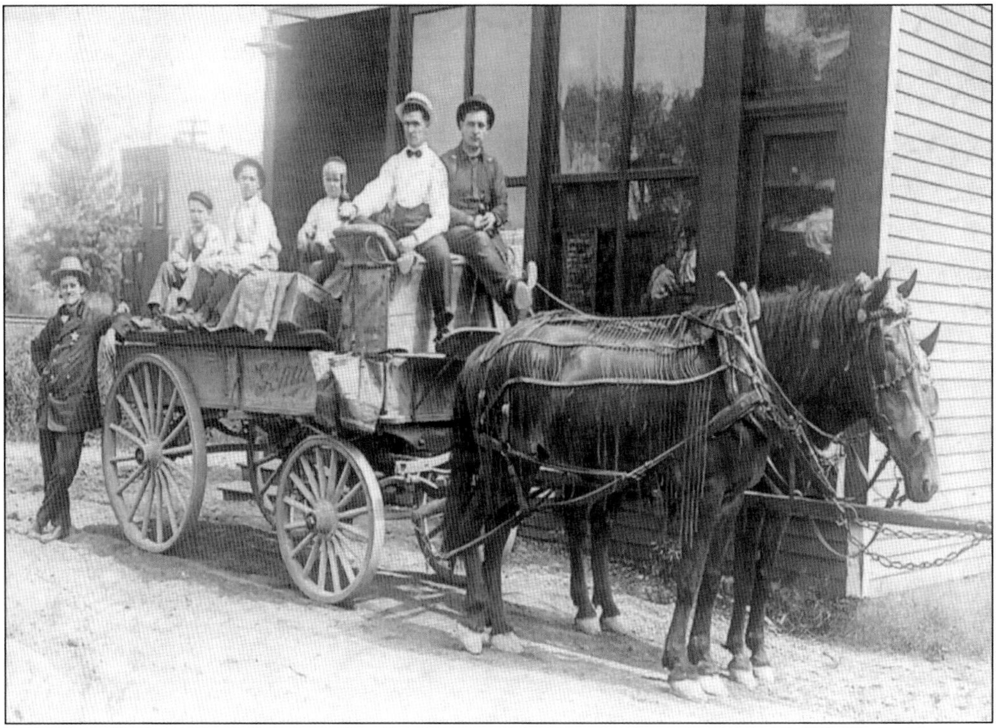

The advent of the B&O Railroad brought both jobs and people to Miller. Around that time, William Cook worked for the Lake Shore & Michigan Southern Railroad, earning $24 a year on top of his $40-a-year salary as Miller's postmaster. More people in Miller meant more beer consumption; here, a Schlitz beer truck gets ready to unload at the Bee Hive Saloon. (Courtesy of Joyce Davis, Lake Street Gallery.)

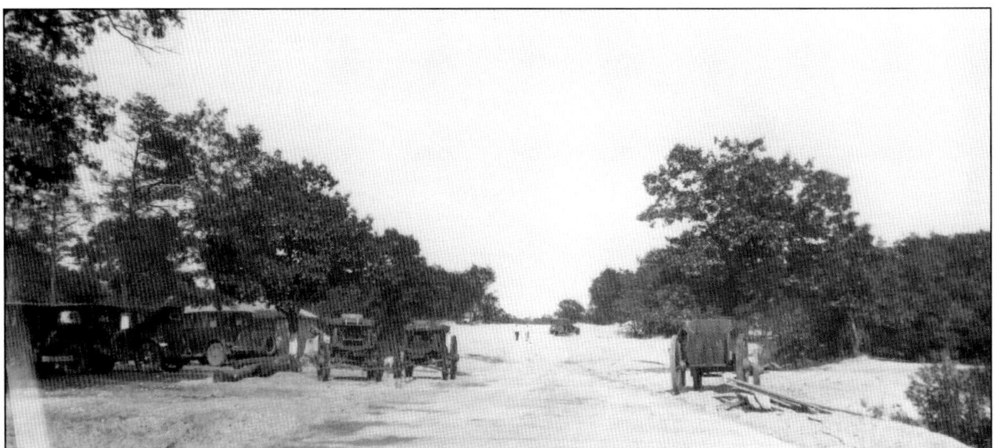

Early Miller pioneer Drusilla Carr used to walk a towpath like this from her two-room pine cabin to Miller with the cranberries she had picked. But by the early 1900s, the beach was changing from a place where hundreds of bald eagles flocked and wolves howled at night to a place where people came for beach recreation. (Courtesy of the Calumet Regional Archives, IU Northwest.)

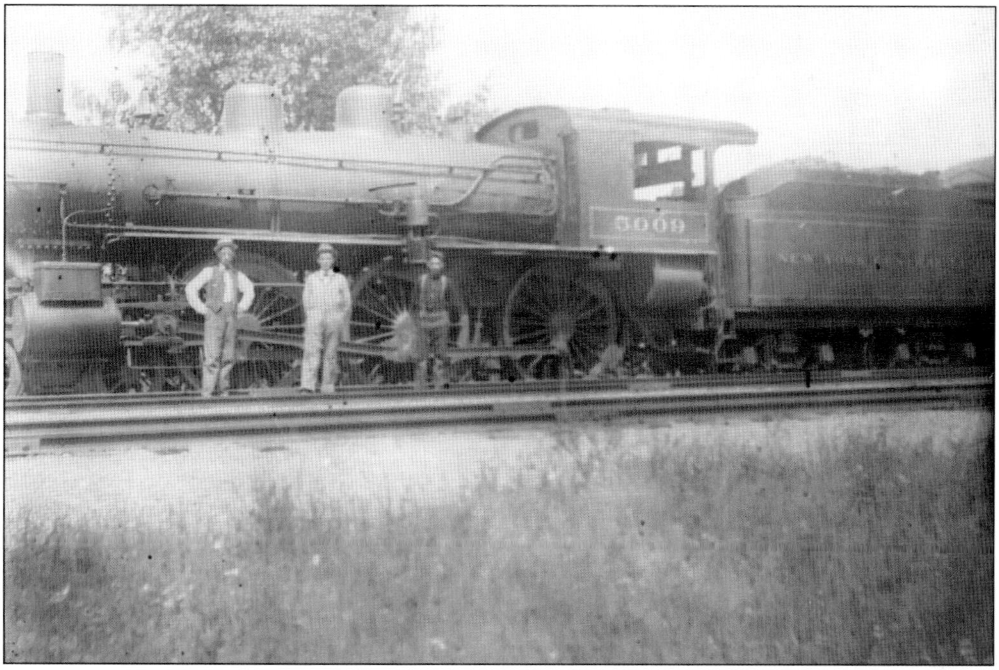

Father Pere Marquette came ashore in 1673 on what is now Miller Beach, making friends with the Native Americans and smoking the peace pipe called a calumet. The mouth of the Grand Calumet River, in Miller, was later the location of a stage house built by a man named Bennett in 1833 to serve the stagecoaches that ran between Chicago and Detroit, a week or more journey at the time, which today can be covered in five hours. But by the mid-1880s, transportation was changing Miller from a desolate outpost to a vacation destination. (Courtesy of the Calumet Regional Archives, IU Northwest.)

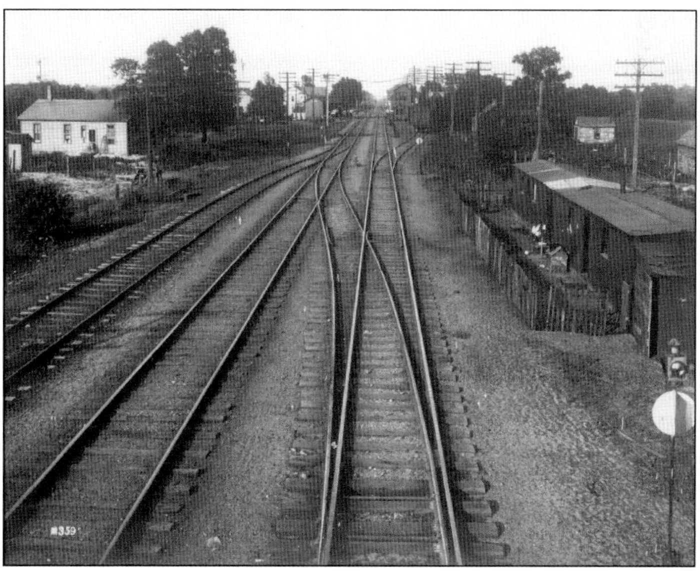

This July 11, 1906, photograph shows the tracks of the Lake Shore & Michigan Southern Railway facing east. The railway, often referred to as the Lake Shore, was one of the main lines of the New York Central Railroad's water level route connecting Buffalo to Chicago, mostly following along Lake Erie's south shore. The line is still a major corridor and is also used by Amtrak passenger trains. (Courtesy of Steve Spicer.)

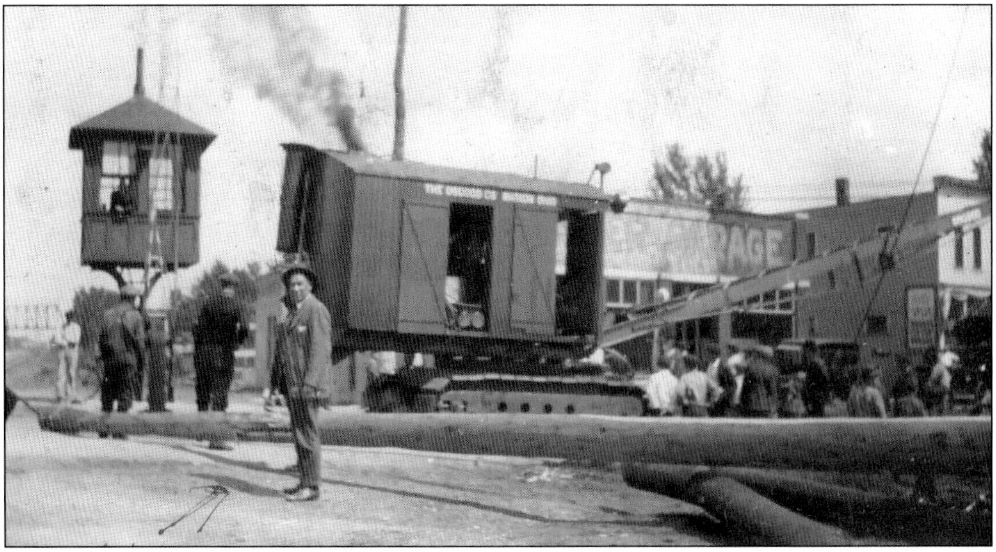

Less than 150 years ago, even a short trip from nearby towns was arduous. While crossing the dunes, families would often have to unload their wagons and carry their possessions until they passed over a dune. Trains quickly changed all that. By 1917, four railroads—the Lake Shore & Michigan Southern, the Michigan Central, the Baltimore & Ohio, and the Pennsylvania Railroads—had daily trains from Chicago heading east to duneland stations like Miller. This May 1922 photograph shows the growth of Miller brought about by the railroads. (Courtesy of the Calumet Regional Archives, IU Northwest.)

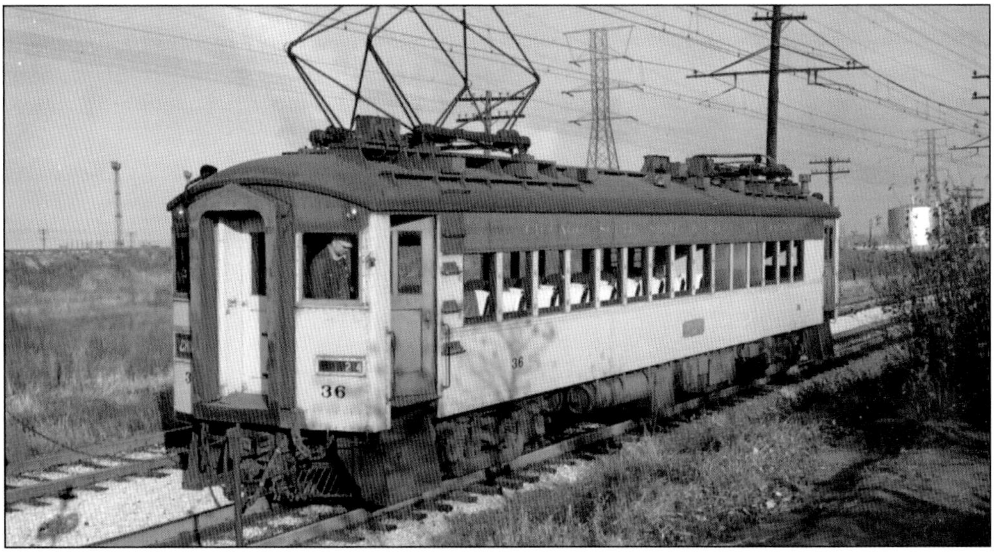

By the end of World War I, some 10,000 interurbans—electric trains—connected towns and cities throughout the country, making traveling between cities much easier. Today, only one remains: the South Shore, whose beginnings trace back to the early 1900s, when it was known as the Chicago South Shore & South Bend Railway Company. The South Shore helped fuel the Miller tourism boom, offering 22 daily routes between Chicago and South Bend with seven Indiana Dunes stops between Miller and Michigan City to the east. This photograph of the South Shore Line was taken in 1938. Information stamped on the back reads, "George Krambles, 2244 Cleveland Ave., Chicago, Illinois." (Courtesy of the Calumet Regional Archives, IU Northwest.)

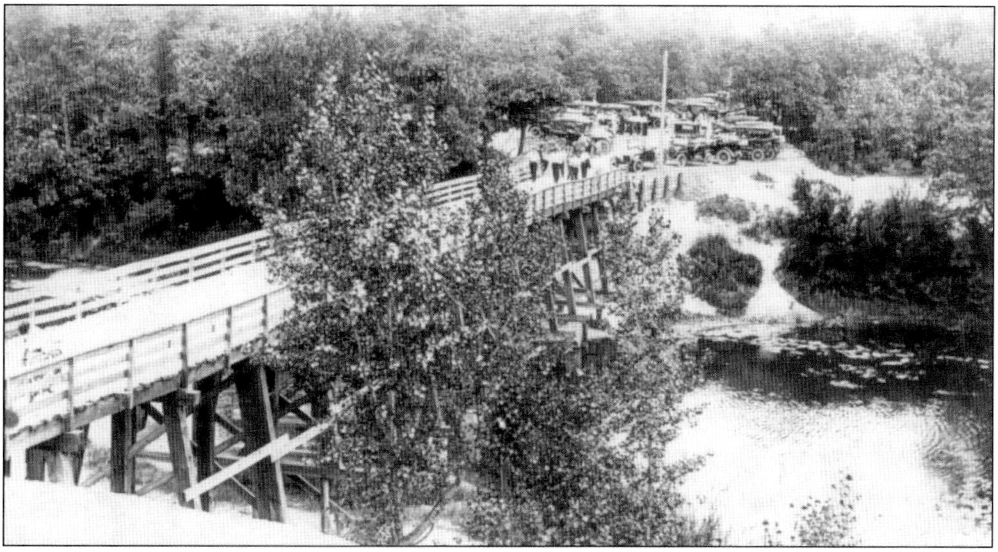

Visitors arriving by car at the Calumet River Bridge at the end of Lake Street had to complete the journey on foot because the wooden bridge could not bear the weight of their vehicles. According to Jim Doyne, whose family rented a cottage from the Carrs beginning in the 1920s, the enterprising Carr family owned two Model-Ts with balloon tires capable of traveling on sand. When vacationers arrived at the bridge, the Carrs transported their belongings and delivered them to the cottage. The water here was very deep, making a great swimming place until Lake Michigan warmed up in the summer. Miller boys liked to dive under the bridge for pennies. (Courtesy of Marilyn Leech and Holly Rodino Breese.)

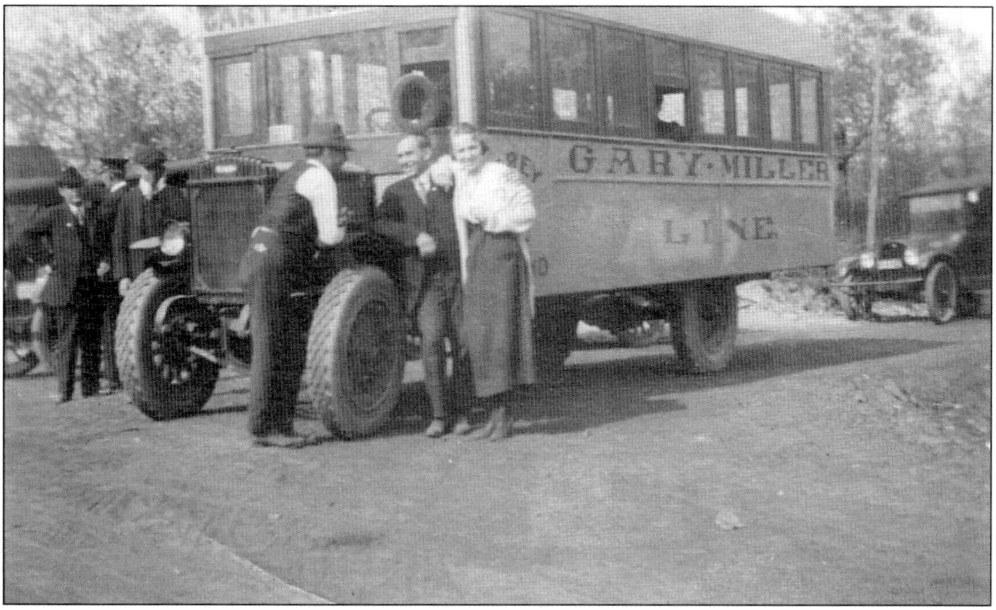

Longtime Miller resident Betty Davin remembers taking a streetcar from Hyde Park to Ninety-fifth Street on Chicago's South Side as a child in the 1920s. Then she caught a New York Central train to Miller and rode a Mack bus down Lake Street to the beach, where her grandmother had a cottage at 9031 Lake Shore Drive. Trolleys like this also covered the short distances between towns. (Courtesy of the Calumet Regional Archives, IU Northwest.)

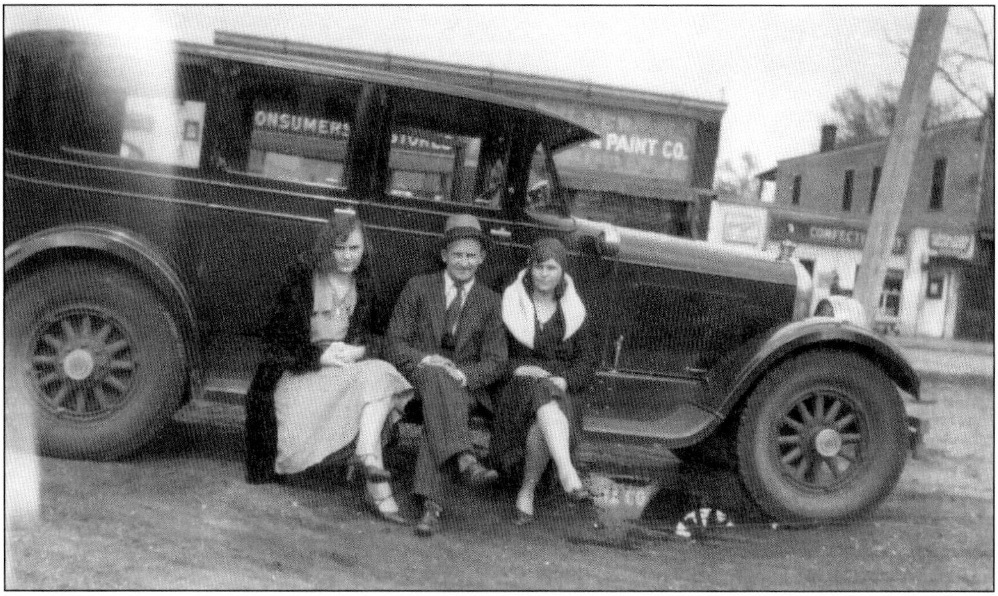

In 1837, Robert Stewart drew up plans for a town called Indiana City in the same location as Miller. Advertising in newspapers out east, Stewart claimed that the harbor at the mouth of the Grand Calumet was wider and deeper than the Chicago harbor. The financial panic of 1837 and 1838 assured that Indiana City never came to fruition. But railroads and the invention of the automobile quickly changed the map of the Calumet Region, adding gas stations, hotels, and new roads to handle all the people flocking here. (Courtesy of the Calumet Regional Archives, IU Northwest.)

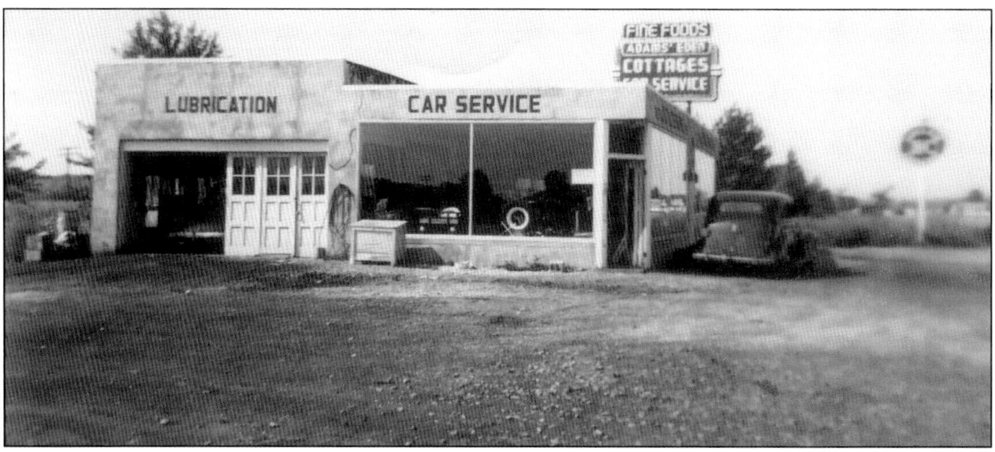

Early on, most roads accessing Miller were dirt, such as this one in a photograph taken between 1918 and 1922. Some remained that way into the early 1930s, particularly those in the country. Dirt roads had to be oiled to keep them from getting too dusty and big oilers, designed for the job and often pulled by horses, helped keep the roads manageable. As more and more people traveled to Miller, there was a boom of roadside cabins and cottages for overnighters, as well as new places to eat. In the 1940s, cabins like the ones advertised here were replaced by motels. (Courtesy of Gene Ayers, Ayers Realtors, Inc.)

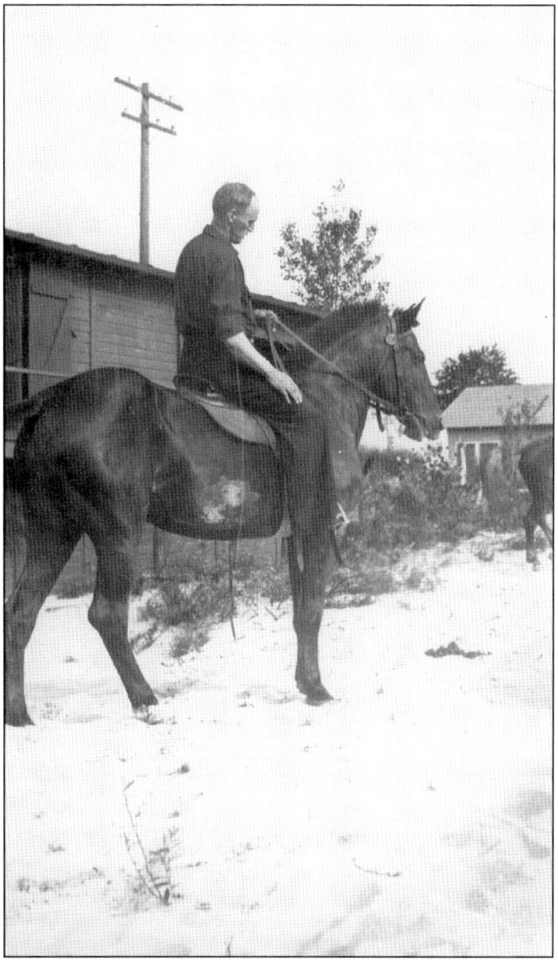

By the end of the 1920s, horsepower had replaced horses. But getting around on horseback was still common. At right, Frank Hough, founder of Wells Street Beach, a privately owned section of the Lake Michigan shoreline in Miller that is open to the public, rides his horse in front of his beach cabin. Hough kept about six horses in a stable near his house. Later Hough's cabin would be expanded and winterized for year-round living. The house still remains in the Hough family, but the stables are gone. Below, Herbert Leech, who moved from Gary to Miller when he was a young boy, stands with his foot on the running board of his spiffy automobile. (Right, courtesy of Alice Pickford; below, courtesy of Marilyn Leech and Holly Rodino Breese.)

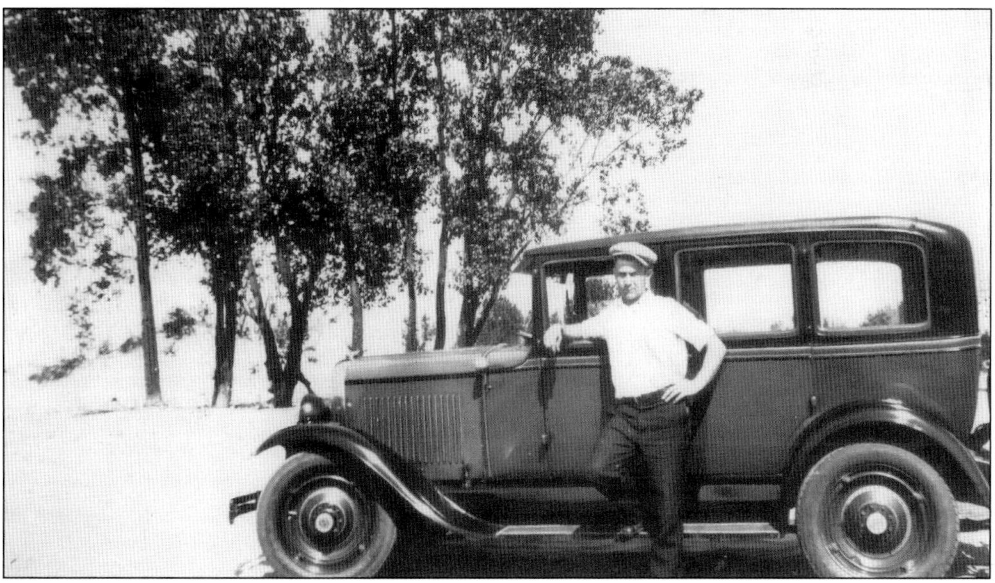

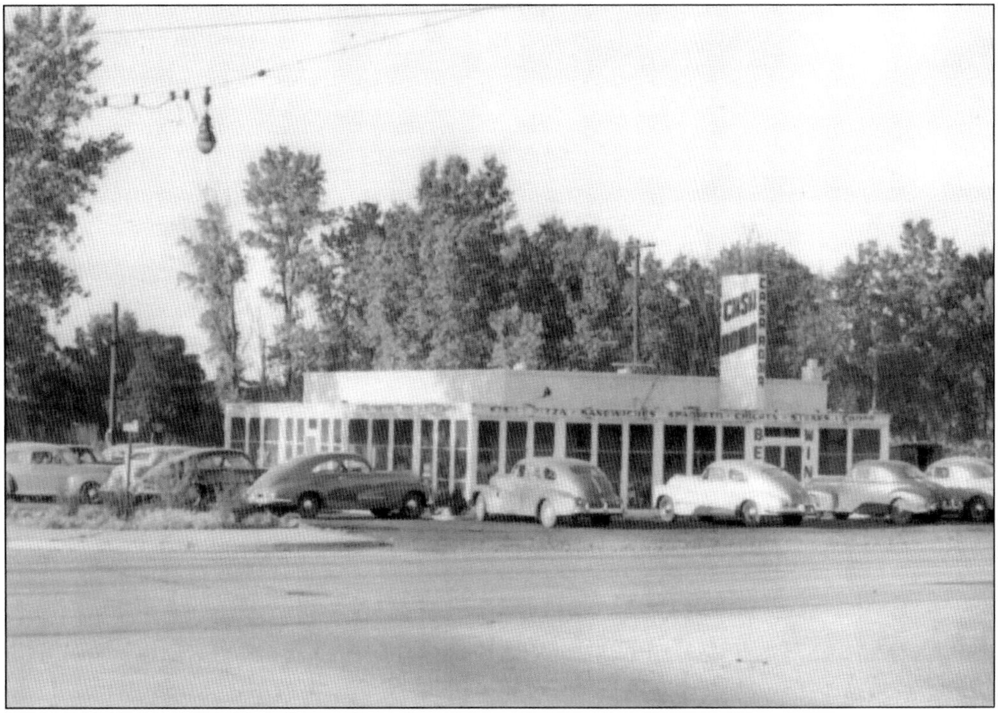

Casa Roma Restaurant, owned by the Iatarola family, was a local favorite for many years. In the book *Miller Memories*, Casa Roma is credited with introducing Millerites to pizza for the first time ever. With good food at low prices, it was also a gathering spot for teenagers. (Courtesy of Joyce Davis, Lake Street Gallery.)

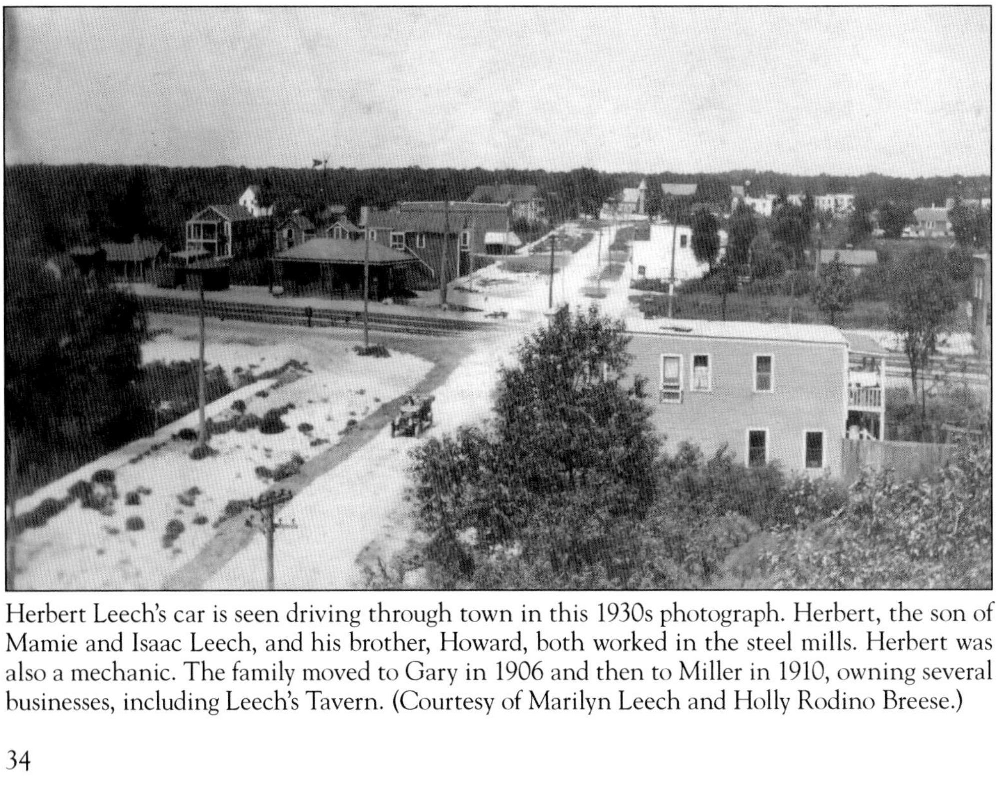

Herbert Leech's car is seen driving through town in this 1930s photograph. Herbert, the son of Mamie and Isaac Leech, and his brother, Howard, both worked in the steel mills. Herbert was also a mechanic. The family moved to Gary in 1906 and then to Miller in 1910, owning several businesses, including Leech's Tavern. (Courtesy of Marilyn Leech and Holly Rodino Breese.)

Three

Lake Industries
Ice, Sand, and Fish

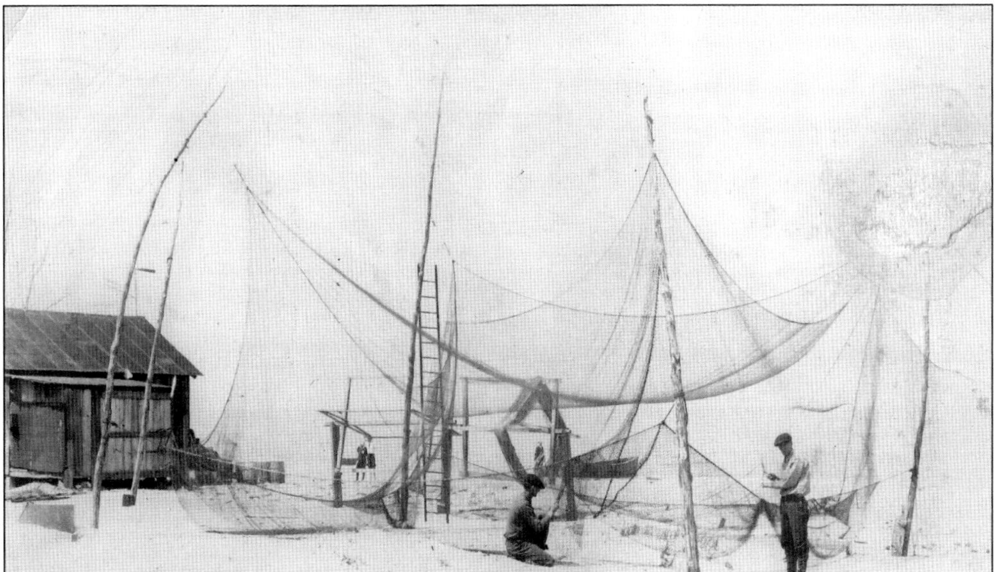

The Anderson family was one of the first pioneer families. Their son, Alfred, recalled that he fished with his father using a 40-rod or fishing net. "A fellow from Hobart had a 106-rod seine and I saw him when he got over 6,000 pounds of whitefish in one haul. He got over 100 sturgeons and one weighed 180 pounds," said Anderson in 1922, almost 50 years after his family moved to Miller. "It was the largest fish I ever saw caught in the lake. The best price we could get for fish was one cent a pound and we were glad to get rid of them for that." Here, the Carr family, who fished these waters for more than a half-century, work on their nets on Miller Beach. (Courtesy of the Calumet Regional Archives, IU Northwest.)

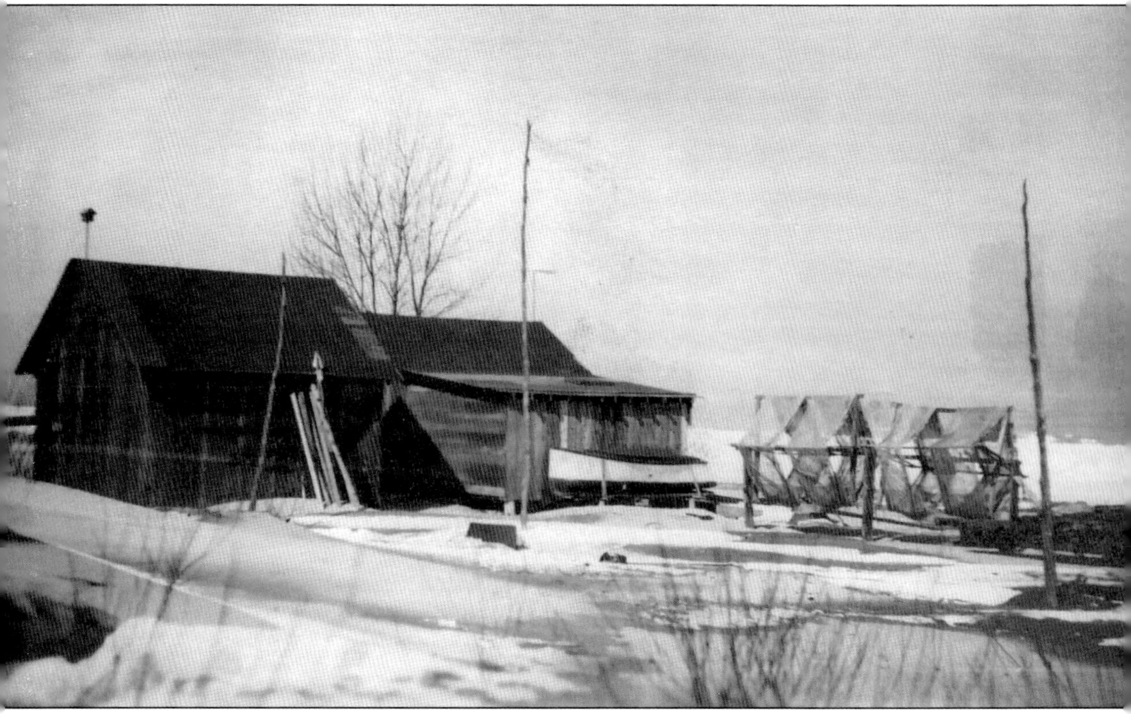

Drusilla Carr, who fished for sturgeon and whitefish with her husband, Robert, remembers waiting for him to return from delivering fish in Chicago one night when the sturgeon began jumping out of the water. "I thought 'My, what a haul we could have if someone was only here to help me.' " Luckily, she found two men to help: John Beaubien and Davy Crockett. They cast their nets, lighting fires on the beach to mark where the nets had gone in and where they needed to come out, and began hauling in their catch. "When the net came in," she recalled years later, "we had 57 large sturgeons." Robert arrived just in time for them to load them on his boat and head back to Chicago. (Courtesy of the Calumet Regional Archives, IU Northwest.)

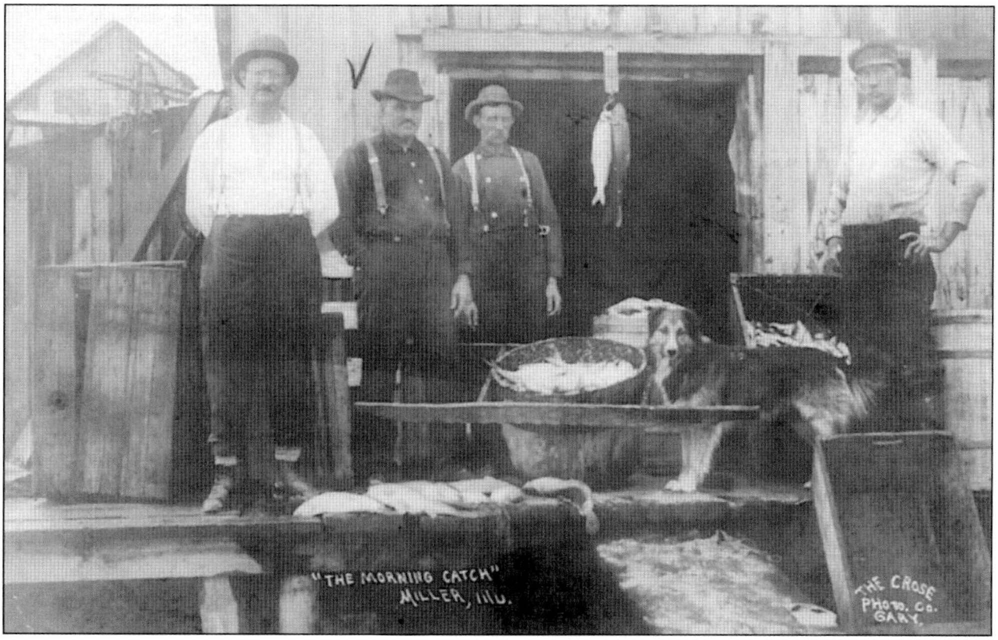

Fishing was the first major industry in Miller. In the mid-1800s, a small commercial sturgeon and whitefish fishery, owned by John and Hank Granger, was built near the lagoon. The fish were tremendously large, with one particular sturgeon weighing almost 200 pounds. Before refrigeration, fish were salted, dried, or smoked to keep them from going bad. (Courtesy of Joyce Davis, Lake Street Gallery.)

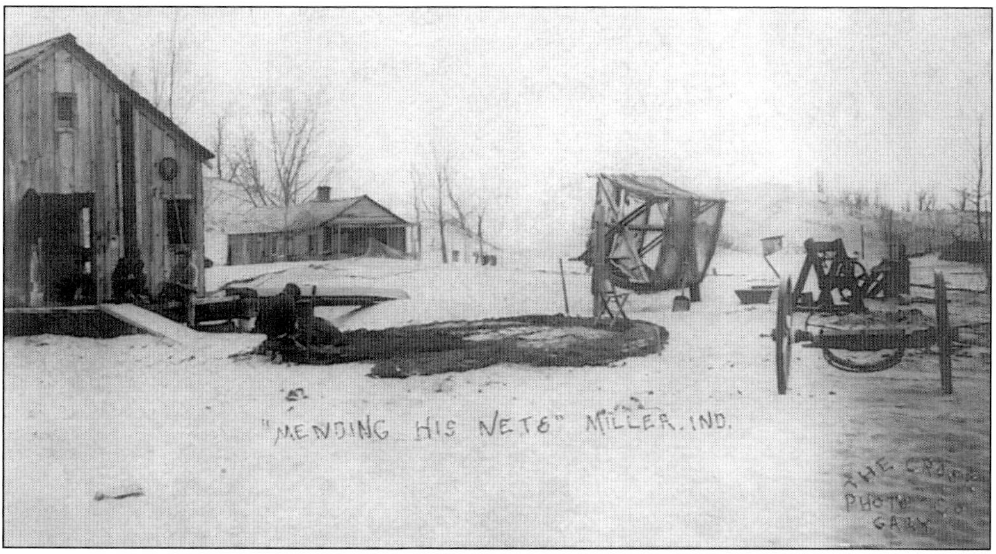

This photograph of the Carr family fishing compound, where the family worked and fished, shows their nets, or seines, rolled up on an apparatus called a windlass. The Carrs fished this land starting in the early 1870s. Before the beautiful lakefront attracted tourists, squatters lived on the beaches and made their living by foraging for wild berries, including cranberries, huckleberries, and blueberries, collecting honey from wild bees, hunting, and fishing. Roe from these fish were considered a delicacy and were shipped to Chicago's better restaurants. (Courtesy of the Calumet Regional Archives, IU Northwest.)

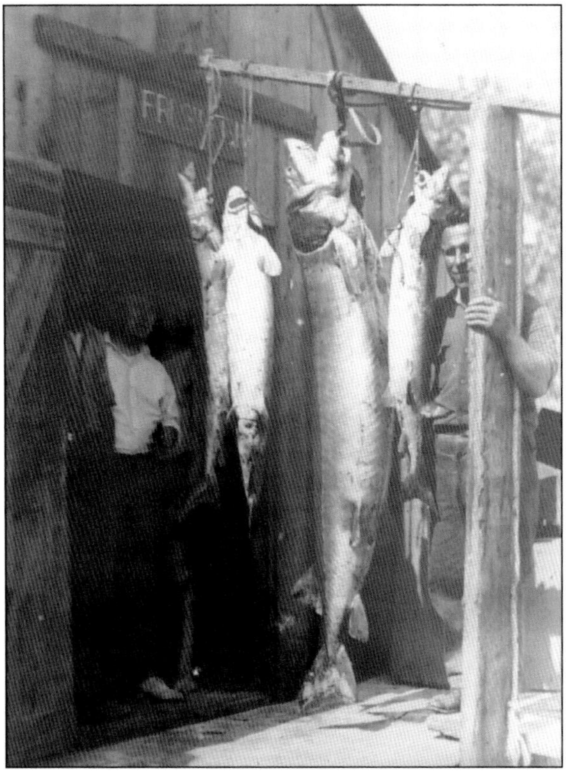

Living off the land was a way of life and those who eked out their living on the beach often bartered their freshly caught bass, pickerel, wild summer berries, or game for foodstuff that could not be gathered, like flour, canned goods, and sugar. Shown here is a display of freshly caught sturgeon in front of a fishery at the end of Lake Street. (Courtesy of Alice Pickford.)

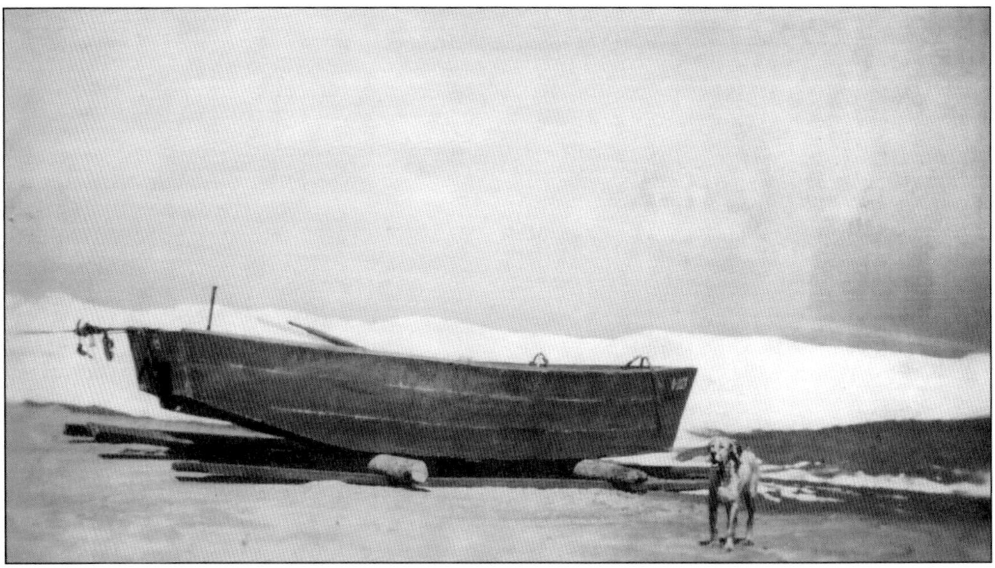

A wet dog stands beside the beached Carr fishing boat. The Carr family and those around them lived an isolated life. Doc Foster tended to the fishing families using herbs instead of anesthetics or surgery. When Drusilla Carr accidentally overdosed her six-month-old baby, Henry, with too much Bochero German cough medicine, Doc Foster told her to take the lids off the stove and get a few teaspoons of soot. When she did, he dabbed the soot on a dampened cloth and placed it under little Henry's arms. Within minutes, Henry had opened his eyes and was laughing. (Courtesy of the Calumet Regional Archives, IU Northwest.)

Early Miller fishermen were tough. At the age of 75, Fred Carr (seen here with a catch) launched a boat into the surf to save his son and two sailors who fell into Lake Michigan's icy waters after their fishing boat was hit by a huge breaker about 200 feet offshore. The three men held on to the side of their boat until Carr reached them. As they clung to his boat, Carr was forced by the high waves to get out of the craft as it neared shore, pulling both the boat and the three men to safety. (Courtesy of the Calumet Regional Archives, IU Northwest.)

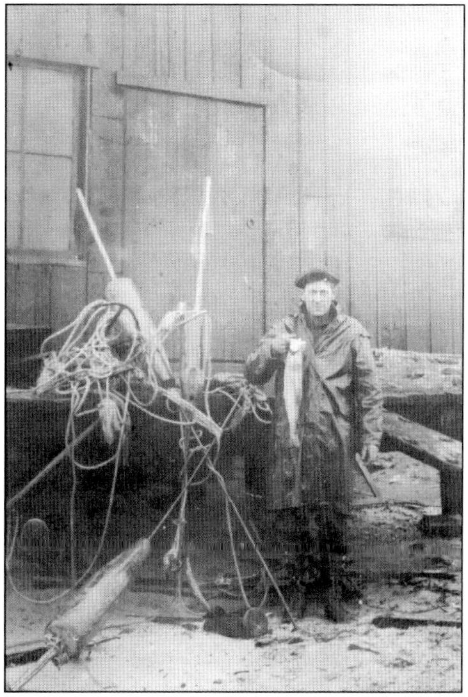

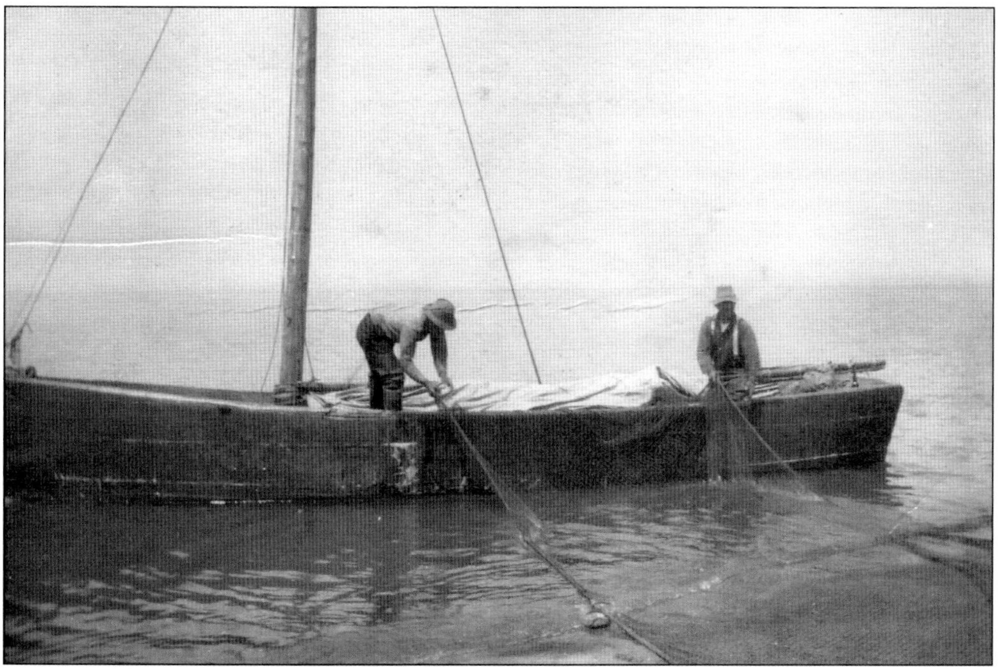

The Sabinskes were also longtime fishermen and beach squatters. Sons August and George Sabinske, shown here in their boat, followed the family tradition. When beach property became expensive, the City of Gary wanted their land and, according to Gus Sabinske, would drive bulldozers up to the doors of his shack and leave them running for hours. Finally, public outcry forced the city to retreat and Sabinske was allowed to remain on his family's land until his death. (Courtesy of Marilyn Leech and Holly Rodino Breese.)

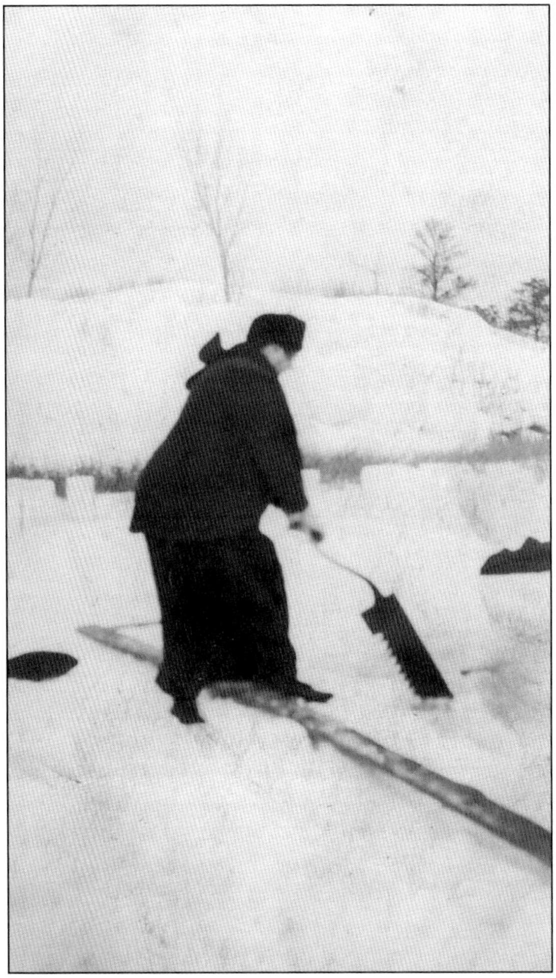

Before refrigeration, inland lakes such as Miller's Long Lake and the slough, fed by a creek running from the lake, were valuable assets in the winter. Ice harvesters cut blocks of ice from the frozen waters and stored them in big warehouses under hay and straw, for use by locals throughout the year. They were also shipped to Chicago, where meatpackers and restaurants used them to keep food cold during the summer. In the 1910s, Mr. White, the only African American in Miller at the time, would deliver the ice harvested from Lake Michigan and drive his horse and wagon down the street shouting "Iceman." He broke it into different sizes, usually 25- or 50-pound blocks, but some people even got 100-pound blocks. White would give the smaller chips of ice created when blocks were cut to children for free. (Courtesy of the Calumet Regional Archives, IU Northwest.)

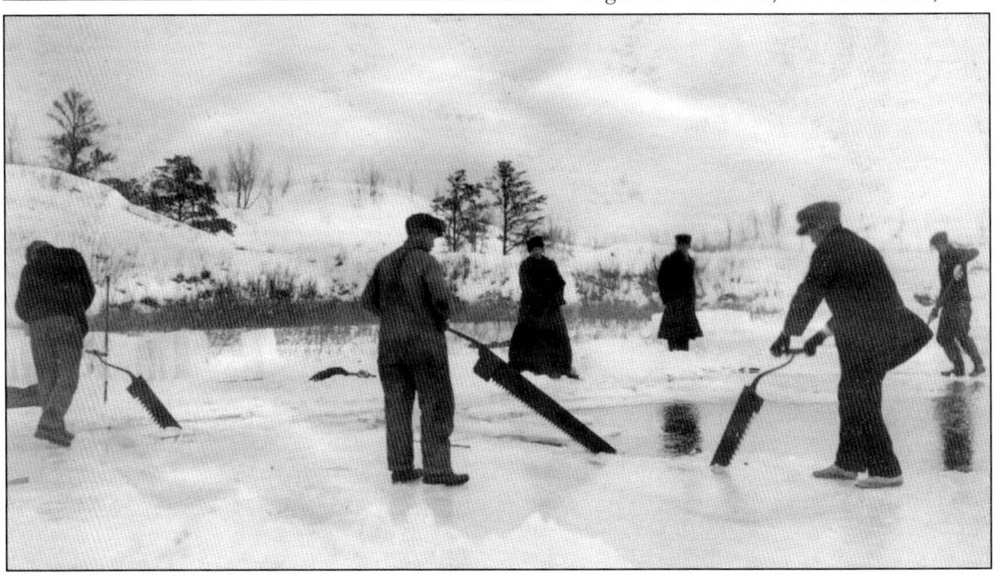

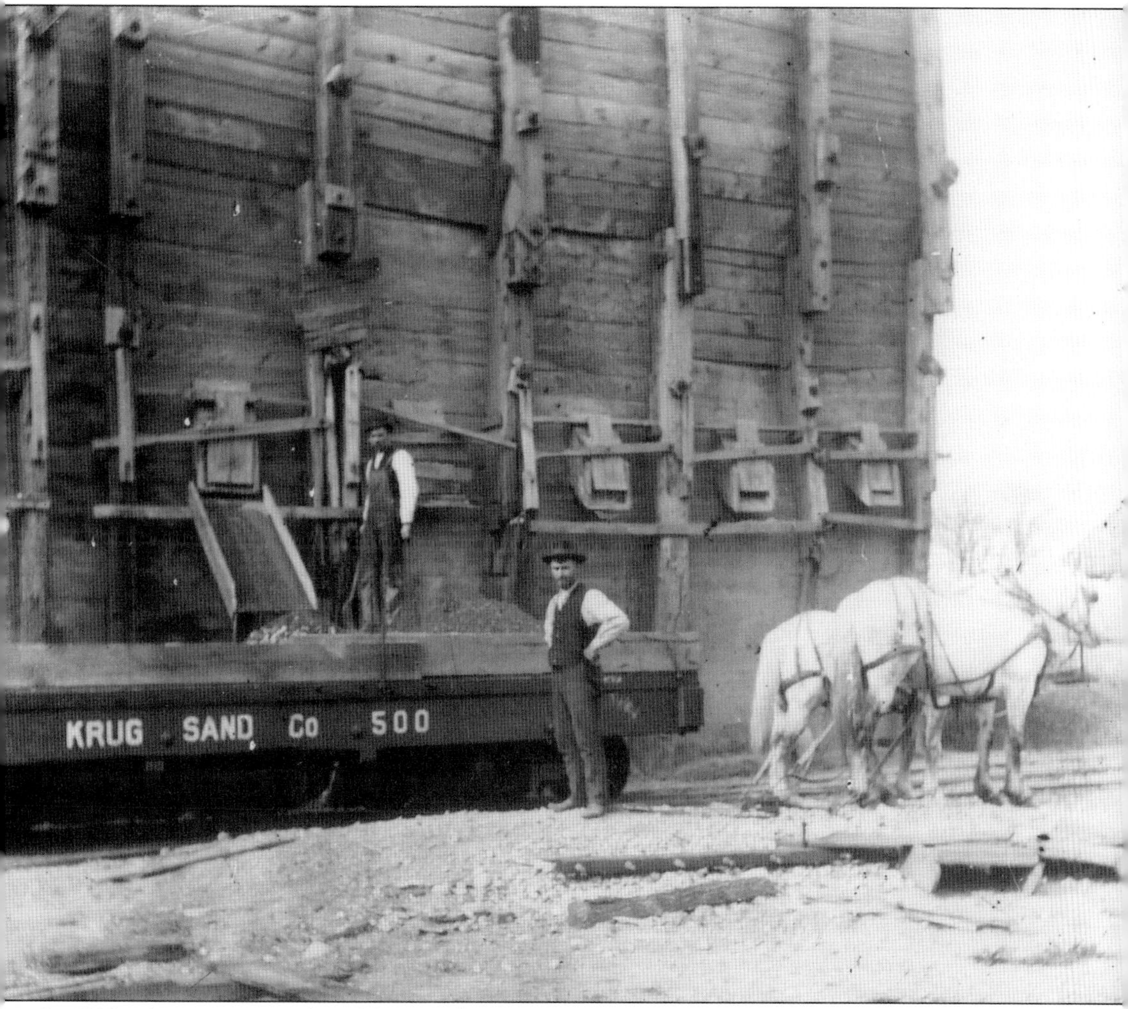

In 1893, a large amount of sand from Miller Beach was used to help fill in part of Lake Michigan for the Chicago World's Fair. The Chicago-based Prairie Club, incorporated in 1911, built a beach house for its members two years later. Prairie Club members and other beachgoers also erected tents and rough wooden cottages on the beach and in the dunes. Loving the area's beauty, they were outraged at the industrial sand mining, which was destroying the dunes, and that great swaths of beach were being purchased by the steel mill. A coalition of people joined together to save the area by turning it into a national park. Despite extensive publicity, as well as advocacy by such people as Stephen Mather, first director of the National Park Service, this effort was not immediately successful. (Courtesy of the Calumet Regional Archives, IU Northwest.)

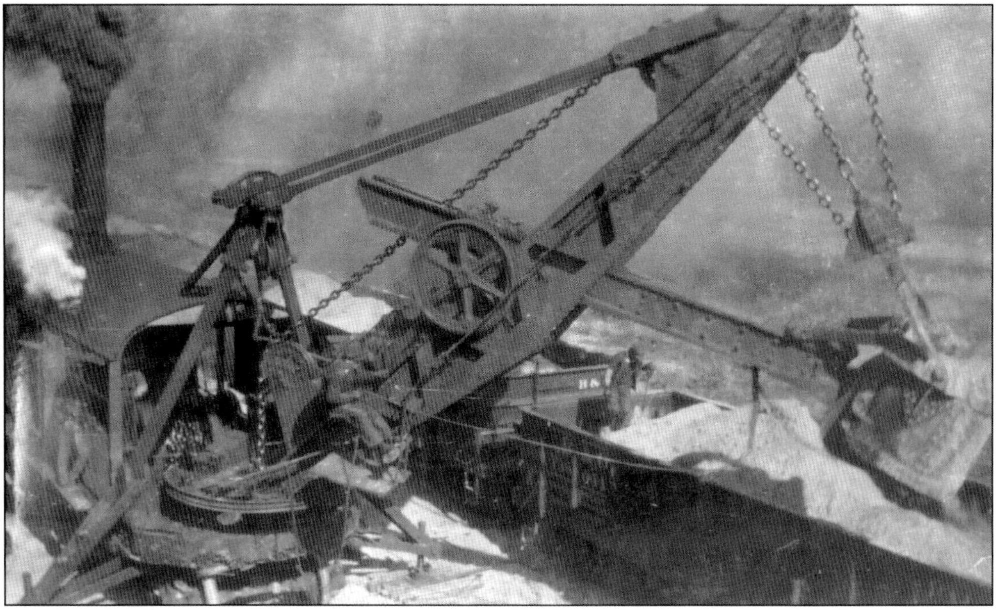

As early as the 1880s, sand mining companies hauled huge quantities of sand from the dunes for use at the steel mills lining the lakefronts of Gary and East Chicago. Sand was also used for Chicago landfills, building industries, and even the Chicago World's Fair. (Courtesy of Gene Ayers, Ayers Realtors, Inc.)

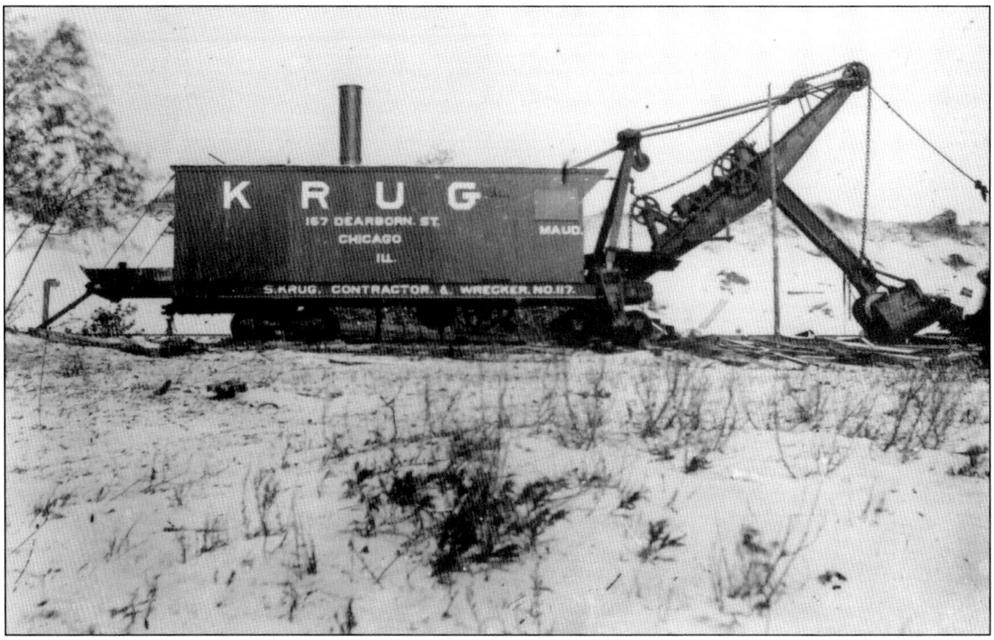

Though some saw the windswept dunes as much less attractive than national treasures like Yellowstone, Yosemite, and the Grand Canyon, others were determined to save them. Today, many longtime residents remember the tall dunes, including the one where Octave Chanute launched his historic flight. Many of those dunes were bulldozed, but environmentalists were ultimately able to save many of the area's beautiful beaches. (Courtesy of the Calumet Regional Archives, IU Northwest.)

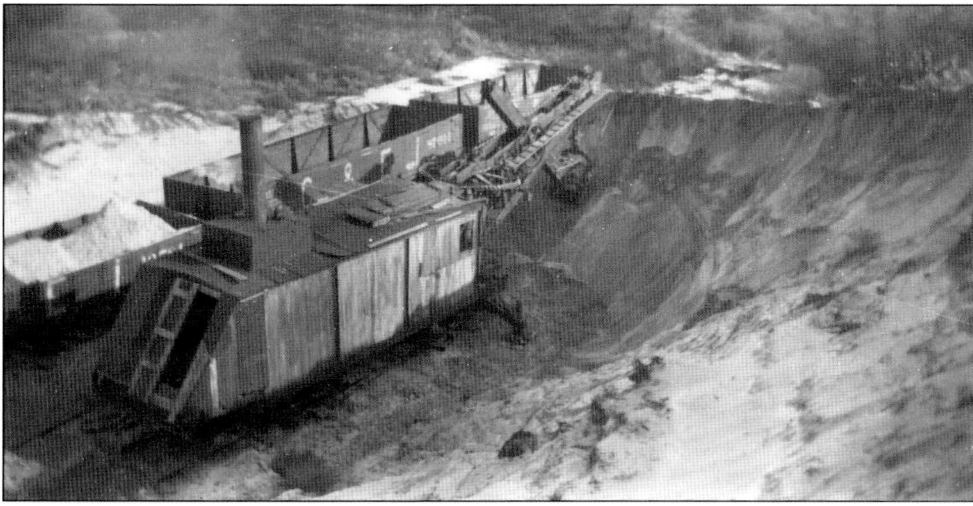

When the train arrived from Chicago with empty boxcars, men from Miller were hired to bring their wheelbarrows and were given a plank. Each man selected an empty car and started working, filling the wheelbarrow with sand, pushing it up the plank and dumping the sand into the empty railroad car. The pay was about $1 per car, with an added 10¢–25¢ for an extra large car. Few men were even able to fill one car per day. (Courtesy of the Calumet Regional Archives, IU Northwest.)

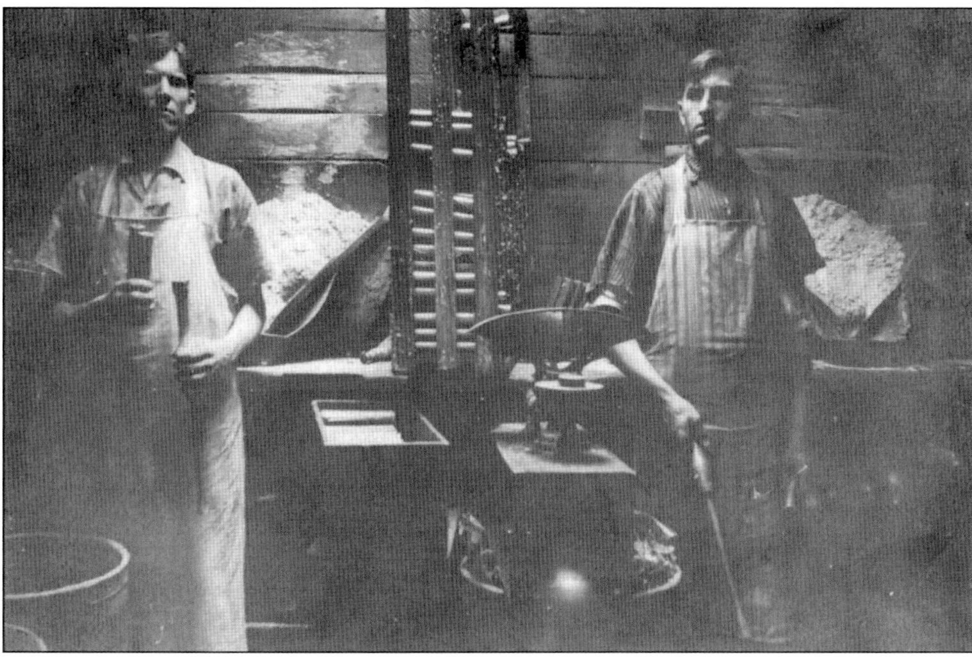

"3,000 Pounds of Nitro-glycerin Accidentally Explodes at the Aetna Powder Works: Three Men Blown Into Atoms and Parts of Their Bodies Found a Mile Away" read the headline of the *Chesterton Tribune* on April 12, 1888. The newspaper, in very graphic detail, told how the jobs of Henry Scott, John A. Gill, and H.L. Jansen, considered the most dangerous at a very dangerous work place, involved mixing nitroglycerin with pulp to create dynamite. One of them dropped a can of nitroglycerin on the floor, causing the explosion that destroyed the building and took their lives. Pictured are Miller residents Mr. Carlson and Andrew Lindstrom packing dynamite at Aetna Powder Works. (Courtesy of Verlaine Wright.)

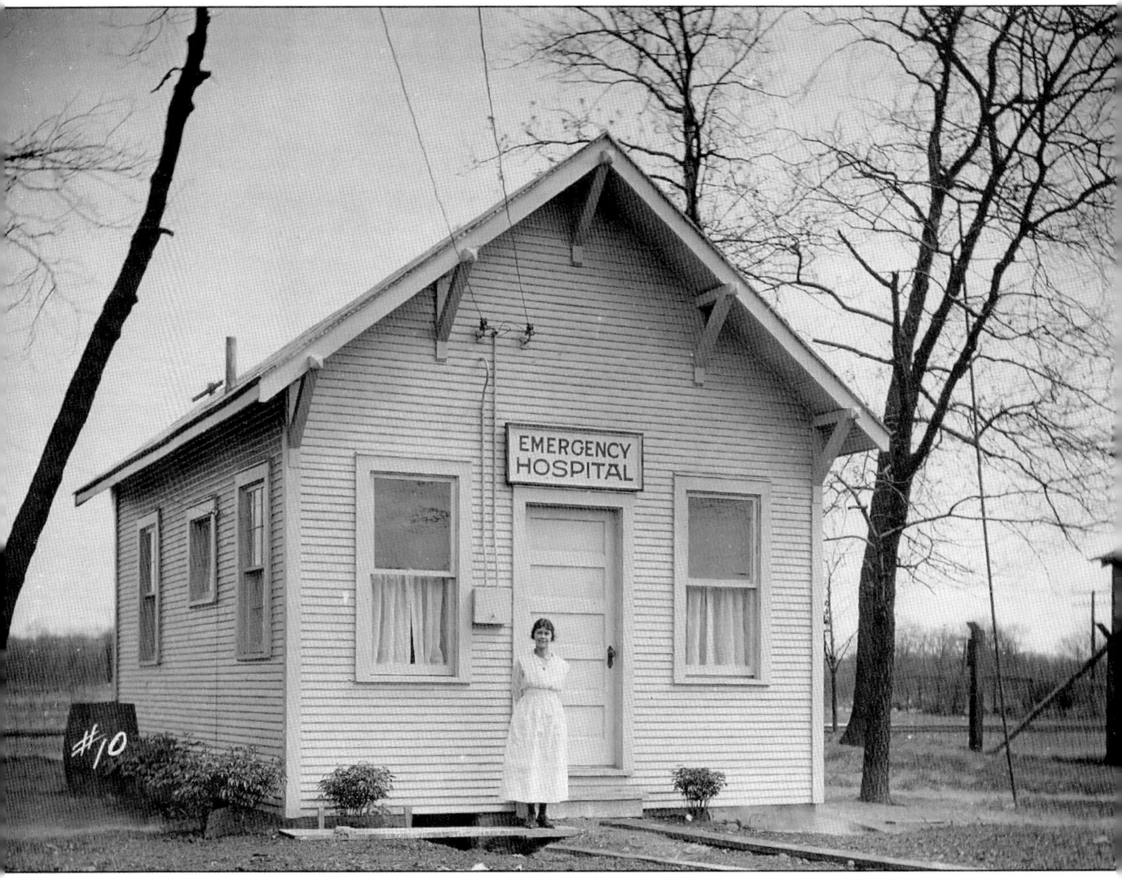

So many explosions occurred at the Aetna Powder Works that they had their own hospital. Six people died and 20 were injured in a 1912 explosion; two years later, a dynamite house perched at the top of a dune exploded with dreadful force, which was felt for miles around. Here, nurse Loretta Nusbaum stands in front of the Aetna Powder Company hospital. (Courtesy of the Calumet Regional Archives, IU Northwest.)

Four

Civic Life

Schools, Churches, and Public Institutions

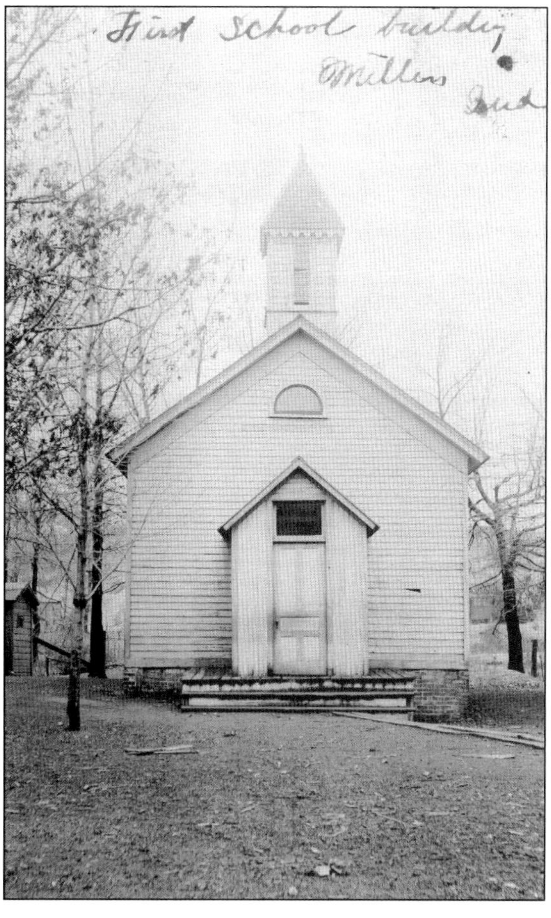

The first schoolhouse, a log cabin, was built in Miller in the late 1860s on South Henry Street. The building also housed the Swedish Evangelical Lutheran Church (now Bethel Lutheran), the first church established in Miller. It was replaced in the late 1870s by the wooden structure pictured here. (Courtesy of the Calumet Regional Archives, IU Northwest.)

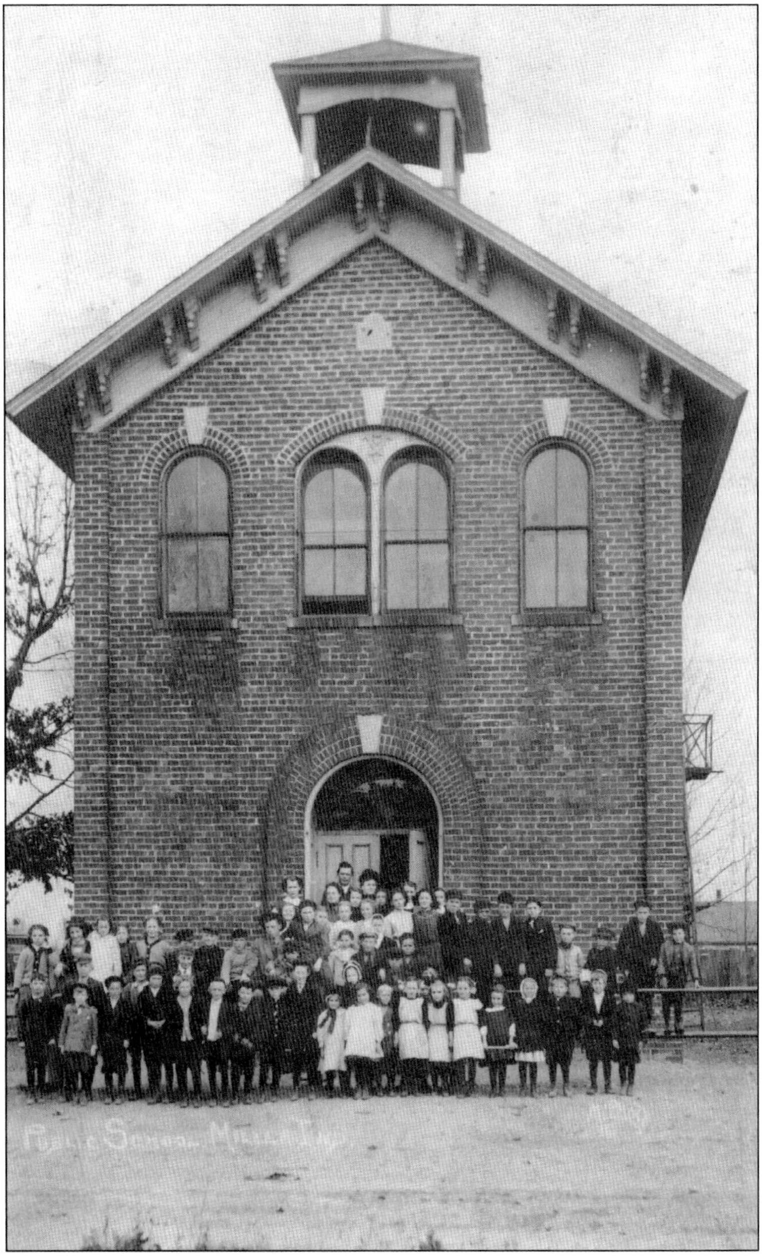

Miller pioneer Alfred Anderson, who moved to Miller in 1864 when he was eight years old, recalled his time at the first school. It was established in 1867, "when a man named Osterman came to Miller from the head of Long Lake in Porter County and built a five-room house, with a saloon on one side and a school on the other." Their first teacher was Mrs. Davis, the wife of a boat captain. Anderson remembered, "Sometimes when we were in school, 30 or 40 wood-choppers would come to the saloon and start a fight. We could hear them bumping against the walls, then the teacher would tell us all to get out and go home." The second school building was built about 10 years later at Sixth Avenue and Lake Street and was replaced by a brick building in the 1890s, shown here with students posing in front of it, and finally by a larger school building in 1910. (Courtesy of Verlaine Wright.)

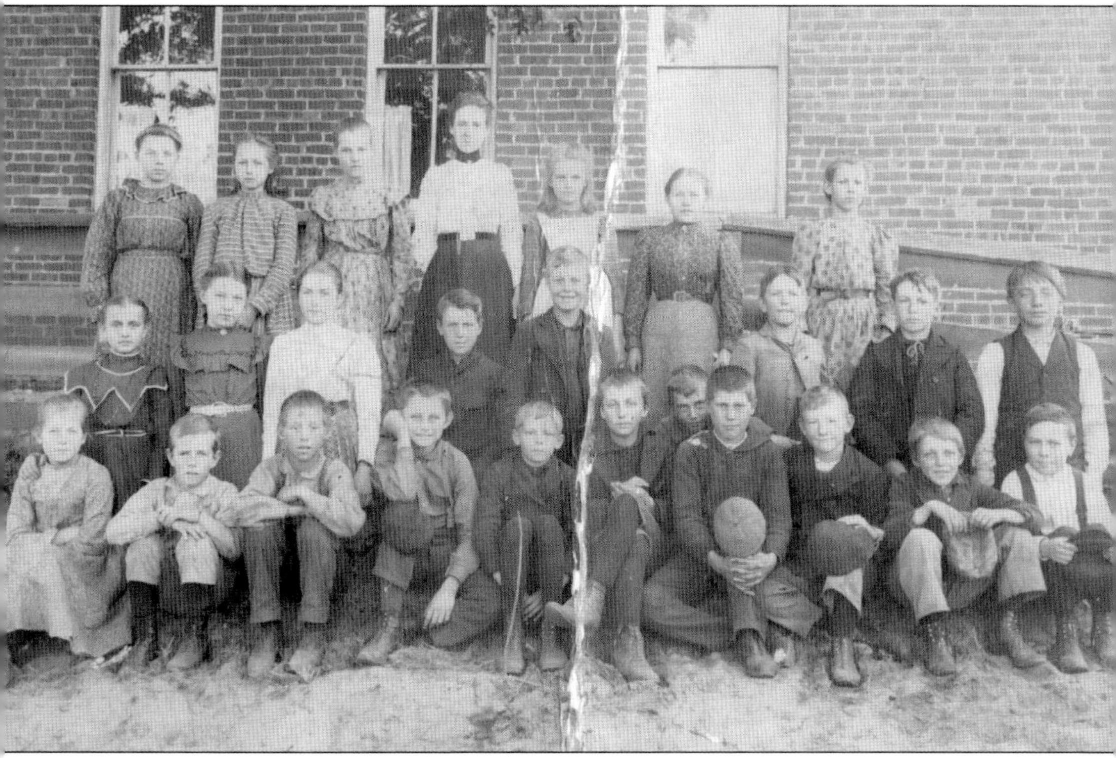

The third school building in Miller was in use from the early 1890s to 1909 and was replaced by the still-standing Miller School building, which was closed in the 1990s and later used as a dance studio. In front of the third building are fourth- and fifth-graders in 1901 or 1902, from left to right, (first row) Edith Carlson, Clyde Kenney, Andrew Johnson, Jack Ryan, Earle Kohler, Martin Nicholson, Algert Peterson, Axel Carlson, Adolph Nicholson, and Roy Cook; (second row) Theresa Mayhak, Teresa May Johnson, Ruth Nicholson, Albin Gustafson, Floyd Olson, Gilbert Nelson, Edwin Johnson, William Graham, and Warren Barnes; (third row) Lizzie Hippi, Clara North, Tina Johnson, Teacher Lena Triebess, Esther Johnson, Emma Johnson, and Hattie Sabinske. (Courtesy of Verlaine Wright.)

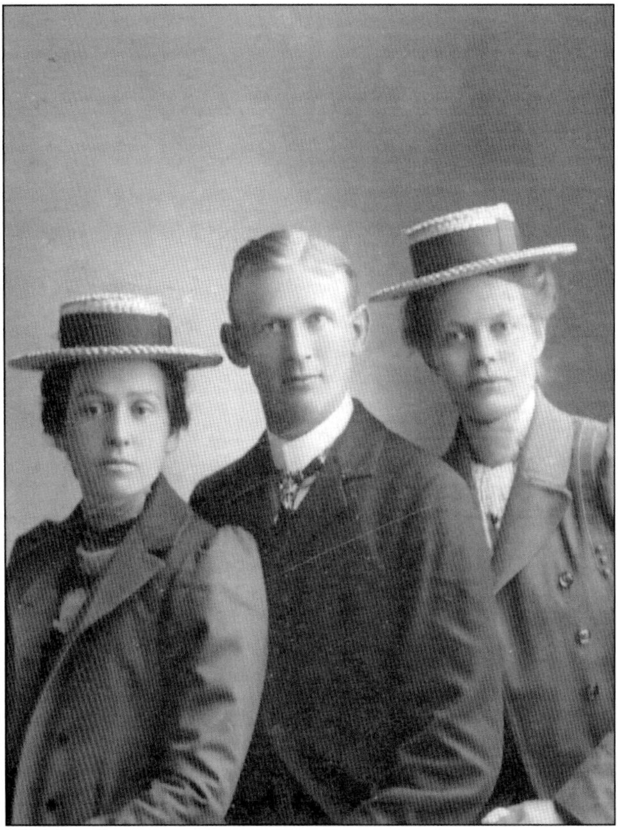

At left, from left to right, is the faculty of the Miller School from the early 1900s: Lena Triebess Peterson, George F. Peterson, and Clara Hazel Green. The booklet for the "Annual Commencement Exercises of the Eighth Grade of Miller School" (below) from 1898 lists seven graduates: Hannah Johnson, Mae Sperb, Emma North, Carl Olander, Clara Peterson, Esther Nelson, and Arthur Carnduff. Also, six students are noted for completing their second year of high school: Lillie Blank, Esther Blank, Frank Cook, Banard Peterson, Clara Peterson, and Laura Johnson. A 1903 commencement program lists Miller as District No. 8 of the Hobart Township Public Schools, with the following seven Miller graduates: Hannah Peterson, Hattie Anderson, Elnore Olson, Agnes Carlson, Myrtle M. Barnes, Agnes North, and Francy Carlson. (Courtesy of Linda Simon.)

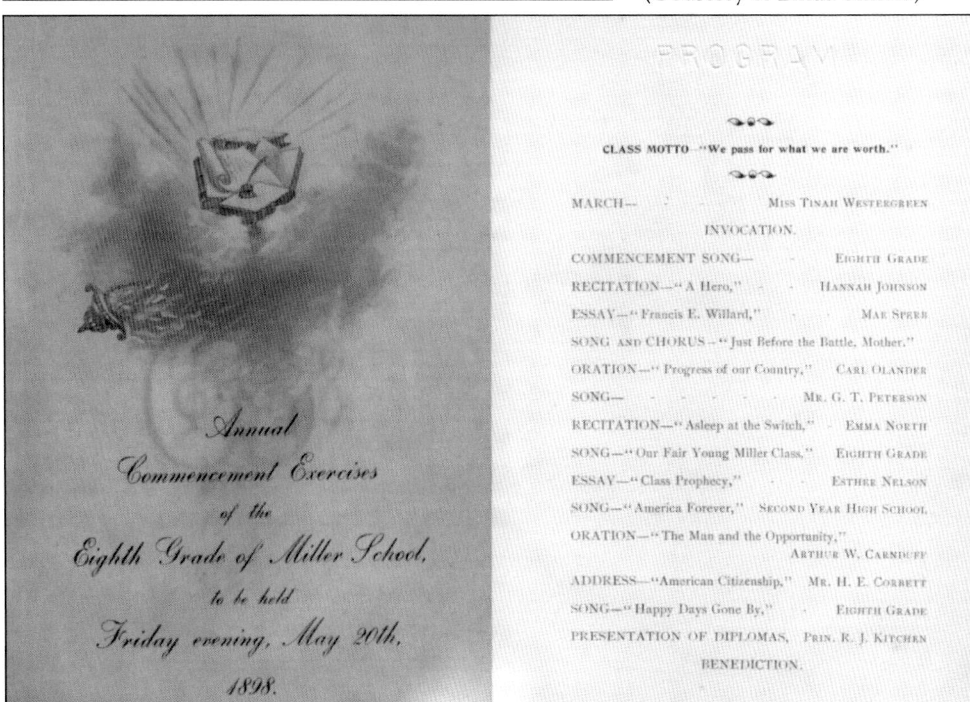

Annual
Commencement Exercises
of the
Eighth Grade of Miller School,
to be held
Friday evening, May 20th,
1898.

PROGRAM

CLASS MOTTO—"We pass for what we are worth."

MARCH— Miss Tinah Westergreen

INVOCATION.

COMMENCEMENT SONG— Eighth Grade

RECITATION—"A Hero," Hannah Johnson

ESSAY—"Francis E. Willard," Mae Sperb

SONG and CHORUS—"Just Before the Battle, Mother."

ORATION—"Progress of our Country," Carl Olander

SONG— Mr. G. T. Peterson

RECITATION—"Asleep at the Switch," Emma North

SONG—"Our Fair Young Miller Class," Eighth Grade

ESSAY—"Class Prophecy," Esther Nelson

SONG—"America Forever," Second Year High School.

ORATION—"The Man and the Opportunity,"
Arthur W. Carnduff

ADDRESS—"American Citizenship," Mr. H. E. Corbett

SONG—"Happy Days Gone By," Eighth Grade

PRESENTATION OF DIPLOMAS, Prin. R. J. Kitchen

BENEDICTION.

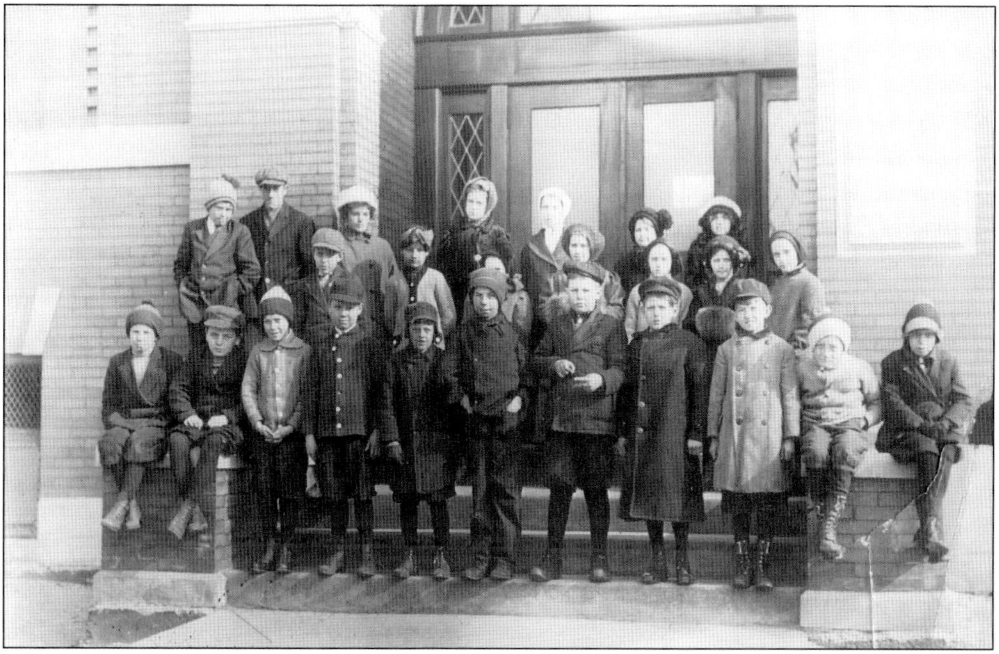

The third Miller School building was torn down to make room for a larger three-story brick structure, which was opened in 1910. It eventually became part of the Gary public school system and served for many years. Above, a group of students stands on the steps of the Miller School at Sixth Avenue and Lake Street in the late 1910s. Below, students stand in front of the Miller School in 1920. Students include Ethel Bowgren, Esther Carlson, Eleanore Nelson, Aldean Myers, and Charlene Bailey. The children's teacher, Miss Carlson, stands in the back row. The school became home to the South Shore Centre for the Arts in 2007. (Above, courtesy of Marilyn Leech and Holly Rodino Breese; below, courtesy of Laura Valentine Jones.)

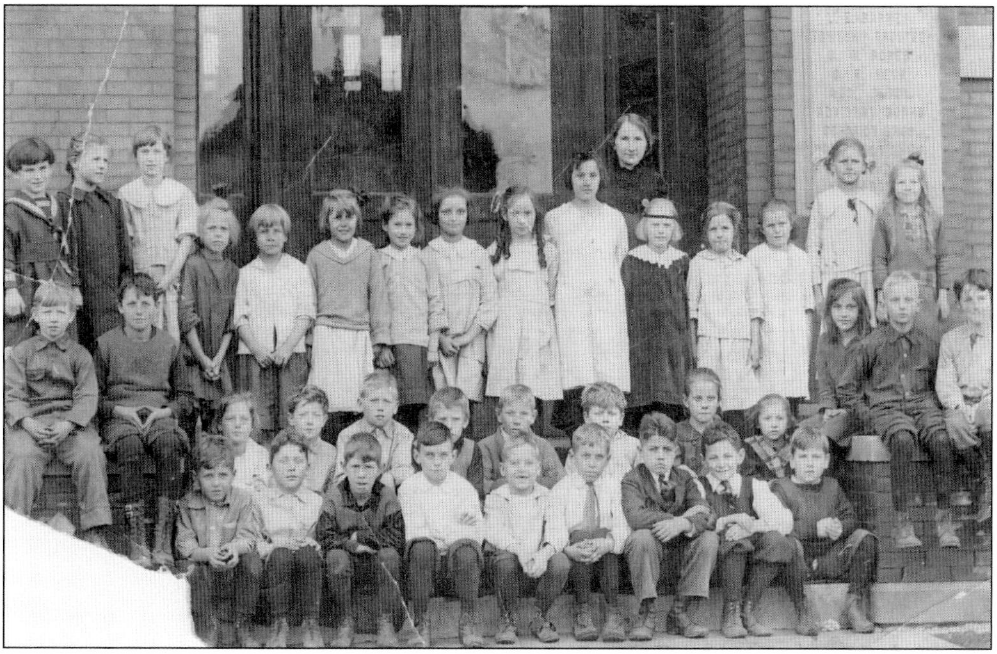

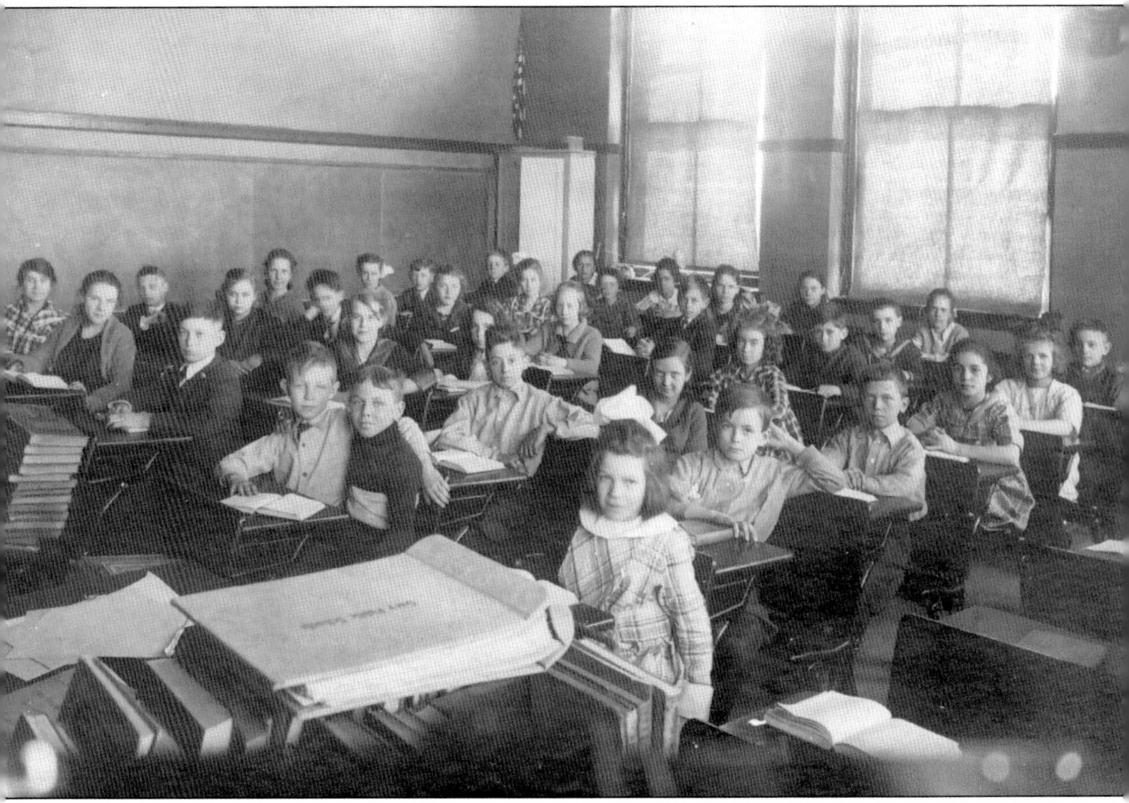

Students posed at their desks inside Miller School at Sixth Avenue and Lake Street in the late 1910s or early 1920s, shortly after Miller was annexed by Gary and the school became part of the Gary system. In the front row, sharing a seat with another boy, is Samuel O. Jones, whose father, A.H. Jones, was the director of visual education for Gary Public Schools. The visual education program was part of the auditorium period of the platoon—or work-study-play—system established by William A. Wirt, the first superintendent of schools in Gary. As part of their education, students spent time in the auditorium watching educational films and slides or practicing public speaking, among other things. (Courtesy of Laura Valentine Jones.)

Eugene Cantwell and Laura Valentine (right) are dressed up for a play at Miller School featuring "Kinskie and his little sweetheart, Louisa." Plays were put on through the school's auditorium department. The Miller School faculty, pictured below in the early 1930s, included, from left to right, (first row) Mrs. Kirby and four unidentified; (second row) Miss Erwin, the sewing teacher, who also ran the cafeteria; Mildred Kelly, the gym teacher; Helen Huber; Principal George Russell; Edward Goforth, who taught math and manual training; unidentified; and Bertha Ramsey who, in 1923, became the first kindergarten teacher at the Miller School. (Courtesy of Laura Valentine Jones.)

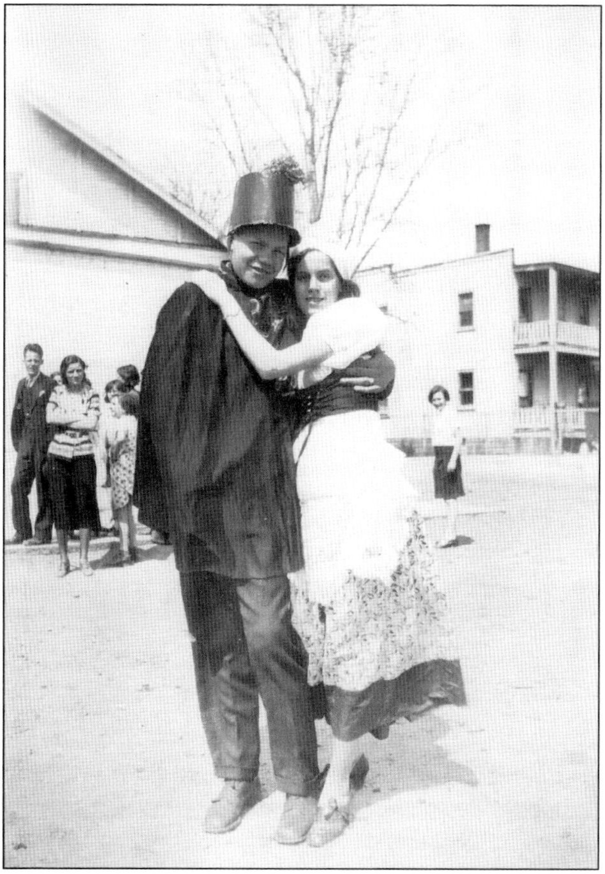

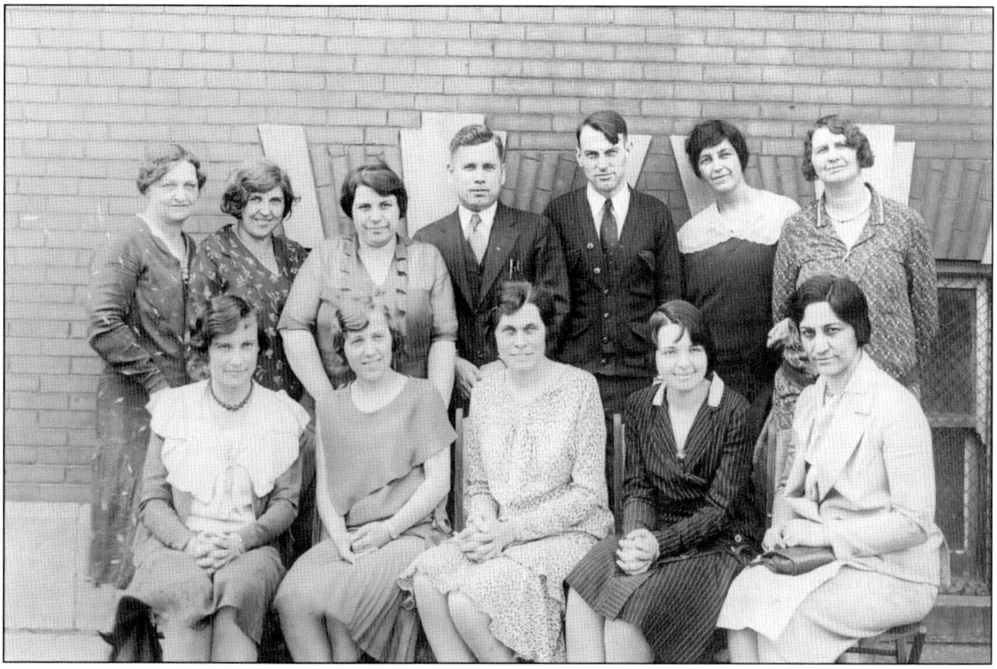

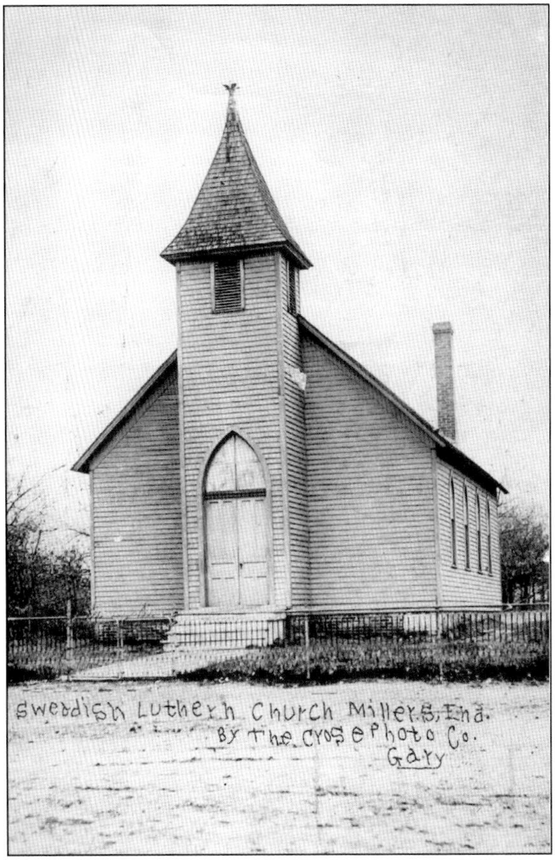

In the 1860s and 1870s, Swedish immigrant Svanti Nordstrom often acted as lay-preacher to the Swedes in Miller. Occasionally, ministers from nearby Lutheran churches in Baillytown and Hobart came to perform sacraments. In 1874, Nordstrom determined that Miller needed its own church and worked hard to help establish the Swedish Evangelical Lutheran Church. The church conducted services in the first and second Miller School houses until moving to its own building (left) at Fourth Avenue and Lake Street in 1894. Services continued in Swedish until 1929, when the congregation added an English-language service every Sunday morning to go along with its Swedish services in the afternoon. The postcard below shows the old church decorated for Christmas in 1907, with a distinctly Swedish flair. (Left, courtesy of the Calumet Regional Archives, IU Northwest; below, courtesy of Bethel Lutheran Church.)

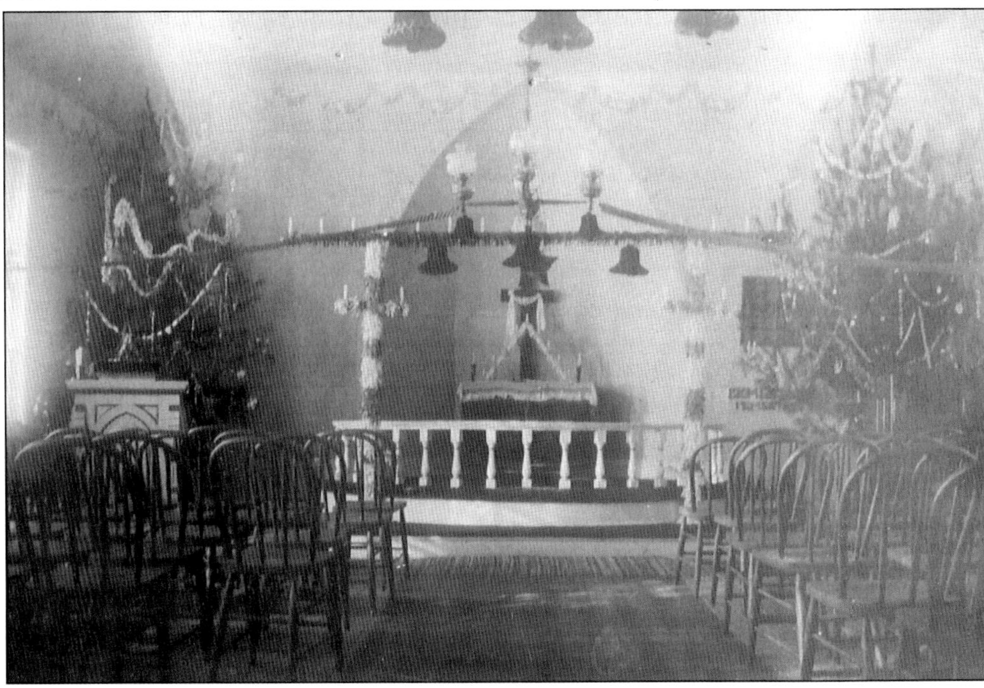

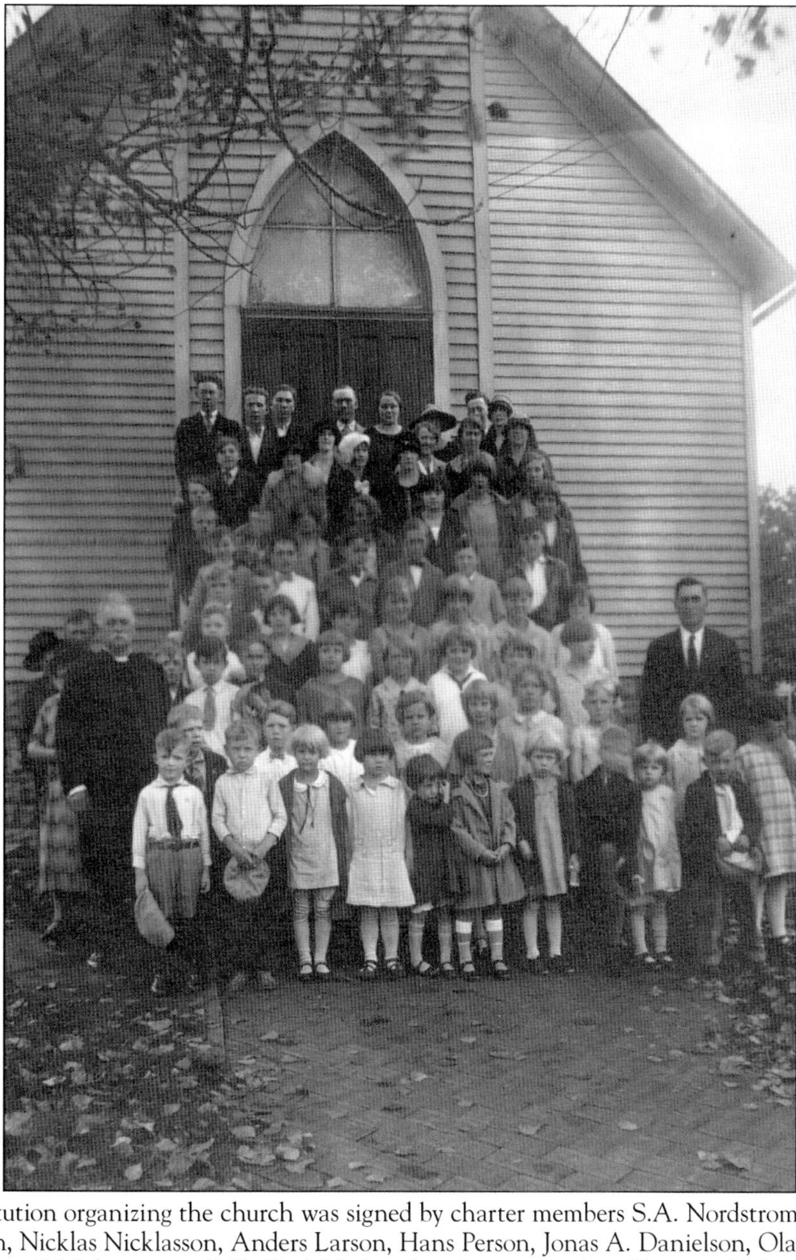

A constitution organizing the church was signed by charter members S.A. Nordstrom, Magnus Anderson, Nicklas Nicklasson, Anders Larson, Hans Person, Jonas A. Danielson, Olaus Olson, J.W. Jonson, C.J. Johnson, and Nils Sjodahl. Another charter member, Christina Nelson, was not allowed to sign because she was a woman. At its founding, the church combined efforts with the Lutheran Church in Hobart and shared its minister. The first regular pastor of the church was J.A. Berg, who arrived in 1905. The first confirmation class from Miller's Lutheran community consisted of Jennie and Alfred Anderson, who traveled to the Lutheran church in Bailllytown for instruction under Rev. C.H. Sodergren in 1872, before Bethel Lutheran was founded. According to church records, the two siblings either walked, ice skated across Long Lake, or occasionally hitched a ride on the train to reach their confirmation classes. These Bethel Sunday School students gathered on the church steps in the 1920s. Rev. J.G. Dahlberg, the pastor at Bethel Lutheran from 1924 to 1933, stands at left. (Courtesy of Verlaine Wright.)

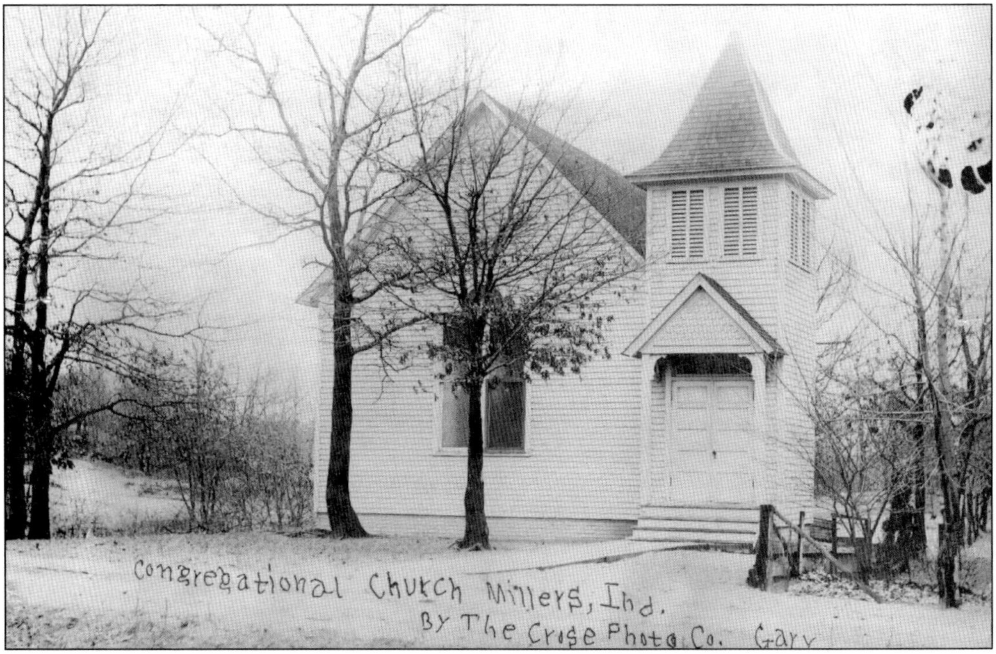

The Chapel of the Dunes (above, in the early 1900s) was established as the First Congregational Church of Miller in 1901. At the time of its founding, Miller included a general store, two saloons, a one-room primary schoolhouse, a two-room schoolhouse for the upper grades, and one church, Bethel Lutheran, which conducted its services in Swedish. The need for an English-language church was plain and Chapel of the Dunes started with Sunday School classes and services with ministers from neighboring Hobart churches. Eight individuals—six women and two men—signed the charter for the Congregational Church on May 16, 1901. The churchwomen formed the Sunshine Club to help raise funds, holding oyster suppers and other social events. The money was used to build a church on land donated by Simcoe Daly, a surveyor from Kingston, Ontario, who owned real estate in Miller at Third Avenue and Lake Street. Below, Sunday School students pose outside in 1915. (Above, courtesy of Laura Valentine Jones; below, courtesy of the Calumet Regional Archives, IU Northwest.)

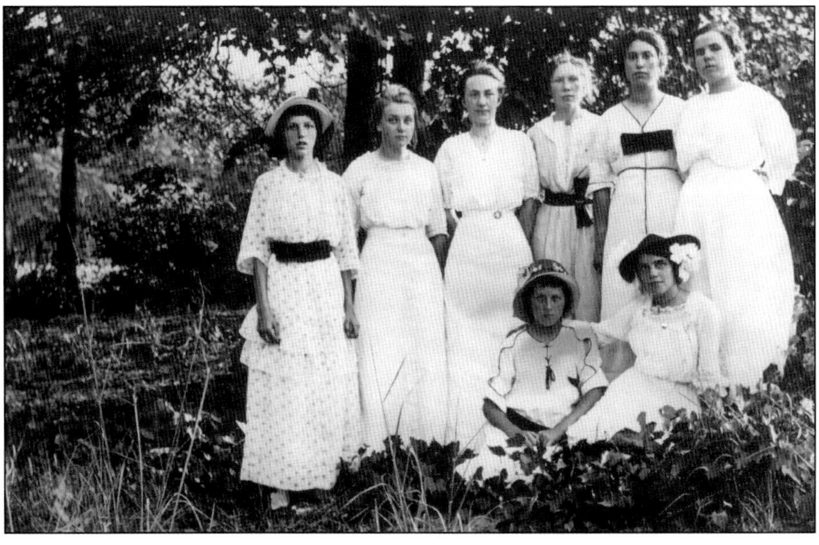

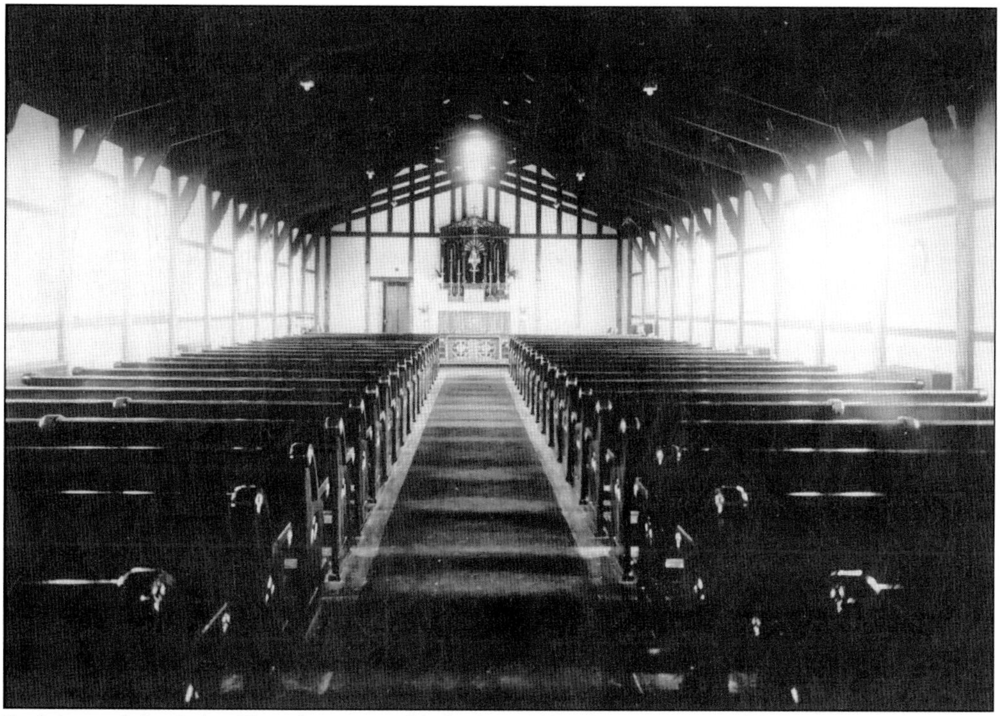

St. Mary of the Lake Church was established in 1929. Prior to its establishment, Catholics in Miller would usually travel to Holy Angels Cathedral in downtown Gary to attend services. The first priest at St. Mary's was Francis Xavier Guerre, who was assistant pastor at Holy Angels Cathedral before being assigned to St. Mary of the Lake. Miller also served as the vacation home of the first Catholic priest in Gary, Rev. Francis Thomas Jansen, who lived in an early cottage on Lake Shore Drive starting in the 1930s. Father Jansen headed up a mission in Gary when the city was founded in 1906 and rode on horseback to spread Christianity before helping establish Holy Angels Cathedral in 1909. The interior and exterior of St. Mary of the Lake Church are shown here at its dedication on May 10, 1931. (Courtesy of Chris Papineau Rogers.)

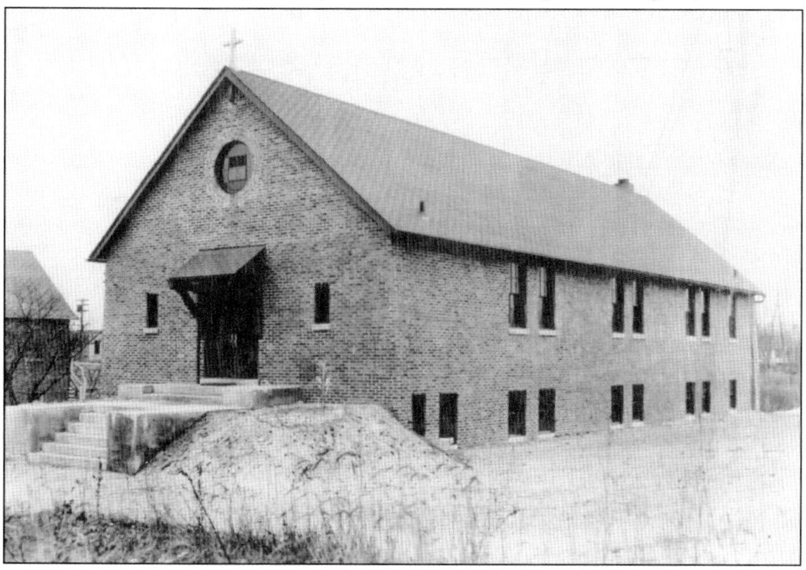

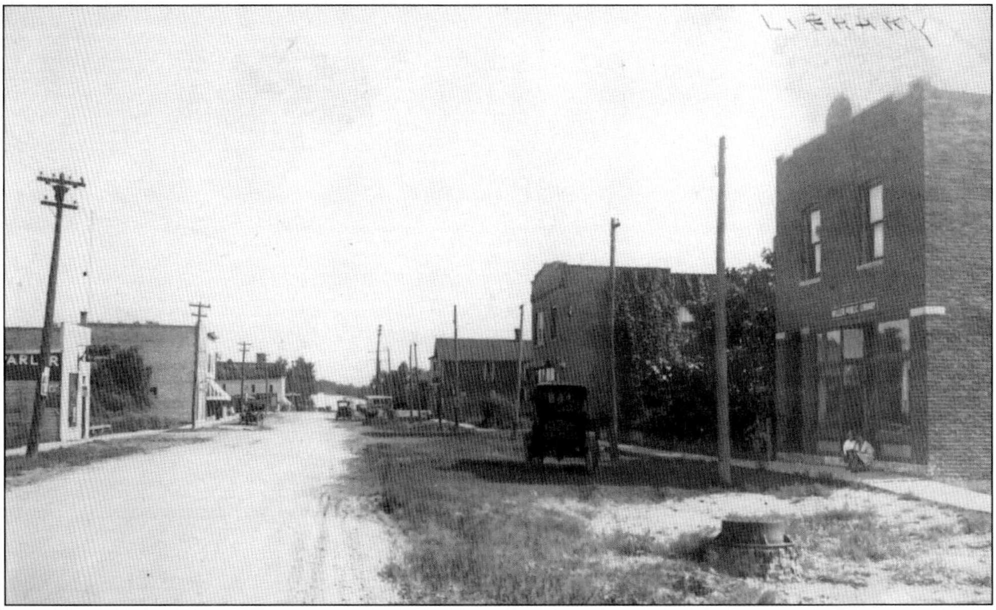

The Miller Library (at right) is seen here in the late 1910s, when it was located on the west side of Lake Street, just south of the original Bethel Lutheran Church. According to some sources, Miller's first library was in a converted home on Sixth Place near Lake Street, just east of the Miller School, with Florence Nelson Graham as librarian. (Courtesy of the Calumet Regional Archives, IU Northwest.)

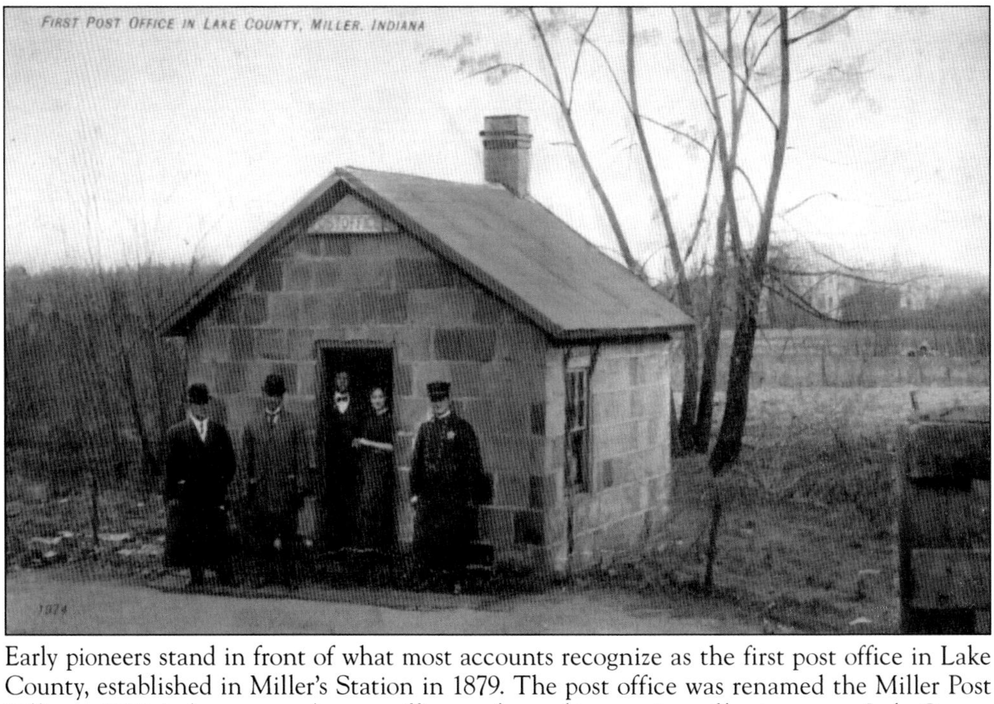

Early pioneers stand in front of what most accounts recognize as the first post office in Lake County, established in Miller's Station in 1879. The post office was renamed the Miller Post Office in 1882. In later years, the post office was housed in a variety of businesses on Lake Street, including Stillson's Grocery and Todd's Confectionery, before getting a new permanent home on Hancock Street. (Courtesy of Laura Valentine Jones.)

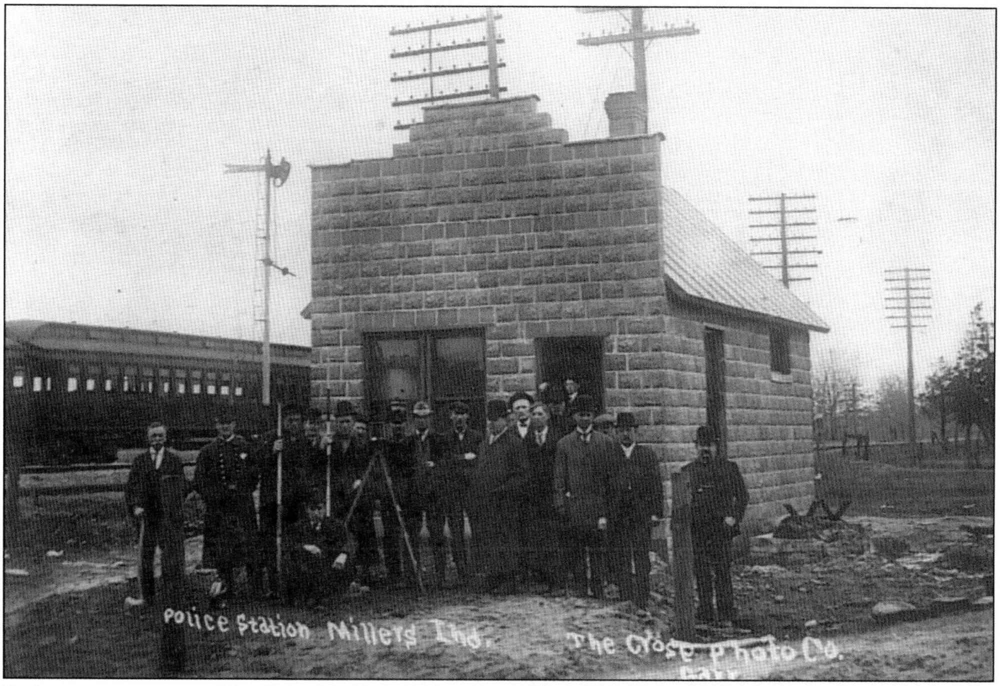

Before it was annexed by Gary, Miller residents established a police station (above) and their own force. After annexation, the Gary police force was responsible for providing police protection. Originally located near the junction of Lake Street and the B&O Railroad and also including a jail, the station was later moved to a spot near the Miller Town Hall on Miller Avenue. Below, Gary policeman Lester Lucas sits on his motorcycle in front of his sister, Lillian Lucas Leech, in the 1920s. Lillian Leech was the wife of Herbert A. Leech, son of the owners of Leech's Tavern on Lake Street. (Above, courtesy of Joyce Davis, Lake Street Gallery; below, courtesy of Marilyn Leech and Holly Rodino Breese.)

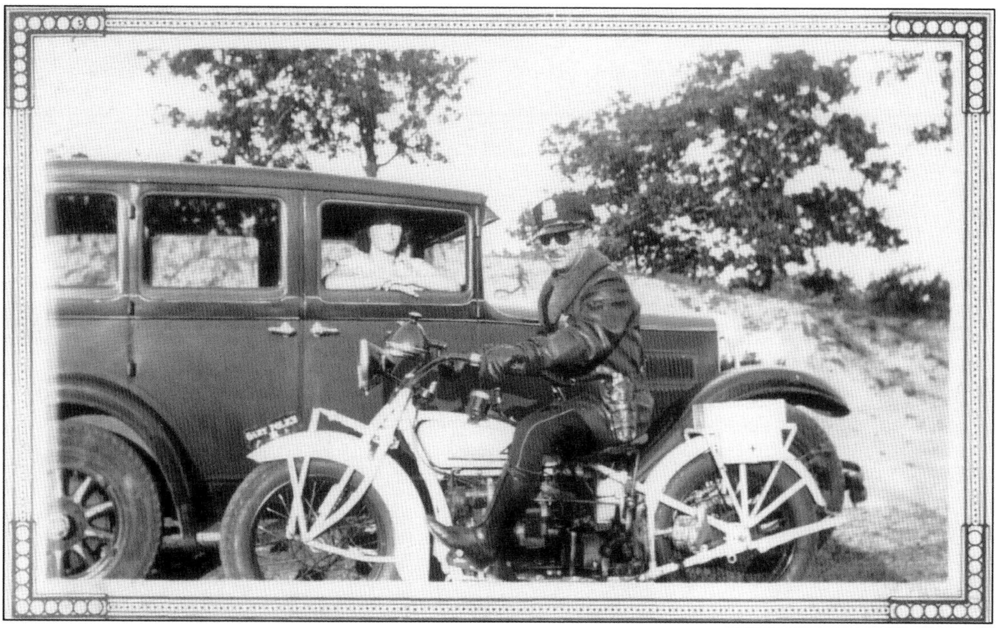

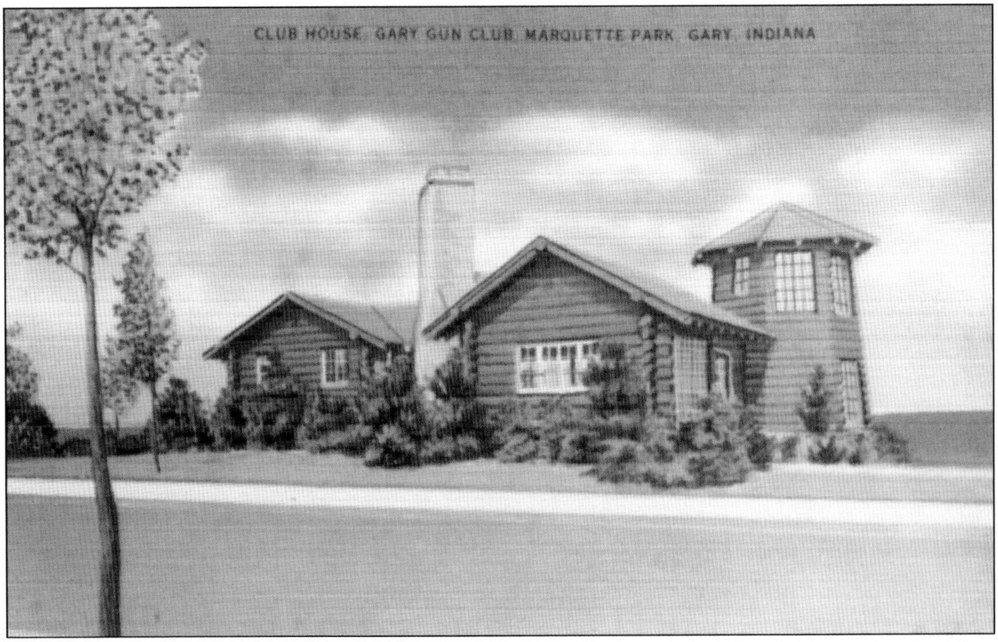

In addition to the pavilion and the bathhouse, Marquette Park included the clubhouse for the Gary Gun Club (above), a municipal rifle range also referred to as the Gun Club of Marquette Park. The clubhouse was located at the east end of the park at Montgomery Street and Oak Avenue. It was a faux log cabin in a lovely setting surrounded by pine trees. In addition to the clubhouse, the club built concrete bunkers in the dunes, from which they practiced skeet shooting over the lake. (Courtesy of Linda Simon.)

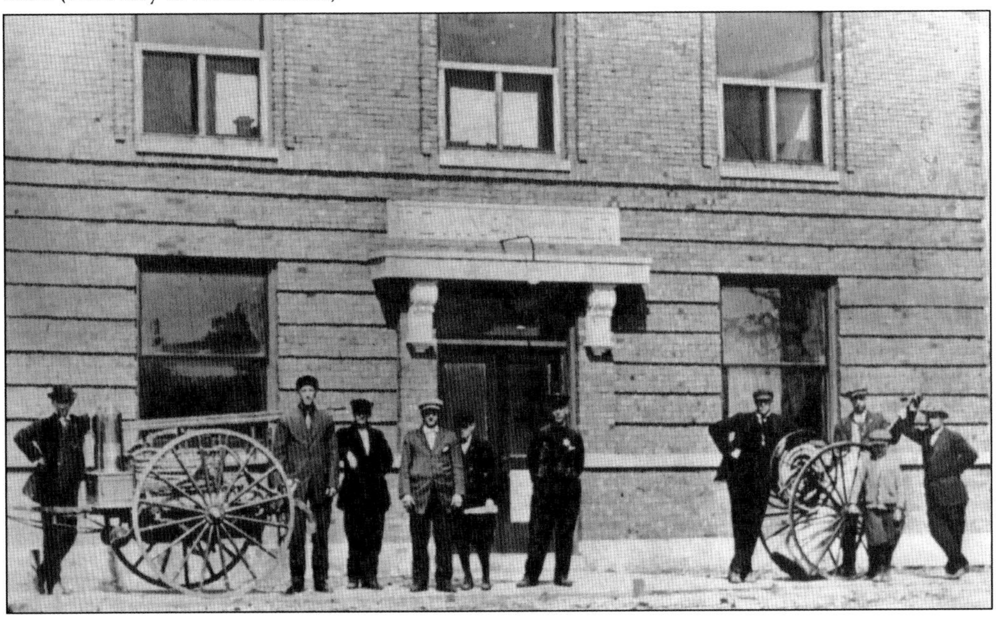

The Miller town hall was completed in 1911 and served in that capacity until Miller's annexation by Gary in 1918. After that, the building was used as a firehouse until 1975. It was listed in the National Register of Historic Places in 1978. (Courtesy of the Calumet Regional Archives, IU Northwest.)

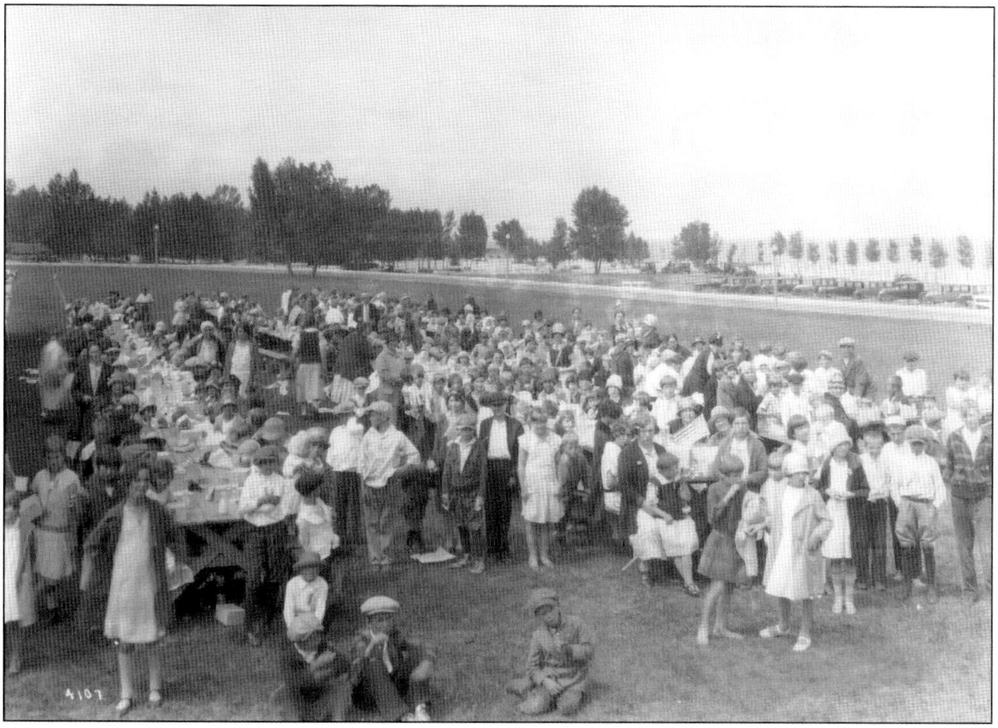

Picnickers enjoy a good meal at Marquette Park in this 1927 photograph titled "Welfare Department Picnic." The image is from the US Steel Collection at the Calumet Regional Archives. (Courtesy of the Calumet Regional Archives, IU Northwest.)

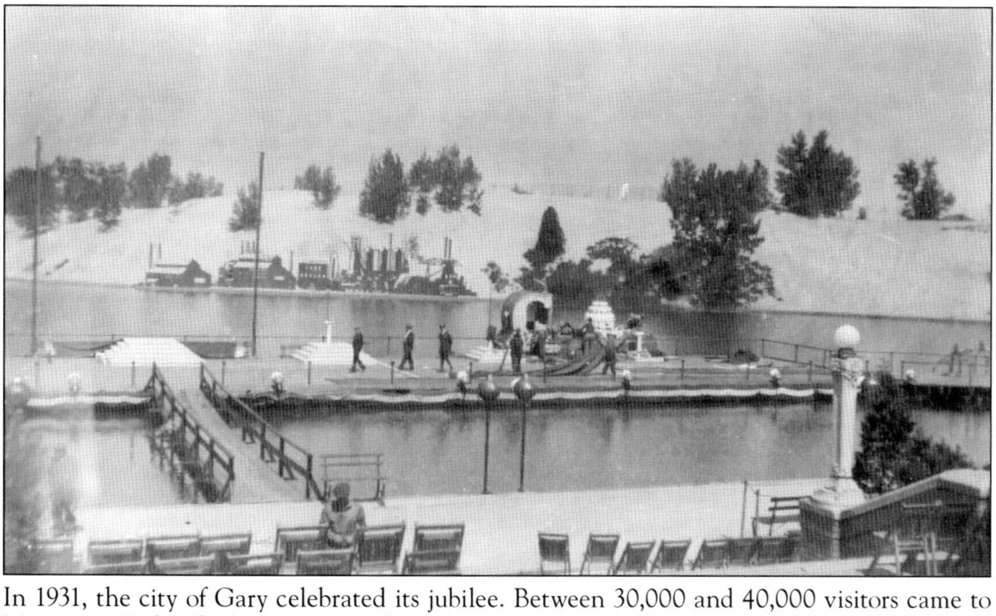

In 1931, the city of Gary celebrated its jubilee. Between 30,000 and 40,000 visitors came to Marquette Park, which was prepared for the occasion with bleachers, floating exhibits in the lagoon, and a miniature replica of a steel mill. Newspaper accounts reported that 10,000 cars came into the park, with bumper-to-bumper traffic stretching from the park entrance all the way to Aetna, several miles away. (Courtesy of the Calumet Regional Archives, IU Northwest.)

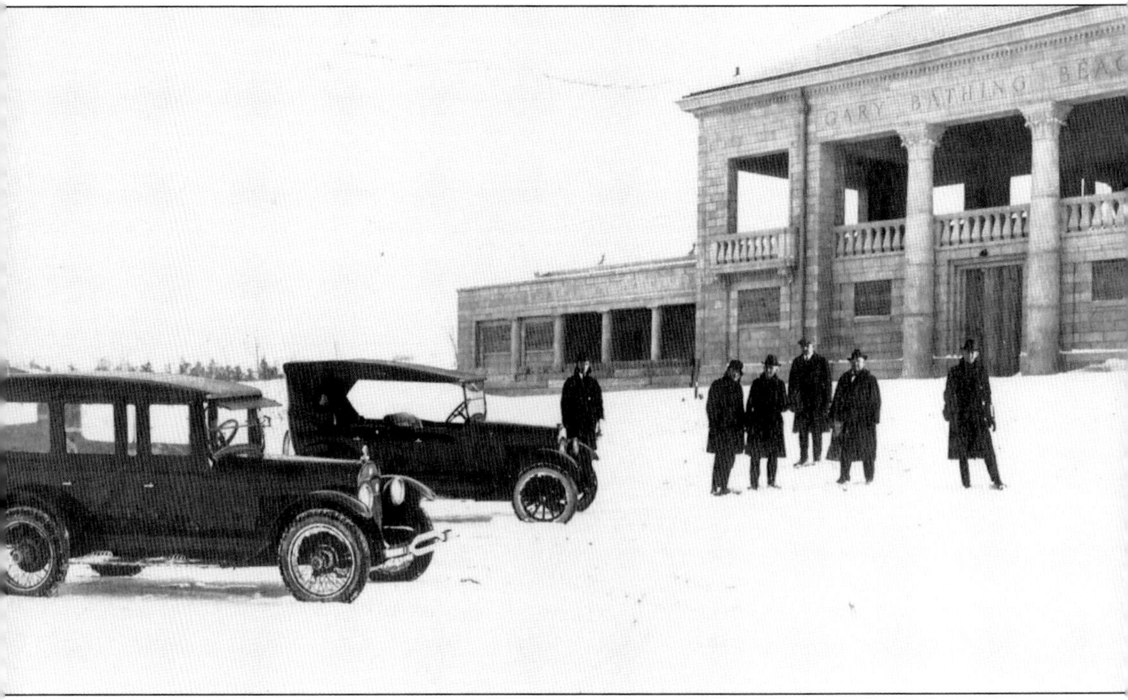

The Gary bathhouse, also in Marquette Park, is another historic Gary structure, designed by Prairie School architect George W. Maher in the Classical Revival style. It opened in 1921 and rented bathing suits for 50¢. It attracted visitors to the lakefront, first by rail and then by car, until it closed in the 1970s. A 1941 postcard describes the bathhouse as containing 2,000 lockers and floodlight towers for evening bathing. The beach was manned by lifeguards and included a special children's section with a playground. The shuttered bathhouse was saved by a group of Miller citizens, the "Aquatorium Society," who have extensively renovated the building, which now offers meeting and party spaces and contains photographs honoring the Tuskegee Airmen, Octave Chanute, and Miller's bygone days. (Courtesy of the Calumet Regional Archives, IU Northwest.)

Five

Flight and Flora

Octave Chanute and Henry Chandler Cowles

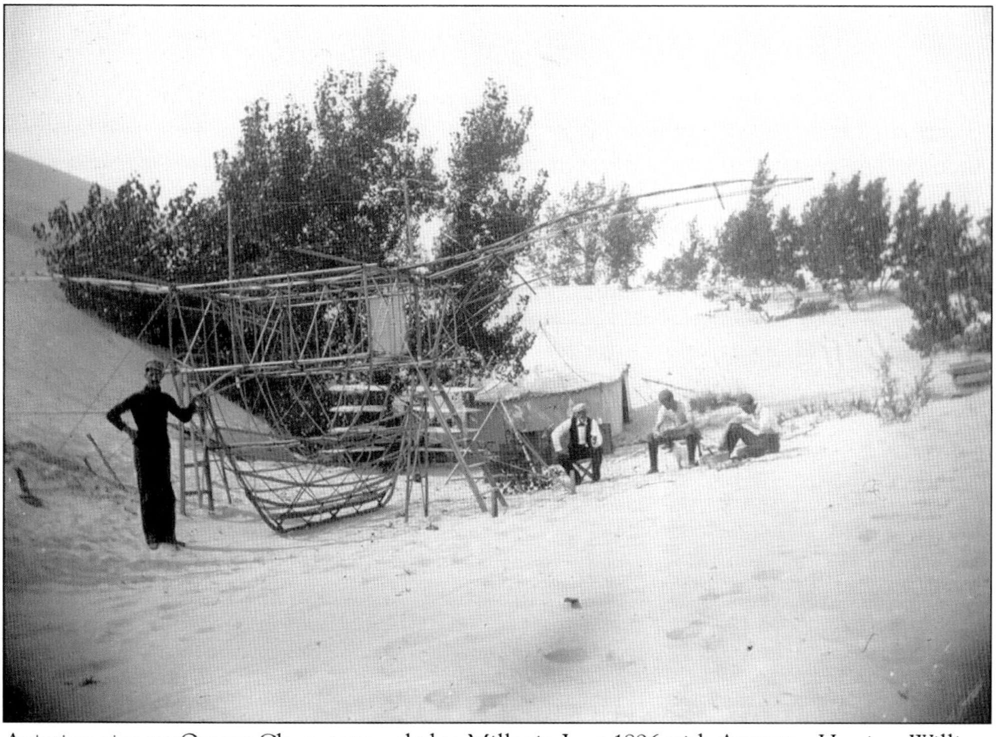

Aviation pioneer Octave Chanute traveled to Miller in June 1896 with Augustus Herring, William Avery, and William Butusov, a Russian who designed the Albatross, another experimental aircraft. They set up camp in the dunes, and while no images of their Miller camp remain, the four men are seen here with the Albatross at the group's camp east of Miller later that summer. From left to right are Butusov, Chanute, Avery, and Herring. (Octave Chanute Photo Album, Manuscript Division, Library of Congress, Washington, DC.)

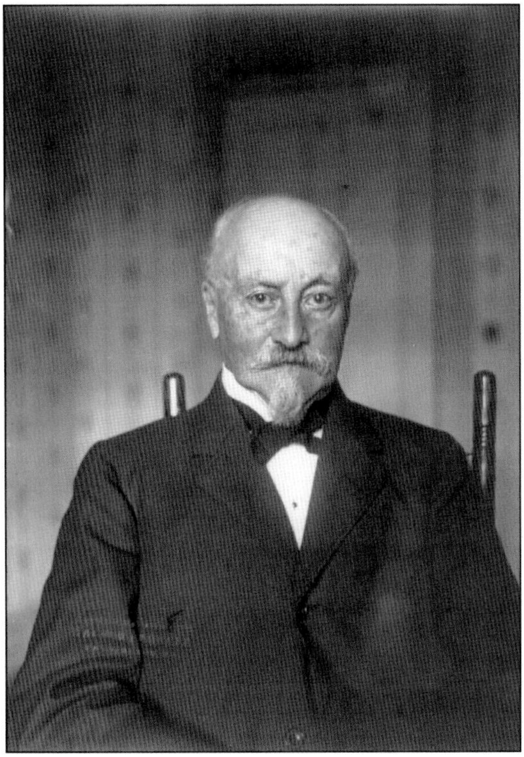

Octave Chanute, seen at left in a 1908 portrait, was born in France in 1832 and spent most of his career in Chicago. He was a self-taught civil engineer who developed innovative bridge designs and invented a process for treating railroad ties to extend their life. However, he was best known for his work later in life as an aviation pioneer. In June of 1896, Octave Chanute and several colleagues traveled to Miller Station to conduct flying experiments in the dunes. Chanute's experiments in Miller were conducted on a high dune just east of Lake Street. Below, Chanute tests one of his aircraft types in Miller. (Octave Chanute Photo Album, Manuscript Division, Library of Congress, Washington, DC.)

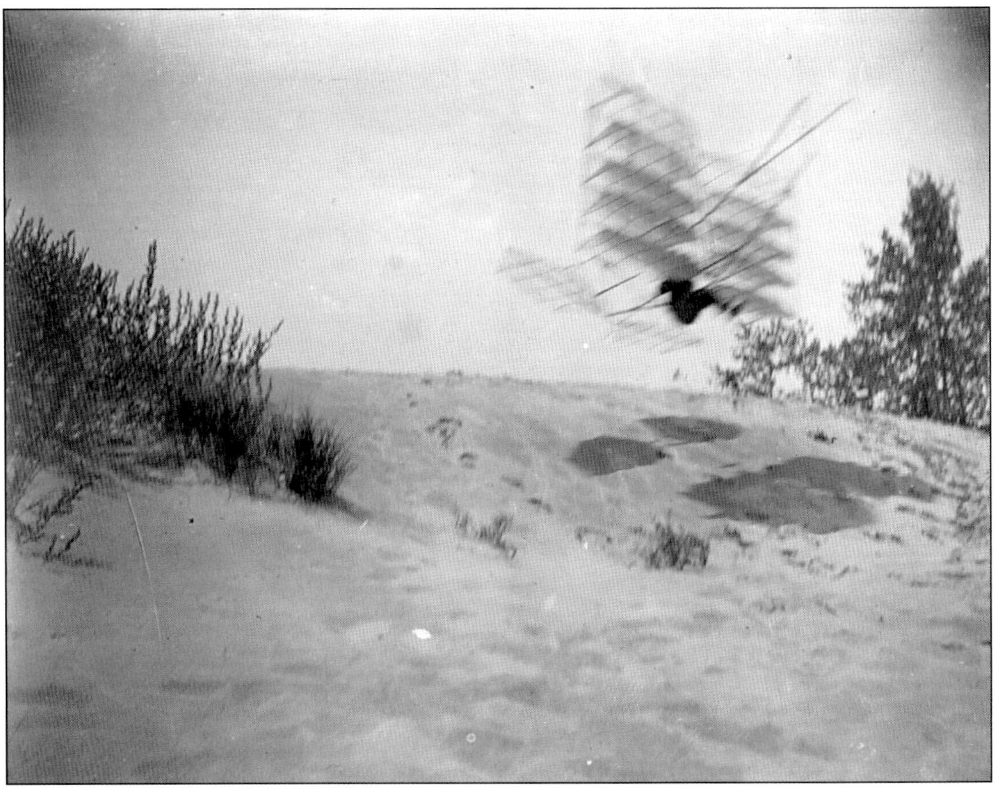

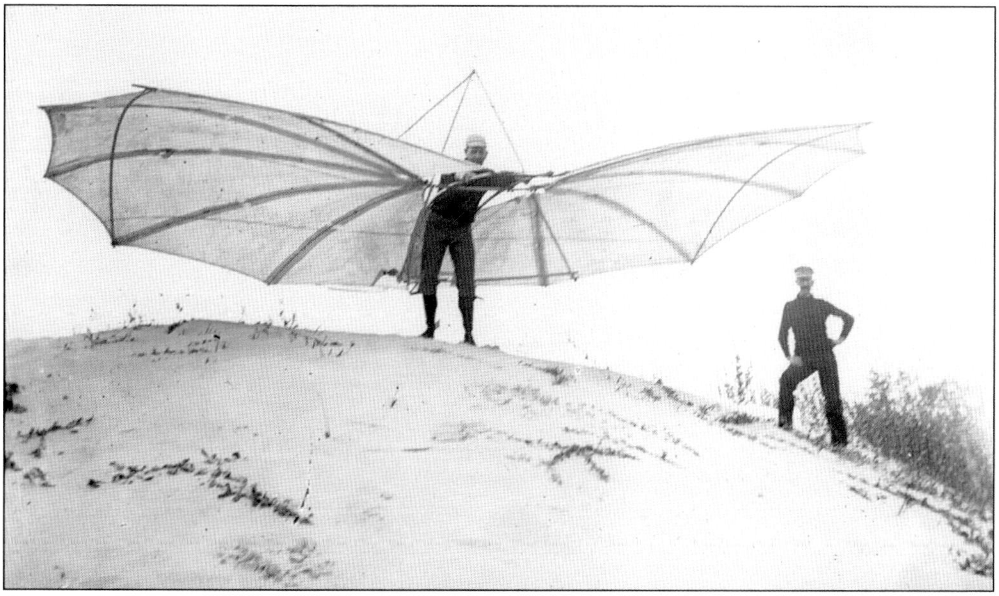

During their two weeks in Miller, the group first experimented with the modified Lilienthal aircraft based on a design by the German Otto Lilienthal. Here, Augustus Herring is ready for takeoff in the modified Lillienthal. The machine weighed 36 pounds and was awkward to fly, but the group made about 100 glides with it in Miller. Just weeks after Chanute's experiments in Miller, Lillienthal was killed while experimenting with his own version. (Octave Chanute Photo Album, Manuscript Division, Library of Congress, Washington, DC.)

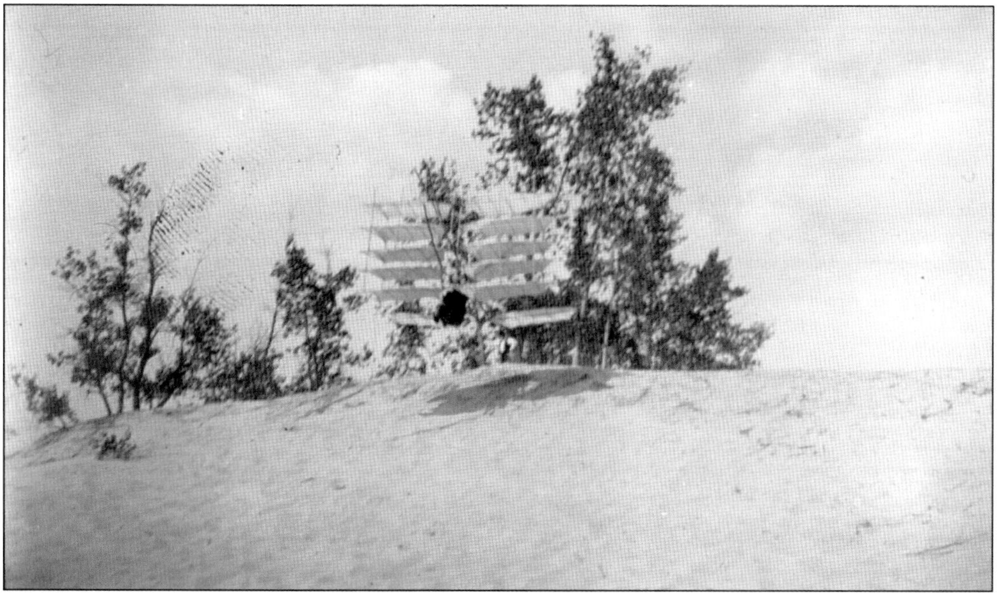

After a hard landing, the Lillienthal glider was discarded and the group experimented with the Katydid, a multiple-wing glider. The aviators made revisions to the machine based on the results of gliding flights and from information gathered after releasing feather down in front of the machine to watch the paths of air currents sweeping past the wings. The Sixth Form Multiple-Wing Machine is seen here in flight. Chanute and his colleagues made about 200 glides in Miller. (Octave Chanute Photo Album, Manuscript Division, Library of Congress, Washington, DC.)

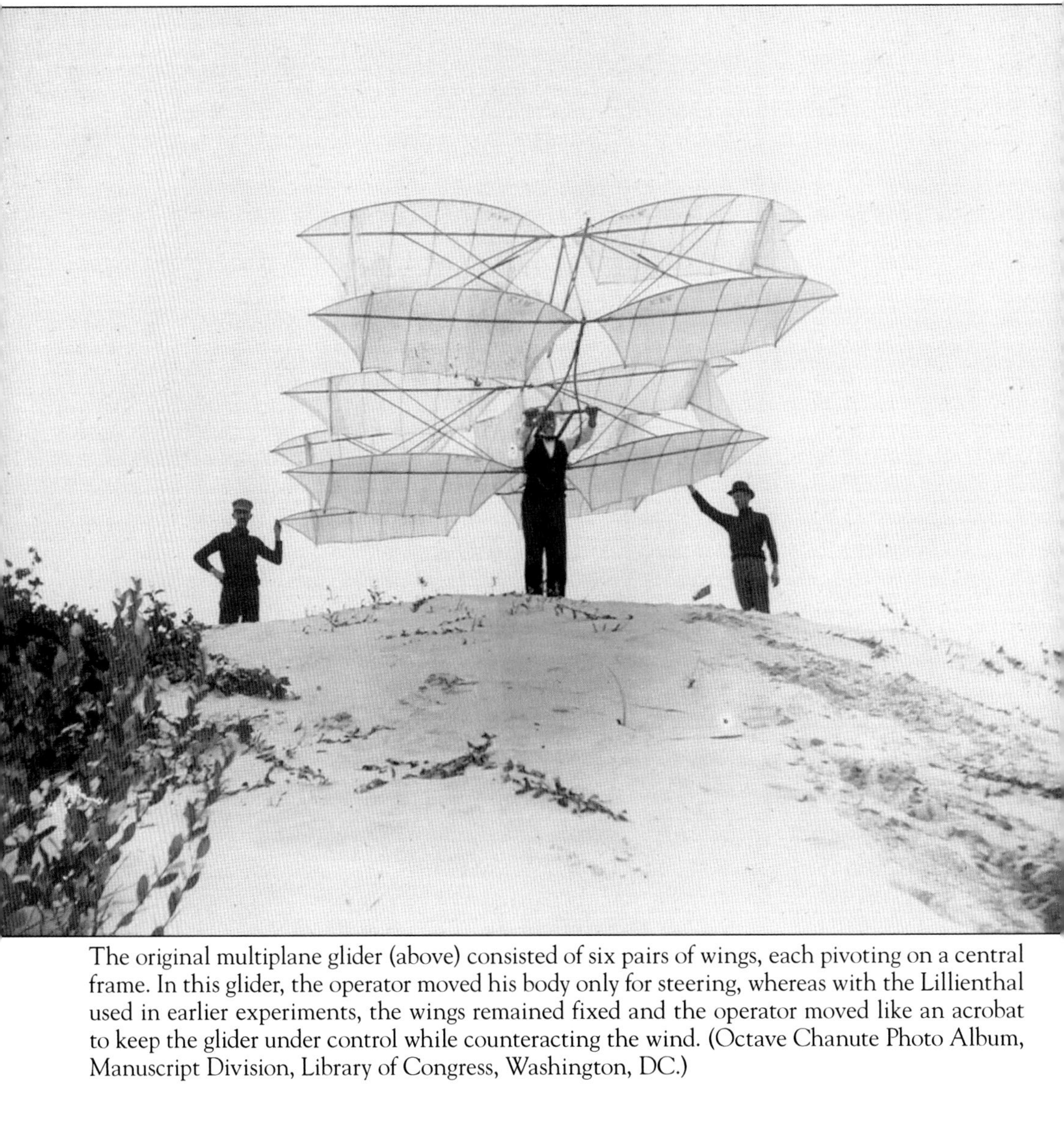

The original multiplane glider (above) consisted of six pairs of wings, each pivoting on a central frame. In this glider, the operator moved his body only for steering, whereas with the Lillienthal used in earlier experiments, the wings remained fixed and the operator moved like an acrobat to keep the glider under control while counteracting the wind. (Octave Chanute Photo Album, Manuscript Division, Library of Congress, Washington, DC.)

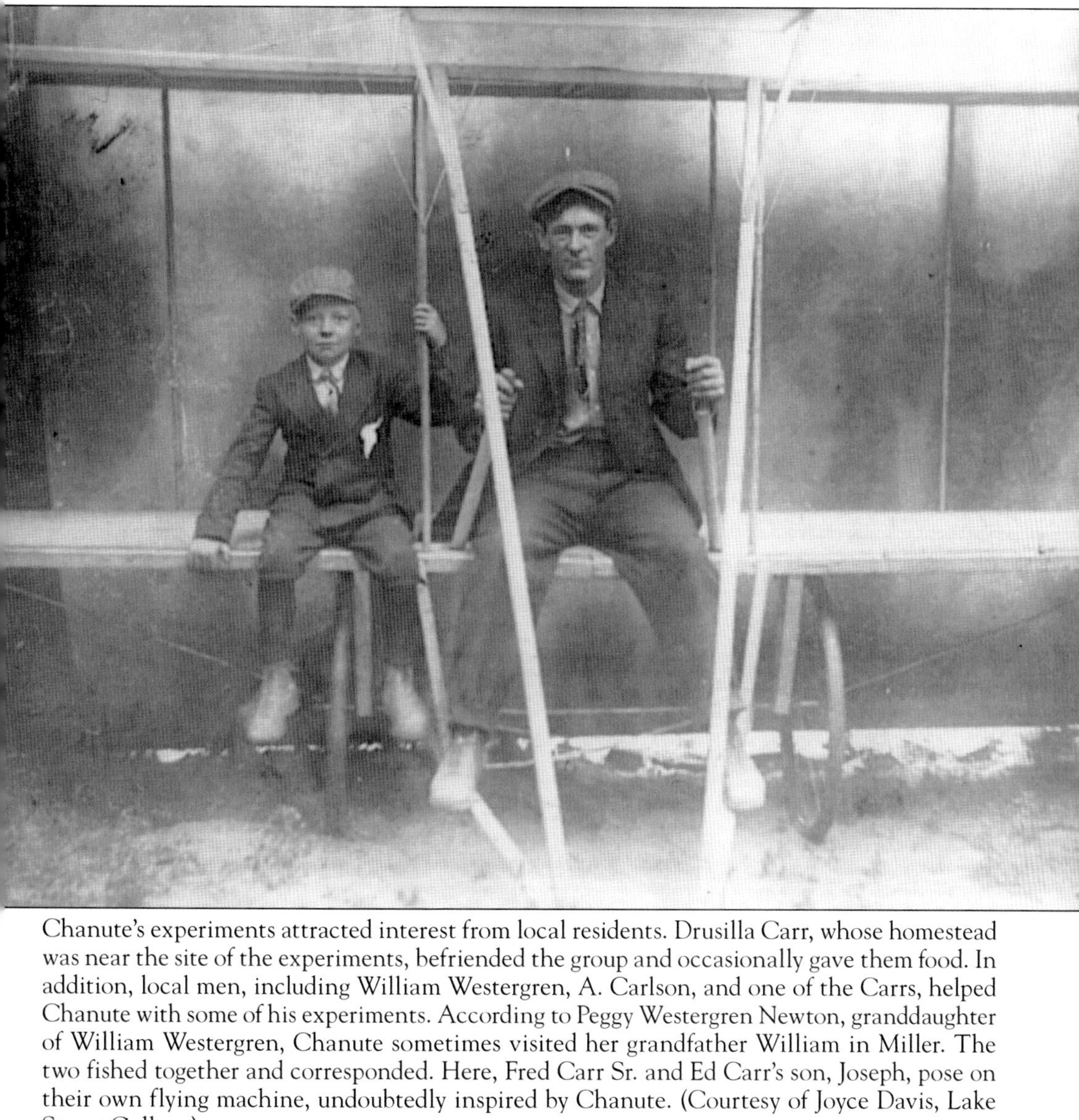

Chanute's experiments attracted interest from local residents. Drusilla Carr, whose homestead was near the site of the experiments, befriended the group and occasionally gave them food. In addition, local men, including William Westergren, A. Carlson, and one of the Carrs, helped Chanute with some of his experiments. According to Peggy Westergren Newton, granddaughter of William Westergren, Chanute sometimes visited her grandfather William in Miller. The two fished together and corresponded. Here, Fred Carr Sr. and Ed Carr's son, Joseph, pose on their own flying machine, undoubtedly inspired by Chanute. (Courtesy of Joyce Davis, Lake Street Gallery.)

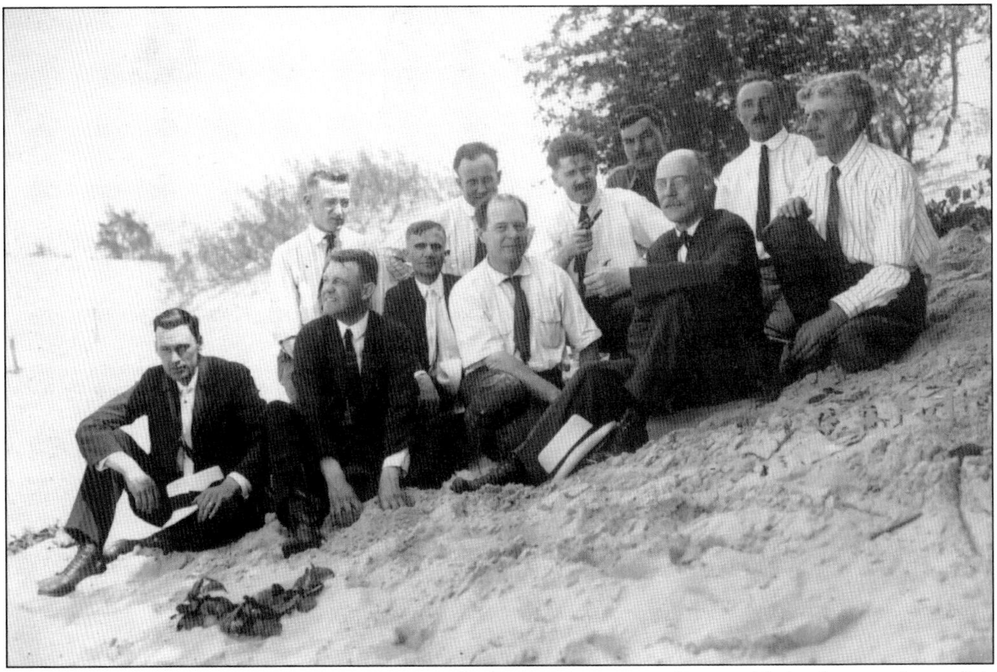

Henry Chandler Cowles was a University of Chicago botanist who established an ecology club and brought groups of students and fellow professors out to study in the dunes. He wrote his dissertation, "An Ecological Study of the Sand Dune Flora of Northern Indiana," in 1898, based on his research in dunes areas including the Miller Woods. Later, Cowles and others, including Jens Jensen, formed the Prairie Club, the first group to propose protection of the Indiana dunes. Pictured are Cowles (above, front row center with no jacket; below, first row far right), George Damon Fuller (above, far right; below, fourth from right), and botanist and professor William Trelease (above, third from right; below, center). (Courtesy of American Environmental Photographs Collection, Department of Special Collections, University of Chicago Library.)

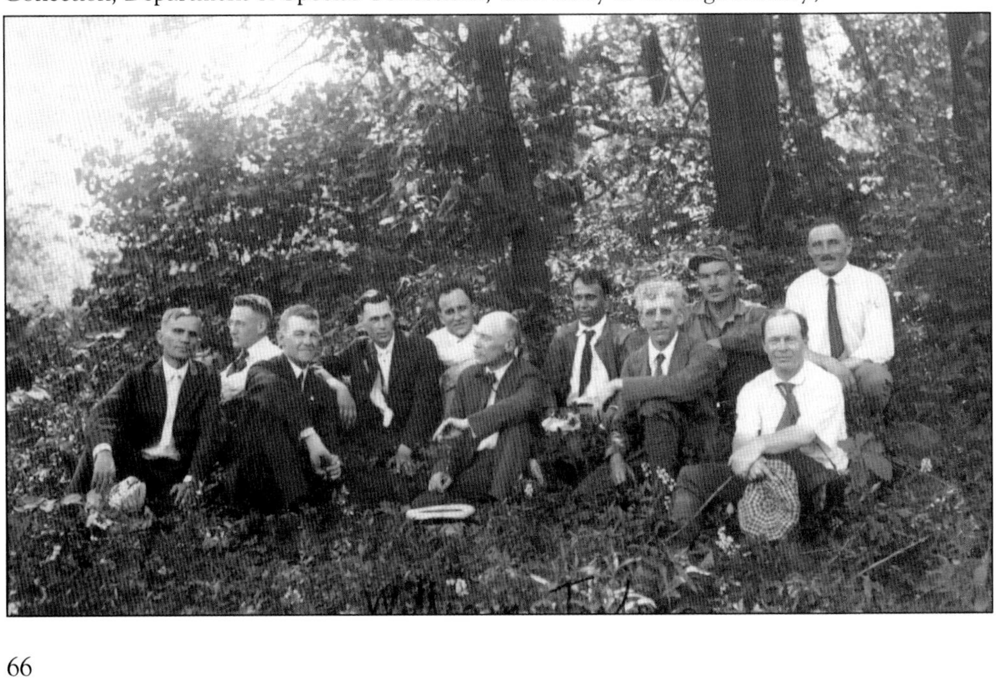

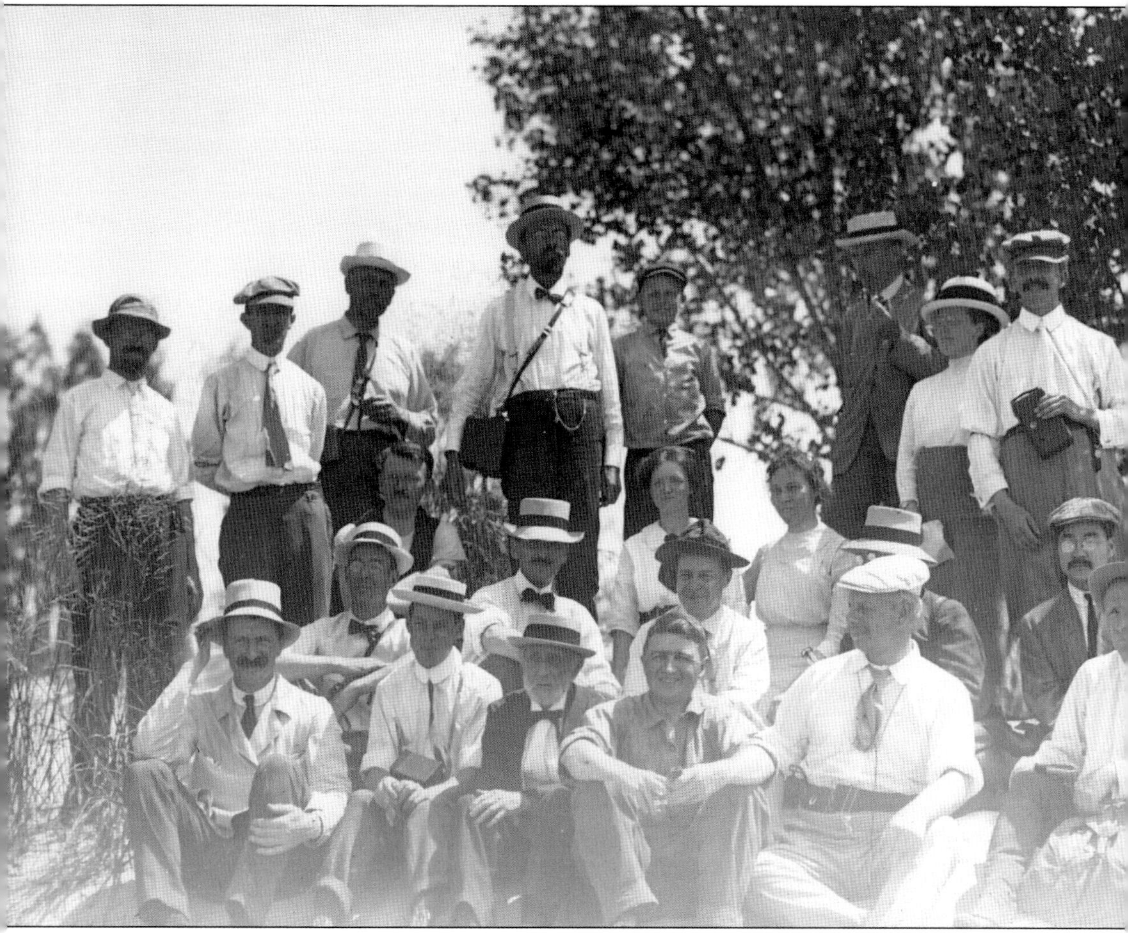

In 1913, American ecologists hosted a group of leading European botanists for a scientific tour called the International Phytogeographic Excursion in America, visiting significant natural environments like Miller, where the group is seen here, across the United States. The group traveled across the country by rail, beginning in New York City and ending in California, stopping at sites along the way. Three days were spent in the Indiana dunes, where the group was led by Henry Chandler Cowles. English botanist and ecologist Arthur Tansley prepared a summary report on the excursion, praising the grand scale of American landscapes and commenting on the need and efforts to preserve it: "Future generations will be slow to forgive us for the wholesale and often wanton destruction that goes on at present almost unchecked by any general feeling that it is an antisocial crime, and quick to applaud the actions and to reverence the memories of those who have done something to preserve their heritage of natural beauty." (Courtesy of American Environmental Photographs Collection, Department of Special Collections, University of Chicago Library.)

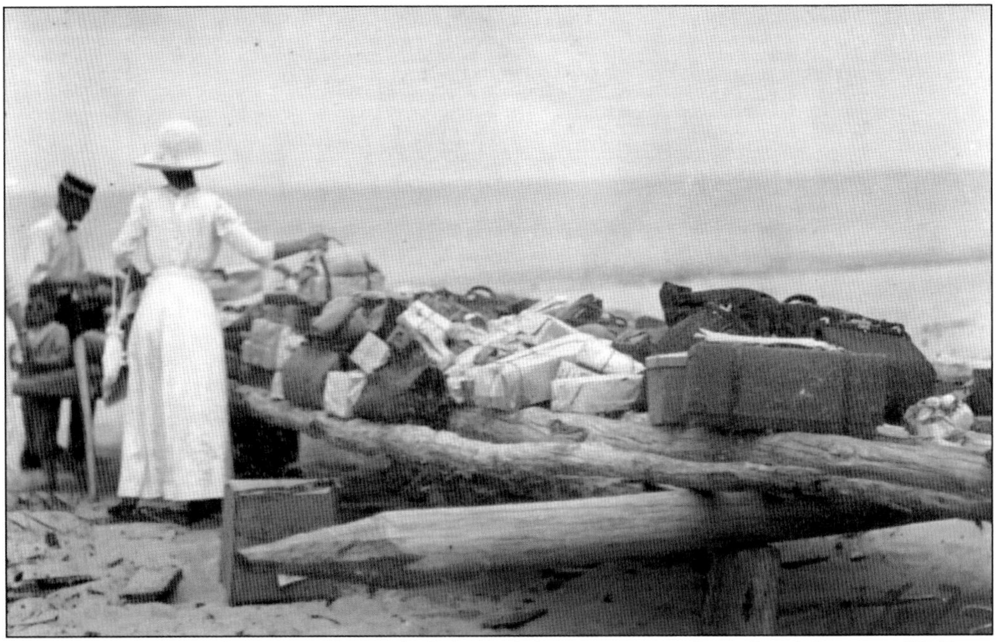

In 1908, a group of Chicagoans formed a hiking club, sponsoring "Saturday Afternoon Walking Trips" to wilderness areas all around Chicago for both men and women. The group, eventually named the Prairie Club, included Cowles, landscape architect Jens Jensen, Prairie School architect Dwight Perkins, and Amalie Hofer, editor of *The Kindergarten Magazine*. Hofer also headed the Playground Association of Chicago, advocating the idea that children should be taught in natural settings. The Prairie Club spent many of their Saturday afternoons in the Indiana Dunes and was the first group to fight to "Save the Dunes" in northwest Indiana. Group members spend time on the Miller beach in these two images from the extensive scrapbooks maintained by the group of their expeditions. (Courtesy of Westchester Township History Museum.)

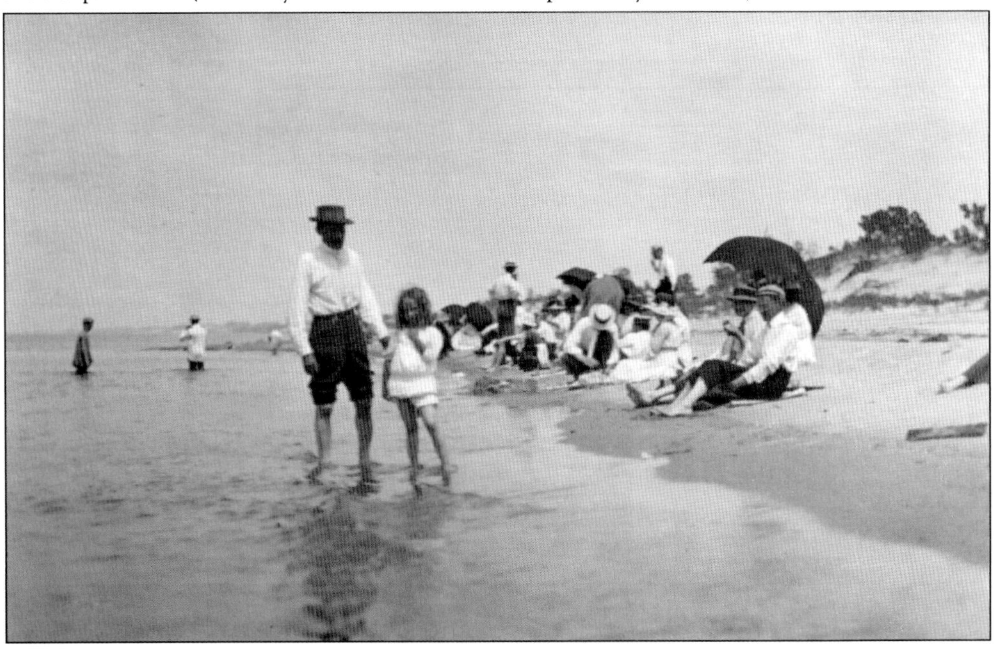

Six

Independent Women

Diana and Beyond

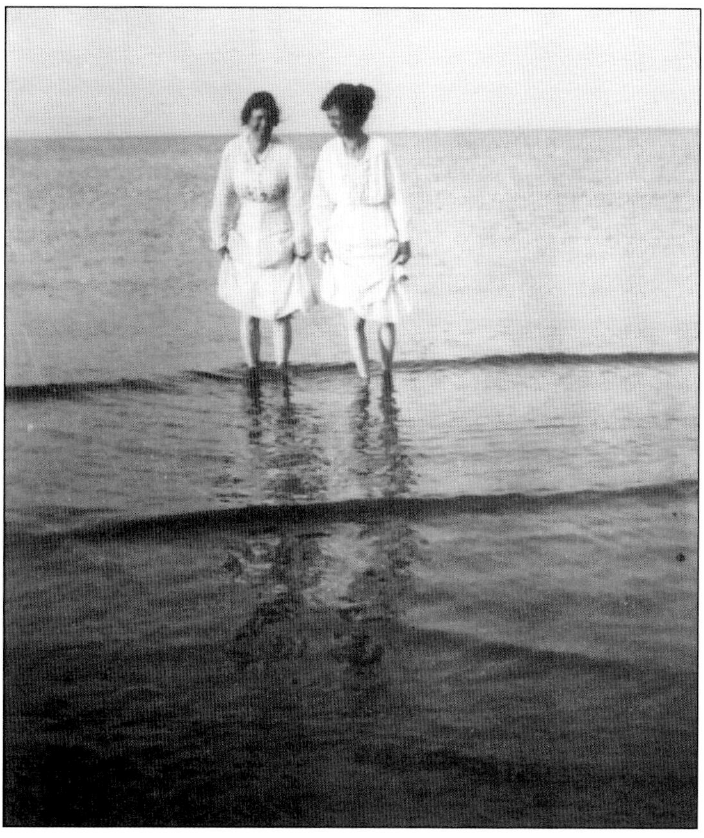

This 1919 photograph likely shows Nelle and Madge Friend, two unmarried sisters who purchased land on the lake in Miller Beach and had a cottage built in the early 1920s. They were not wealthy, but used money they earned in their Chicago jobs to buy the land and build the cottage, which they used to enjoy the wilderness of the Indiana Dunes. (Courtesy of Betty Davin.)

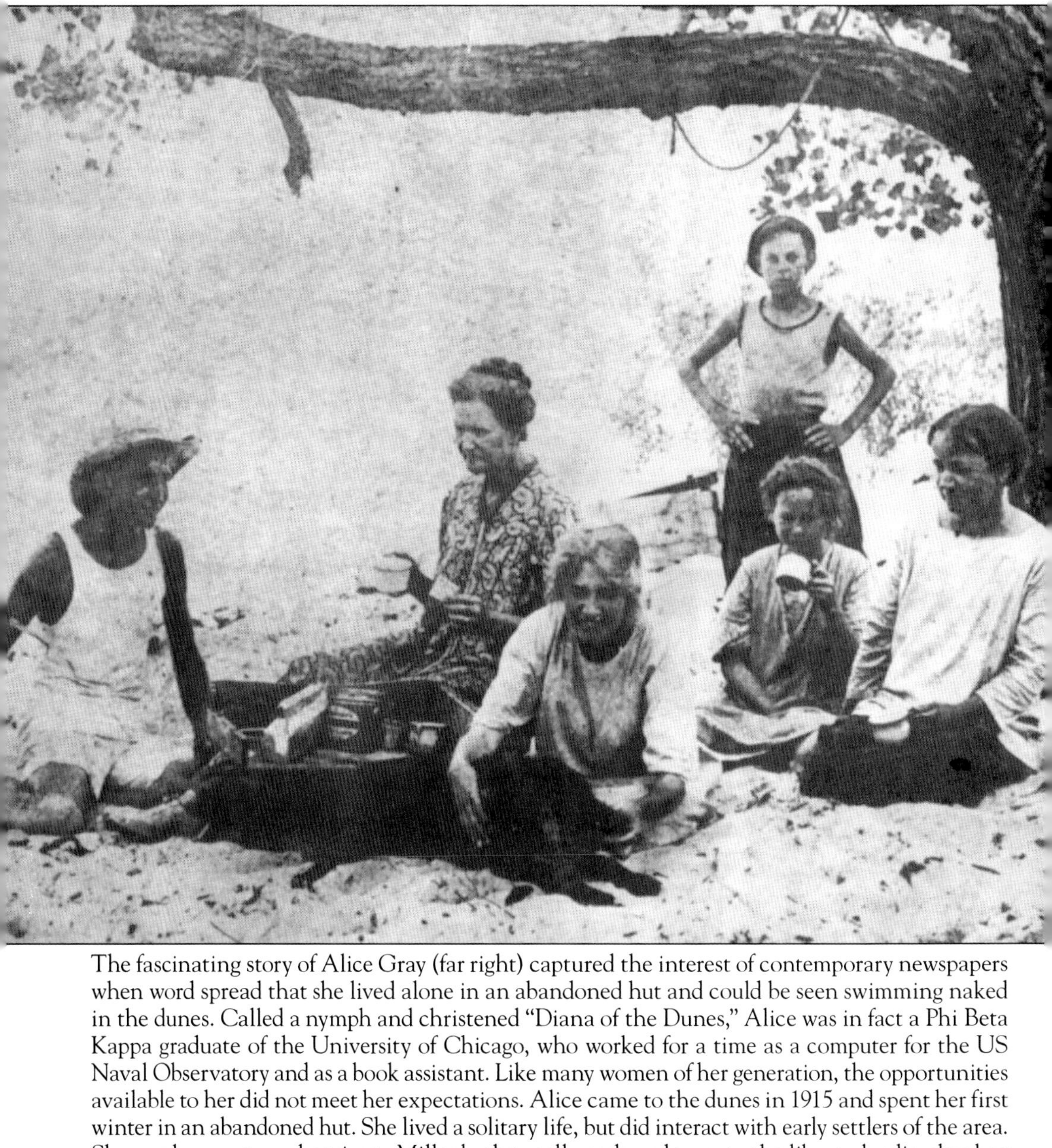

The fascinating story of Alice Gray (far right) captured the interest of contemporary newspapers when word spread that she lived alone in an abandoned hut and could be seen swimming naked in the dunes. Called a nymph and christened "Diana of the Dunes," Alice was in fact a Phi Beta Kappa graduate of the University of Chicago, who worked for a time as a computer for the US Naval Observatory and as a book assistant. Like many women of her generation, the opportunities available to her did not meet her expectations. Alice came to the dunes in 1915 and spent her first winter in an abandoned hut. She lived a solitary life, but did interact with early settlers of the area. She was known to make trips to Miller both to sell perch and to go to the library, loading her bag with magazines and books. (Courtesy of the Calumet Regional Archives, IU Northwest.)

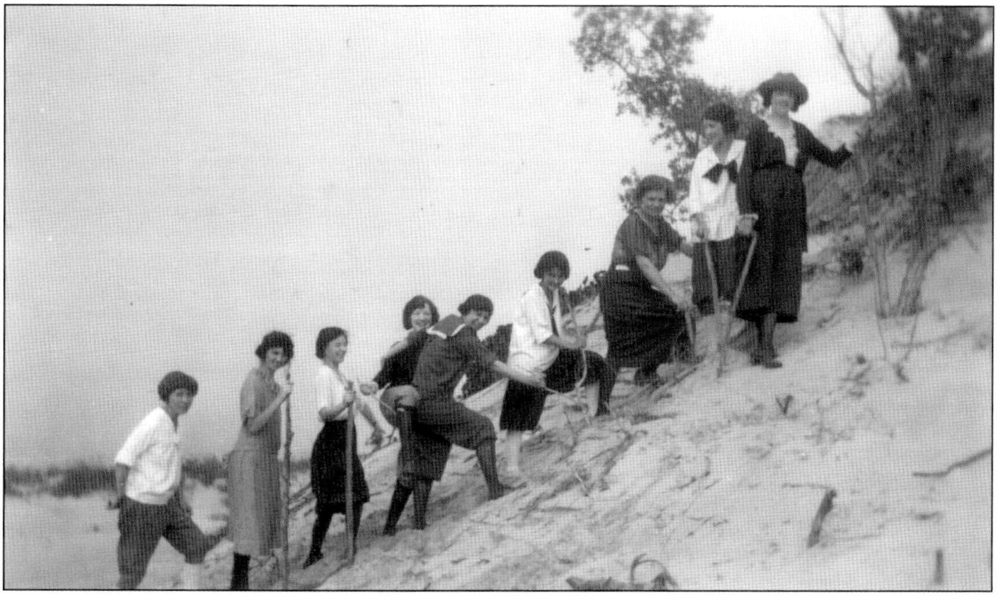

Miller was also home to other independent and adventurous women of the era. Betty Davin, who built her own home in Miller in the early 1950s, recalls that before her "spinster" aunts Nelle and Madge Friend built their cottage, they would come out to Miller, often with a group of friends, to camp on the beach and enjoy the wildness of the dunes. They often hiked on the "moving dune," a large shifting dune just across County Line Road in an area that is now part of West Beach in Porter County. In these images, the sisters and their friends hike the dunes in the 1920s. (Courtesy of Betty Davin.)

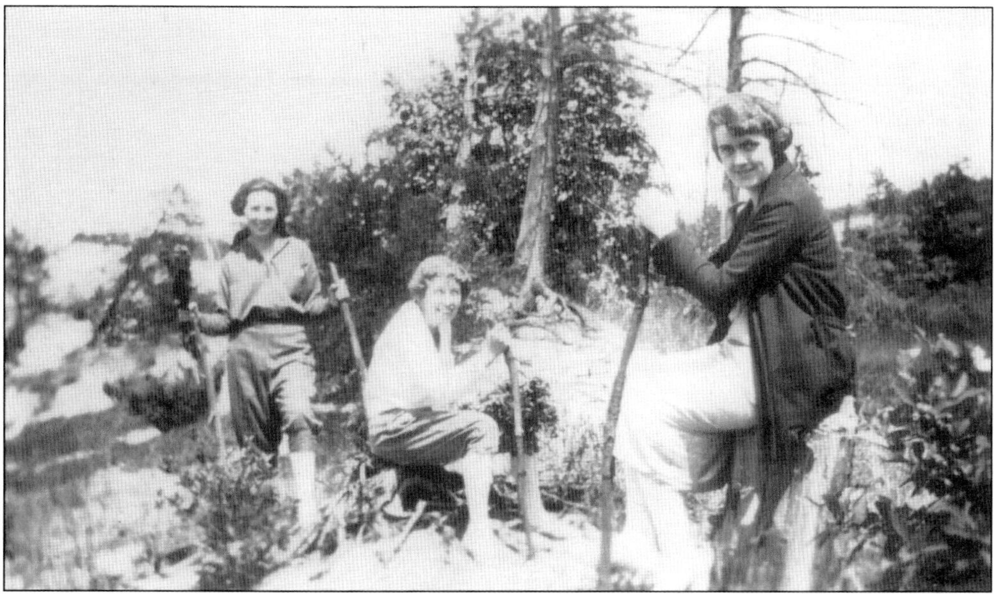

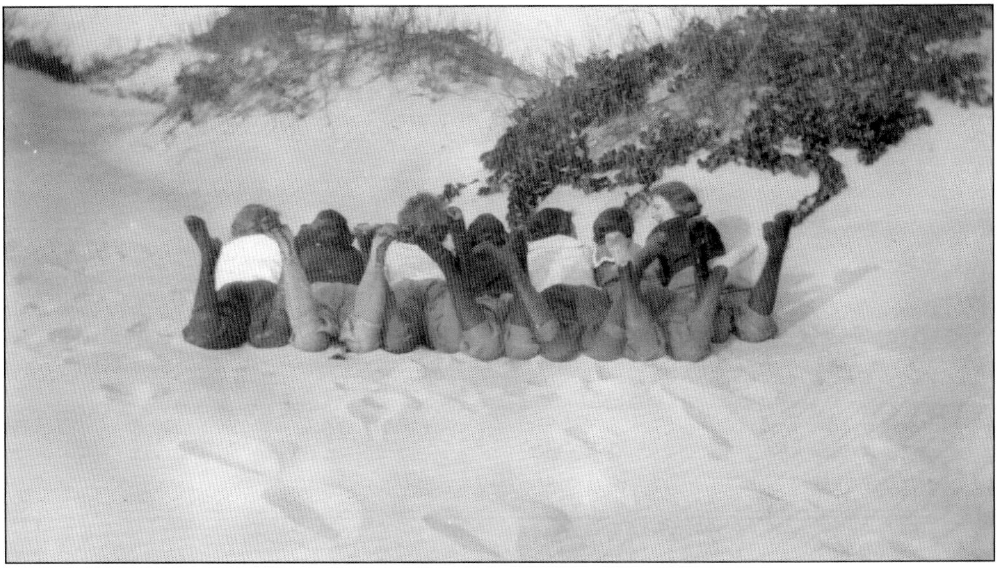

For Nelle and Madge Friend, who grew up in the Hyde Park neighborhood of Chicago, and their friends, the beach was the main attraction. Above, the Friend sisters and their young women friends from Chicago enjoy some downtime in the dunes in the 1920s. Betty Davin and her brother, William, used to spend much of the summer at their aunts' cottage, along with their mother, grandmothers, great-aunts, and other relatives. The Friend sisters built the cottage below in the early 1920s. (Courtesy of Betty Davin.)

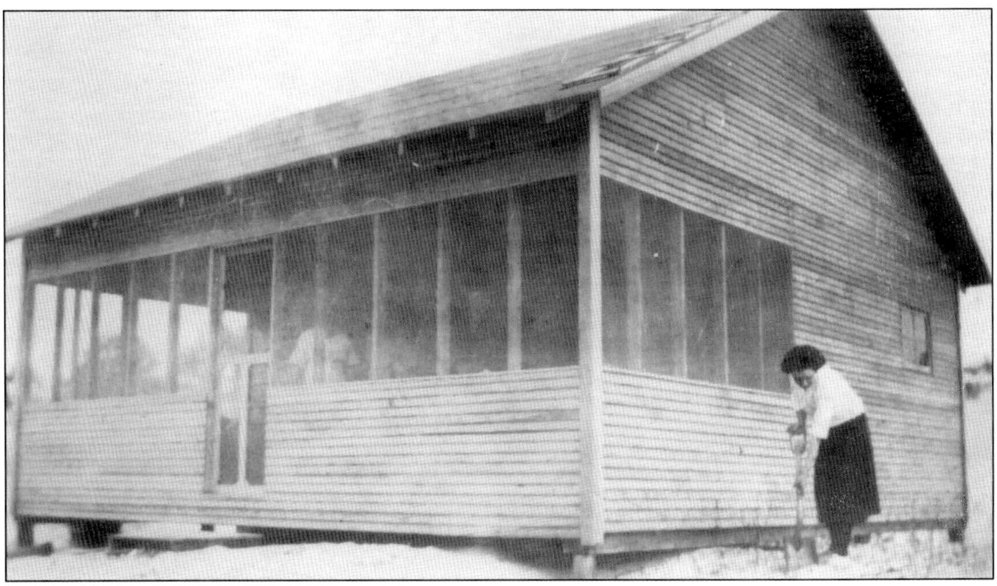

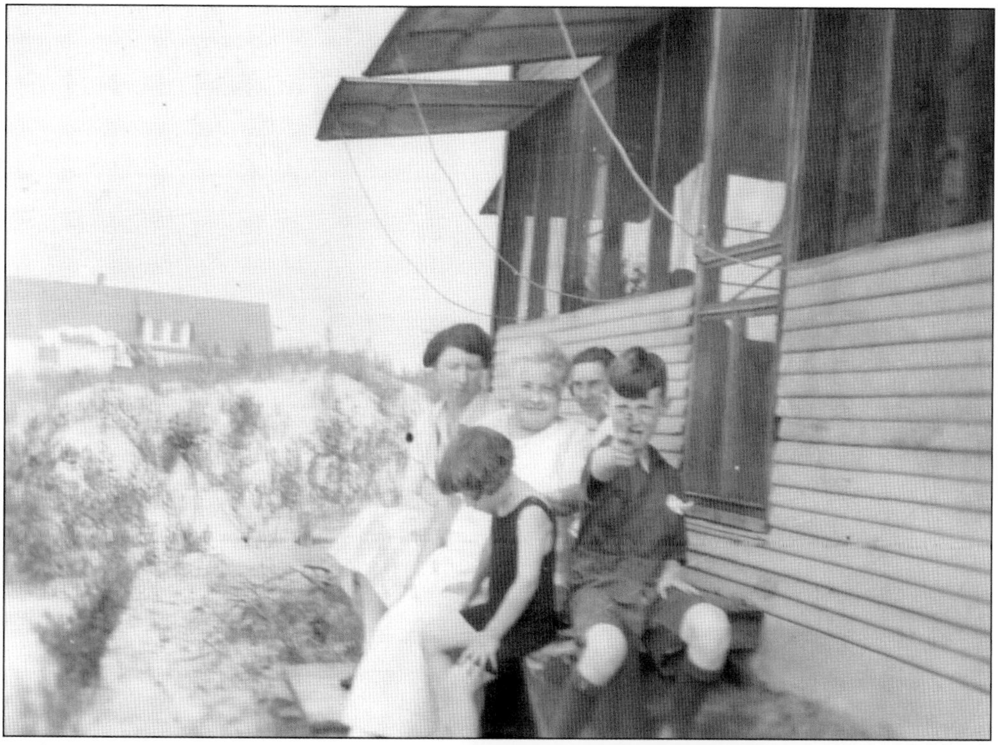

In the late 1910s, Ellen Friend was invited to visit Miller by her friend Martha Coakley. She brought along two of her daughters, Nelle and Madge, who were immediately enchanted with Miller. The sisters went to local realtor Guy Ayers and purchased two lakefront lots from him for $1,000. On their 50 feet of beach, they had a cottage built in 1923. Nelle Friend worked as a stenographer in Chicago and neither she nor her sister ever married. Above, Betty Davin and her brother, William, sit with their grandmother Ellen Elizabeth Friend (center) and their Aunt Madge (rear) in the 1920s. At right, Nelle and Madge Friend and another friend have fun on the front stoop of their Miller Beach cottage in the 1920s. Their mother, who first introduced them to Miller, is in the doorway. (Courtesy of Betty Davin.)

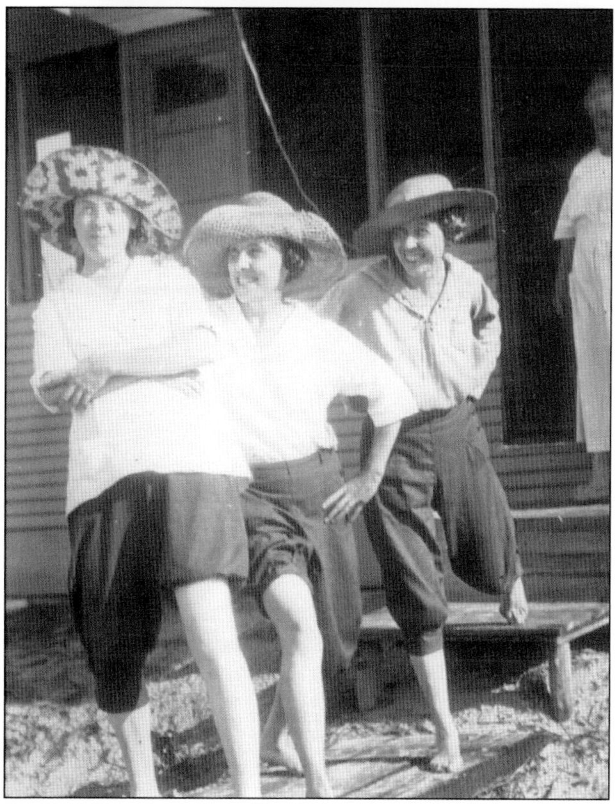

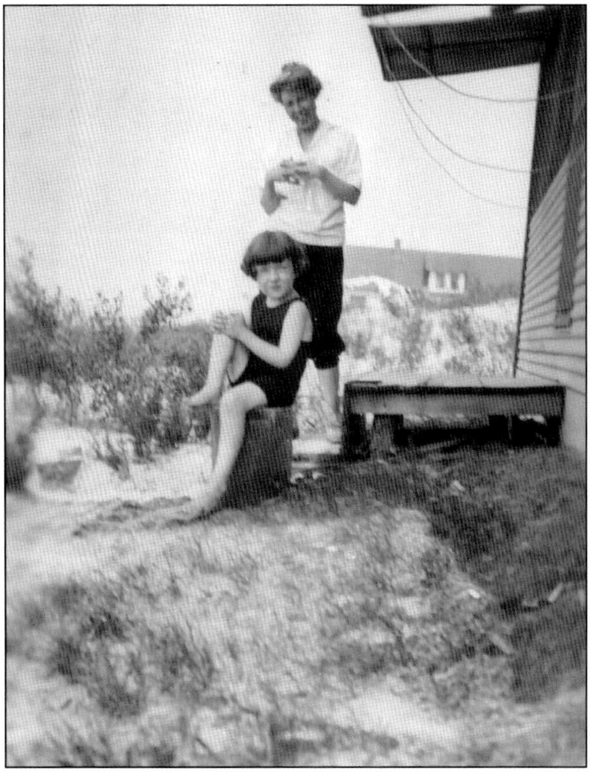

Betty Davin continued to visit her aunts as she grew up, riding the train into Miller where she would take a bus down to the end of Lake Street. From there, she'd walk down the beach, keeping her eye out for the light in her aunts' window in what was then one of the only cottages on the beach. Above, Betty Davin sits with her Aunt Nelle in the early 1920s. Below, Davin, by then a young woman, strikes a pose on the beach in the late 1930s. (Courtesy of Betty Davin.)

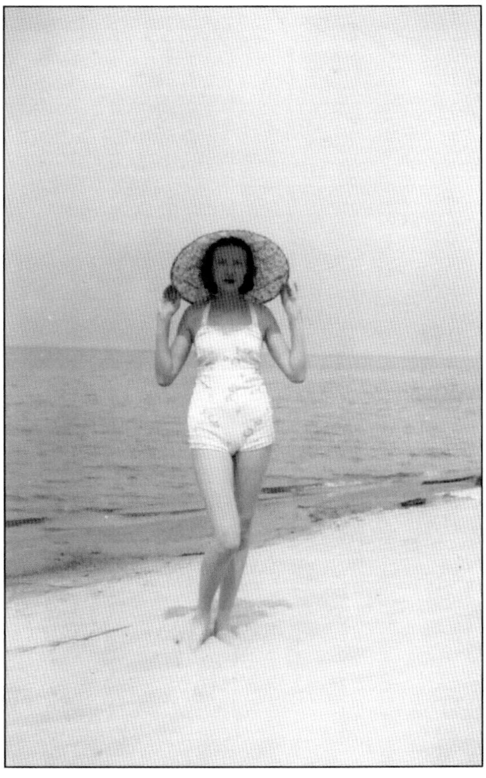

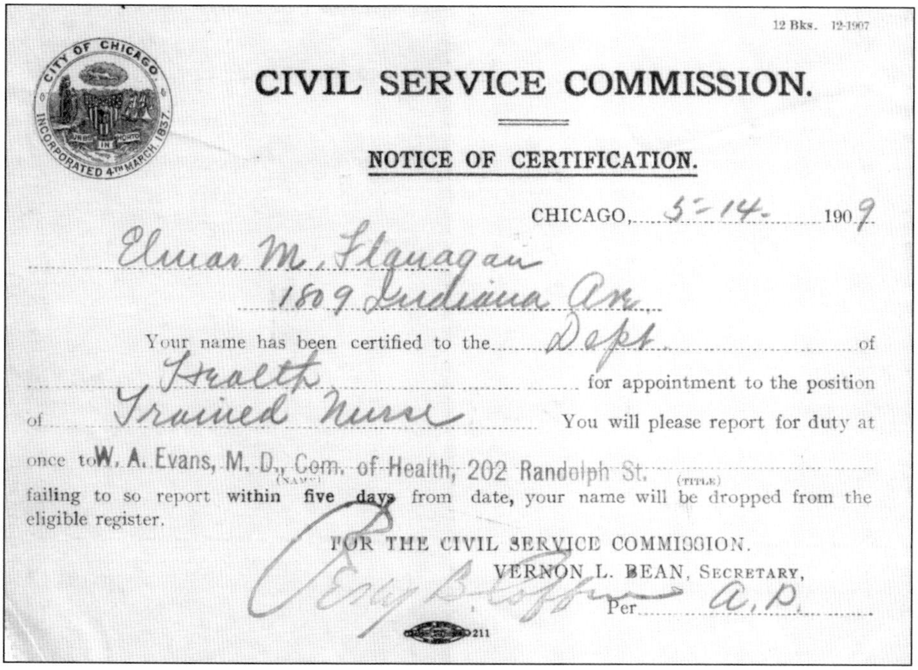
12 Bks. 12-1907

CIVIL SERVICE COMMISSION.

NOTICE OF CERTIFICATION.

CHICAGO, 5-14- 1909

Elmar M. Flanagan
1809 Indiana Av.

Your name has been certified to the Dept of Health for appointment to the position of Trained Nurse You will please report for duty at once to W. A. Evans, M. D., Com. of Health, 202 Randolph St. (NAME) (TITLE) failing to so report within five days from date, your name will be dropped from the eligible register.

FOR THE CIVIL SERVICE COMMISSION.
VERNON L. BEAN, SECRETARY,
Per A. P.

Around the time that Nelle and Madge Friend moved in, Alice Flanagan Pickford's grandmother Elmar Flanagan was settling into the earliest lakefront cottage east of Lake Street. Elmar Flanagan, seen below in her Chicago apartment on South Indiana Avenue, came to Chicago from New York to become the city's second public health nurse, living in an apartment on her own near Hull House and saving her money to build a cottage in Miller. Her nursing license was issued to her in 1909, 11 years before women received the right to vote. Flanagan eventually retired to Miller. (Courtesy of Alice Pickford.)

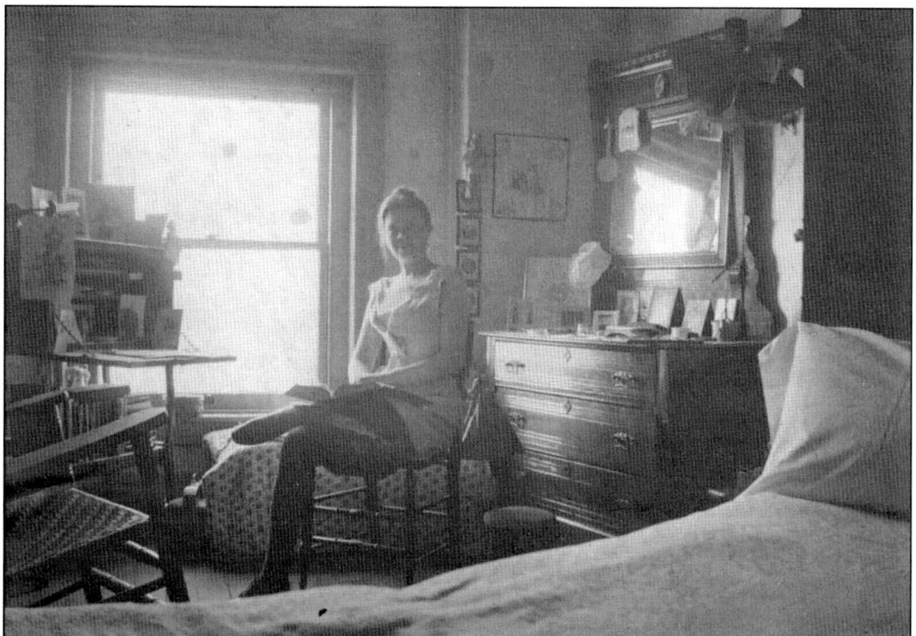

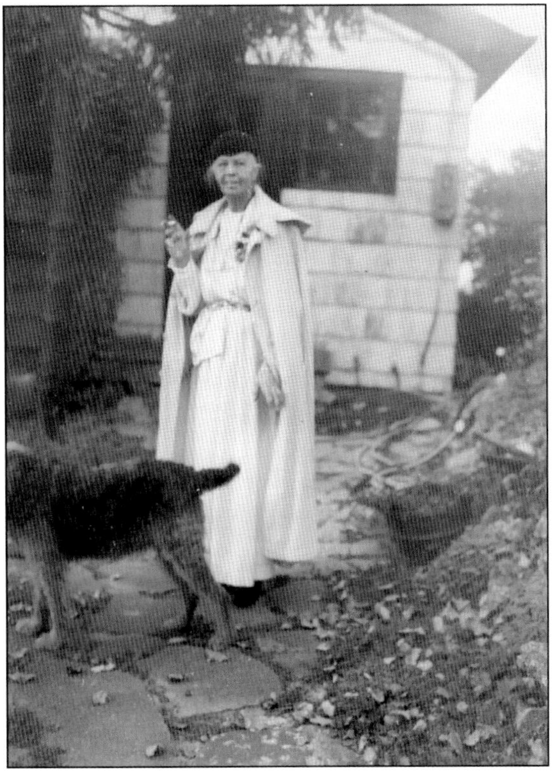

In the early years, most lakefront activity in Miller was focused on the area near Lake Street but with time the residential area of Miller spread eastward. In the early 1920s, Elmar Flanagan built the earliest cottage east of Lake Street in Miller and began spending weekends and vacation time there, often entertaining friends from Chicago. Flanagan is seen here at her Miller home. Her granddaughter Alice Pickford recalls that her grandmother often wore pants, a rarity also attributed to Diana of the Dunes. (Courtesy of Alice Pickford.)

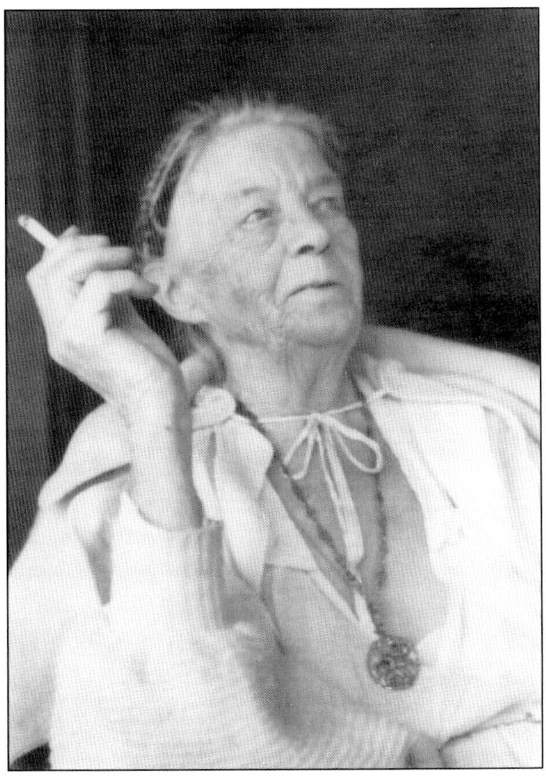

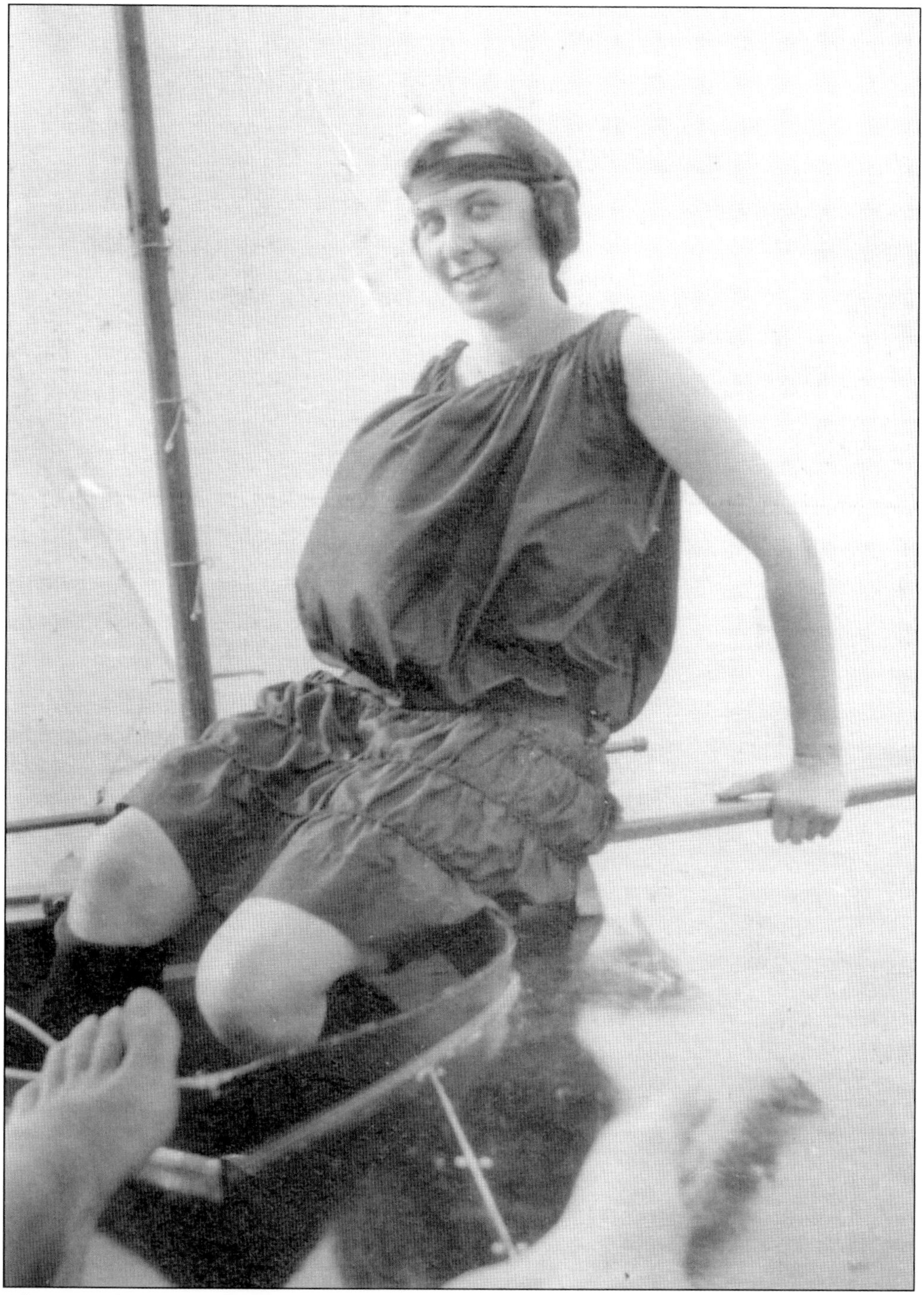

Alice Hough was the daughter of Margaret (Cassin) and Frank Hough, who established Wells Street Beach in 1928, and built one of the earliest cottages off the beaten path of Lake Street. Alice married Philip Flanagan, whose mother, Elmar, also owned a lakefront cottage just east of where Marquette Park ends. The two met on the beach in 1923. Alice Hough Flanagan is seen here in her sailboat in the 1920s. (Courtesy of Alice Pickford.)

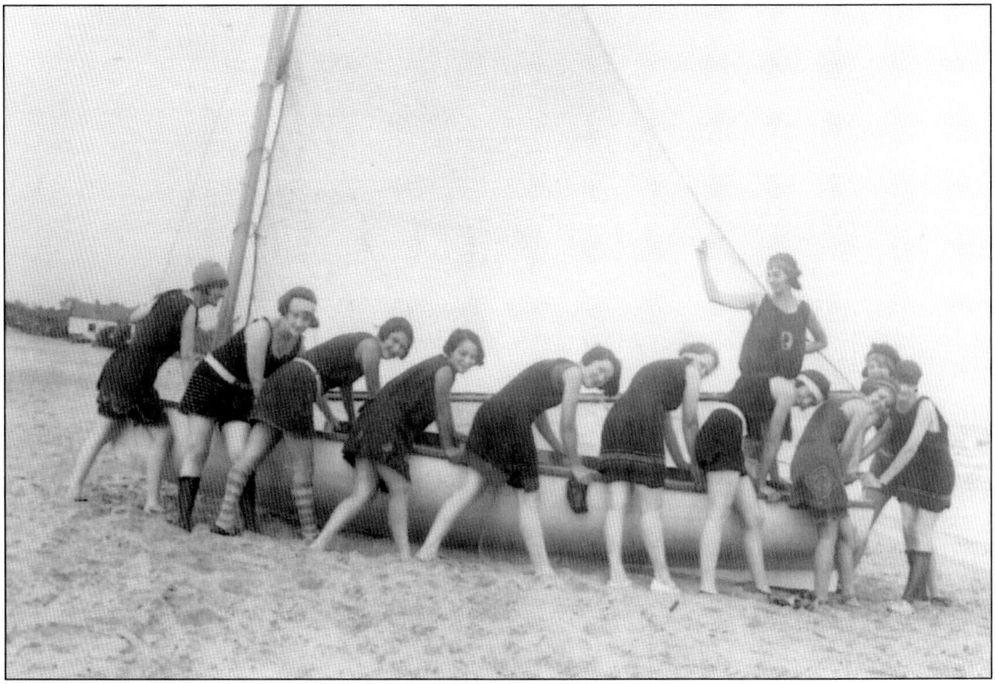

Alice Hough Flanagan and her sister Grace Hough often entertained groups of friends at their parents' cottage on the lake in the 1920s, often sailing on the lake. Their father, Frank Hough, an avid outdoorsman, sailed the Chicago to Mackinac race for many years and his boat, the *Intrepid*, won the Chicago-Mackinac Cup in the 1920s. He taught both Grace and Alice how to sail, which they did often. These images show Alice Hough Flanagan and her friends on the sailboat. (Courtesy of Alice Pickford.)

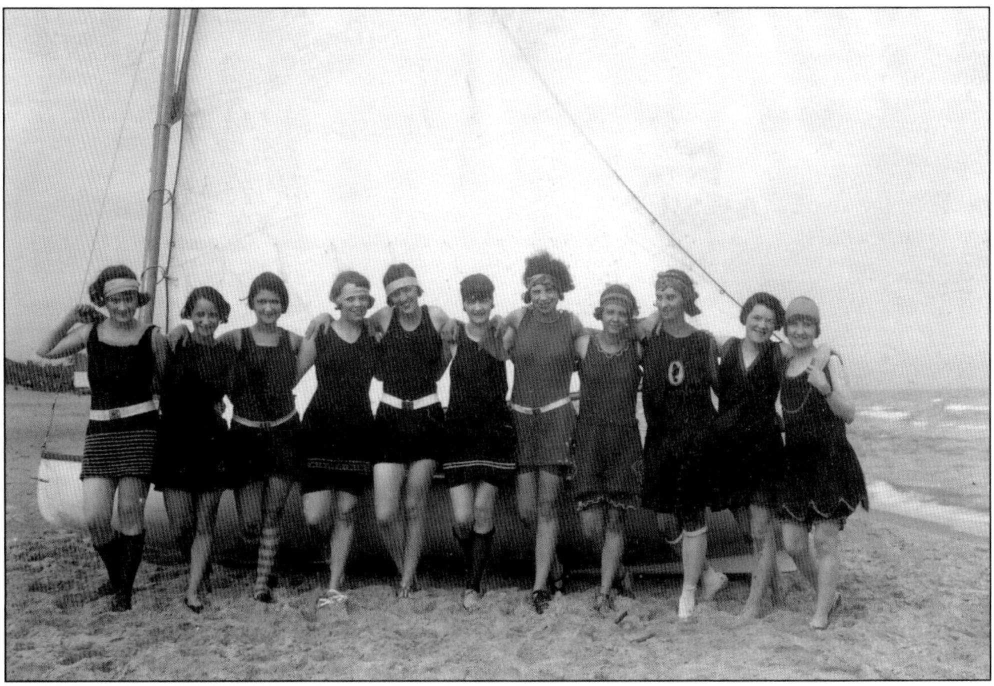

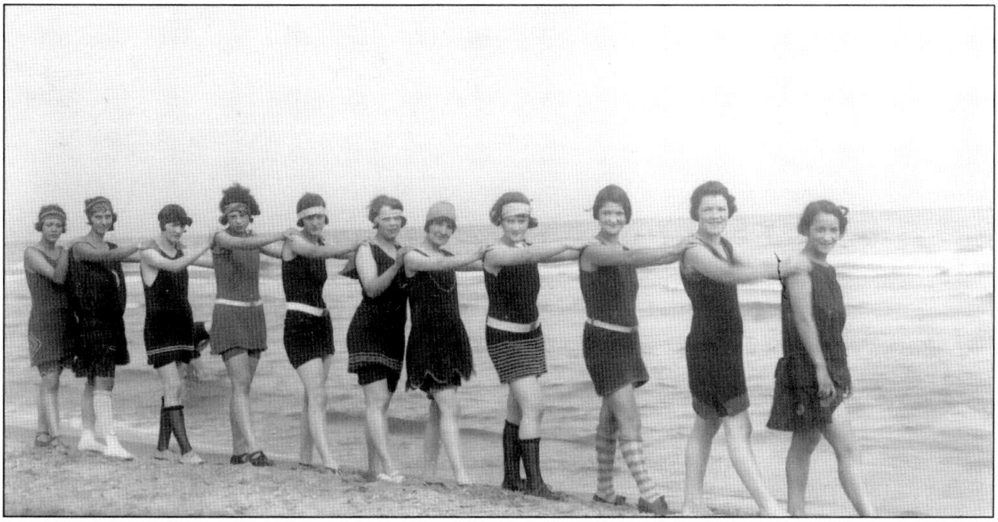

According to Alice Hough Flanagan's daughter, Alice Flanagan Pickford, Frank Hough raised his two daughters like boys, wanting them to be able to do everything that boys could do. In addition to teaching them to sail, Frank taught Alice and Grace to canoe, hike, and fish. Alice Hough Flanagan (second from left) and friends from Chicago have fun on the beach in the 1920s. (Courtesy of Alice Pickford.)

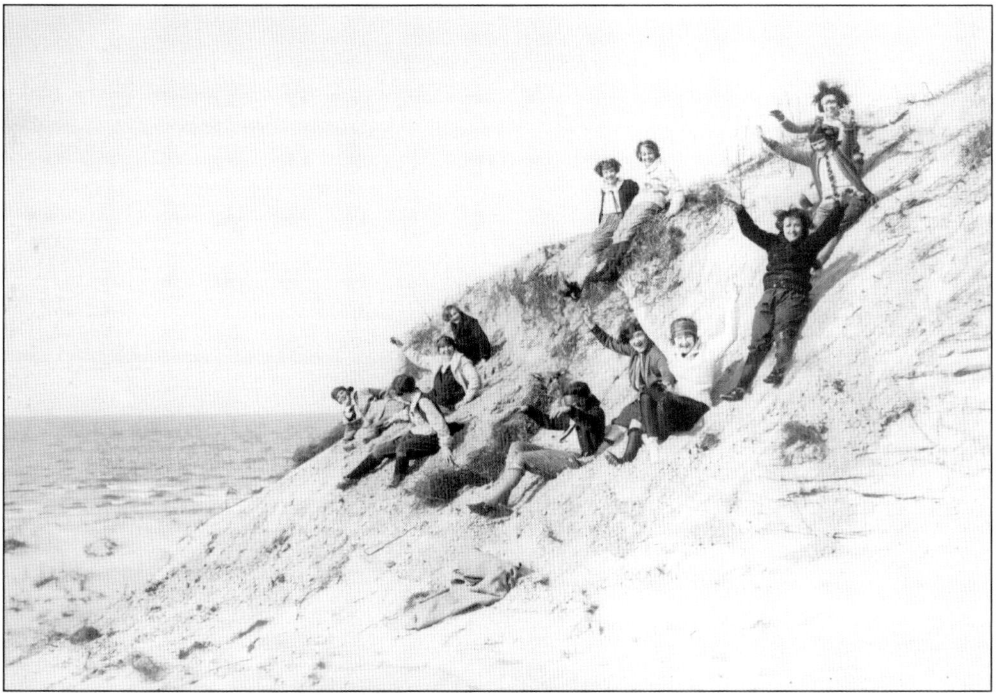

When Alice and Grace Hough's friends would visit from Chicago, the girls would either stay at the family cottage or camp on the beach. The girls' father, Frank Hough, had a boy's tent, a girl's tent, and a cook tent. Alice and Grace both attended college, which was somewhat unusual for the time, and became teachers in Chicago, with Grace teaching art and Alice teaching elementary school. After Alice met her husband, fellow Miller visitor Philip Flanagan, they moved to Miller fulltime. (Courtesy of Alice Pickford.)

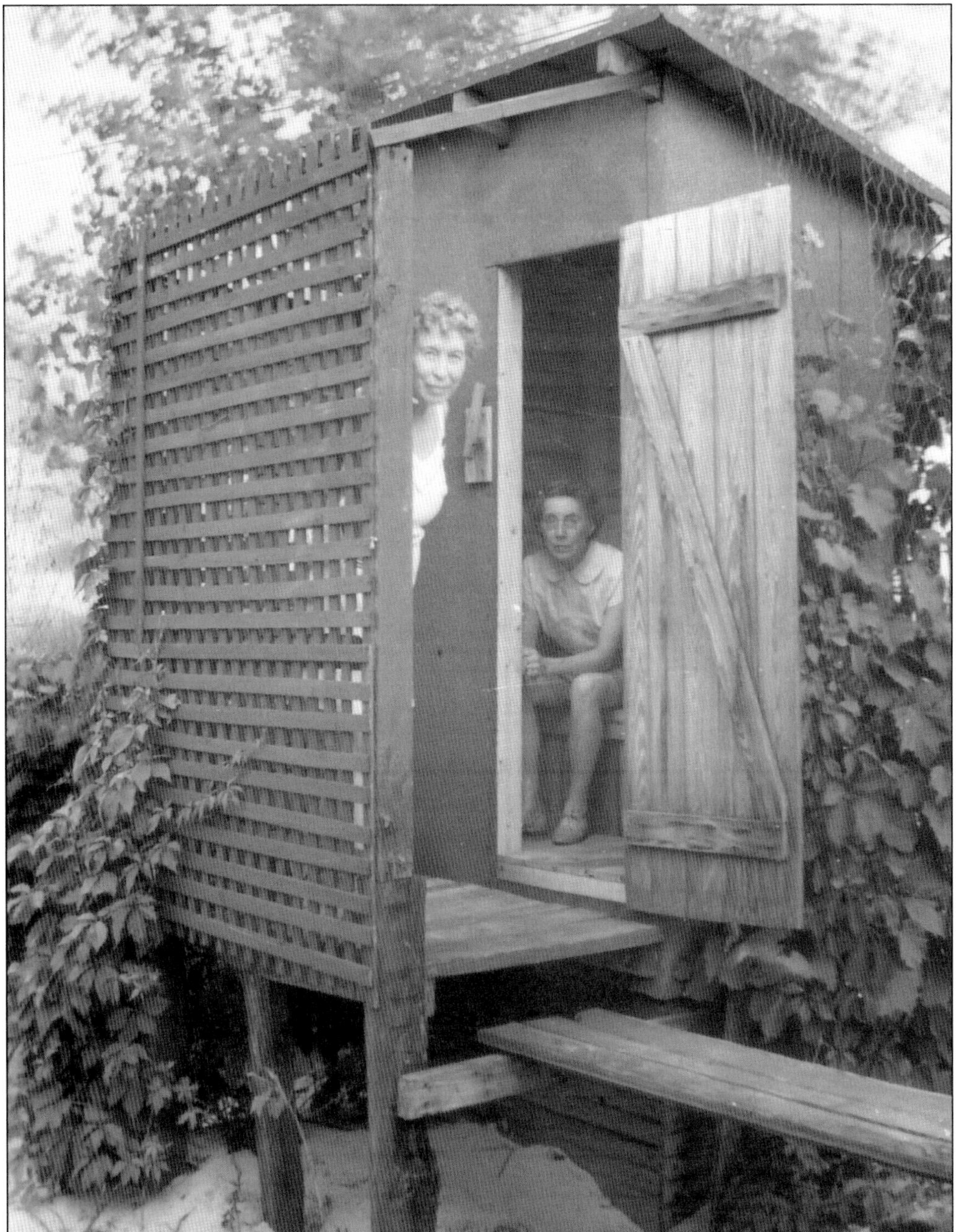

Nelle and Madge Friend pose in front of their "Two-Holer" privy near their lakefront cottage in the 1930s. Even after their cottage was built, the Friend sisters kept their camping equipment in an outbuilding and used it often. The cottage remained rustic for many years, without insulation, heat, or indoor plumbing. Betty Davin, Nelle and Madge's niece, recalls that at one point an optometrist moved to a house near her aunts' cottage and was offended by what he viewed as their unacceptably informal approach to housing and lifestyle, especially their outdoor privy. He circulated petitions to kick them out, but his efforts were unsuccessful and he eventually moved away. (Courtesy of Betty Davin.)

Seven

Miller Beach

Fun in Any Season

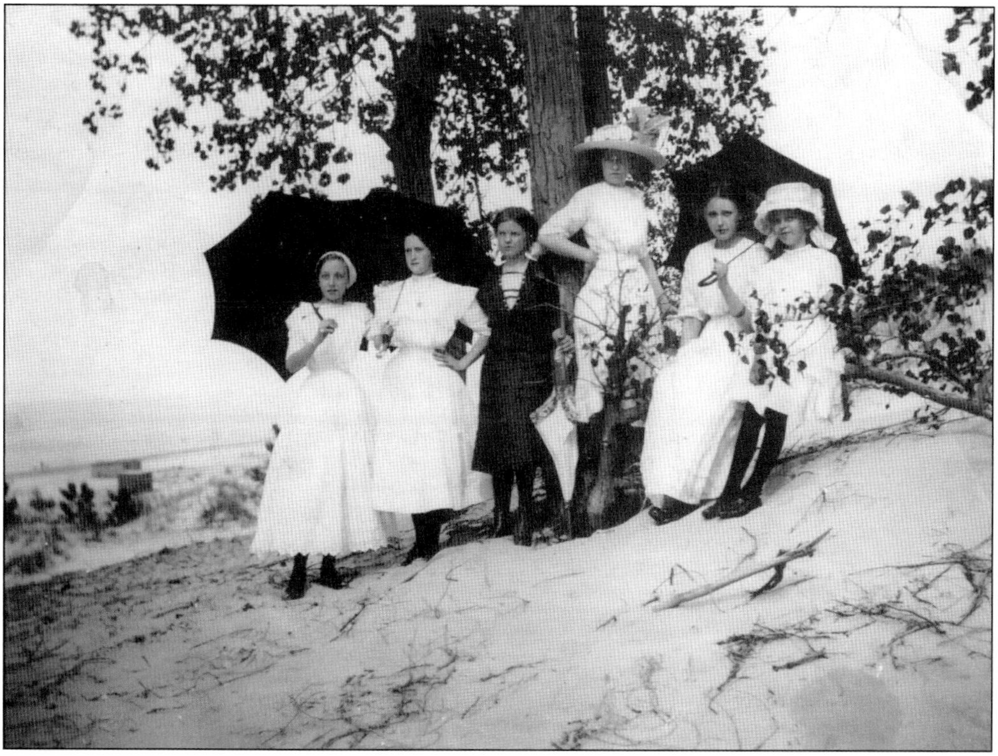

The early settlers used the beach as a place to live and fish, hunt, and forage for a living. But by the late 1890s, the beach was increasingly used for exploration, fun, and frolic. These women stand atop one of the many sand dunes that once lined Miller Beach. Miller was one of the three earliest recreational and residential developments east of Chicago. The other two were Michigan City to the east and the area now known as Porter Beach near the Indiana Dunes State Park. (Courtesy of the Calumet Regional Archives, IU Northwest.)

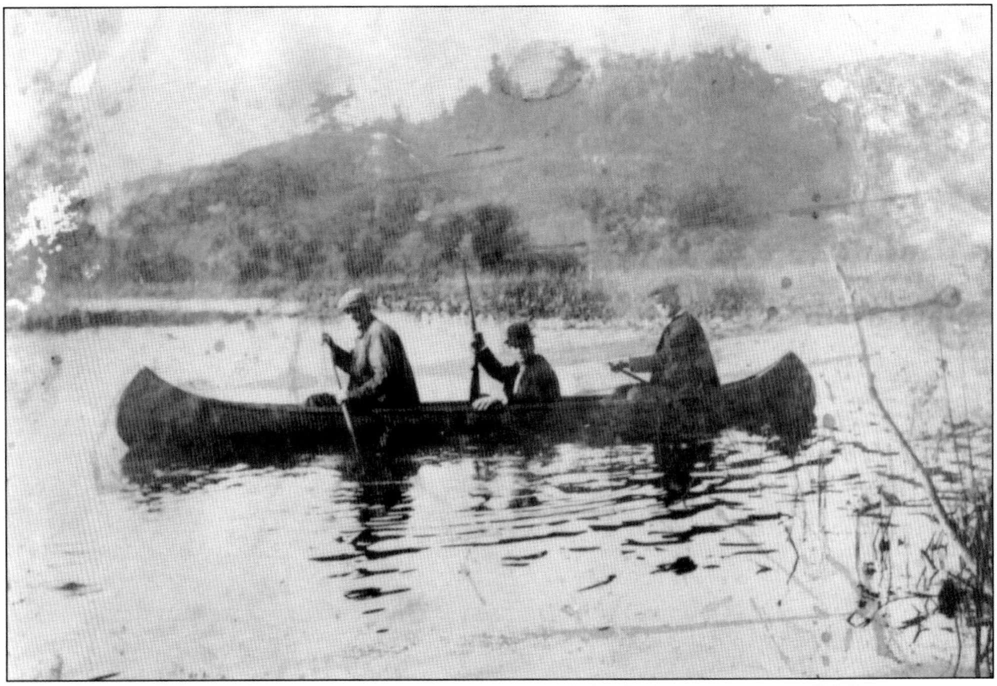

Note the rifle in the hand of the man in the middle of the boat. Hunting and fishing were not only ways of sustaining a living; they were also sport. The wild game available included deer, mallards, wild turkeys, geese, quail, and even beaver. (Courtesy of Clara Harmening.)

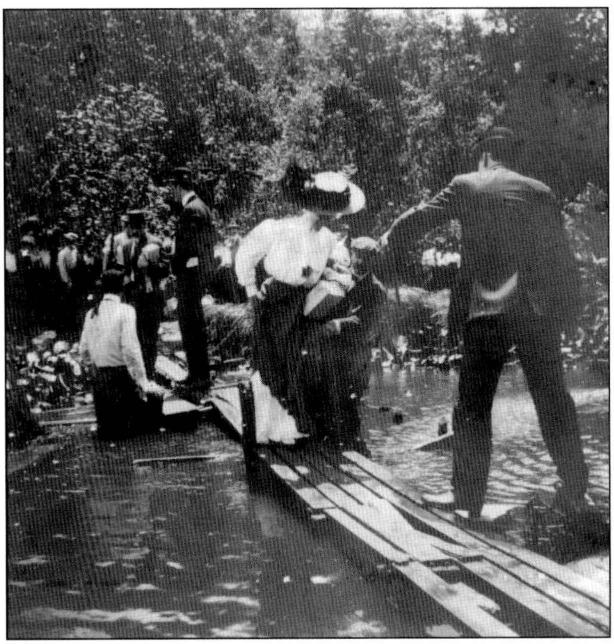

Some people worried that too much time spent in dance halls and other less-than-healthy places could disrupt the social order. Organizations like the Chicago Playground Association, whose mission was to provide outdoor recreation for urban children, started hosting Saturday Afternoon Walking Trips, including their 1908 Memorial Day hike to the Indiana dunes, which attracted 338 people. Other hiking clubs abounded too, lured not only by the beauty of the dunes and the beach, but also its woods and marshes. Pictured is a Saturday Afternoon Walking Trip in Miller in May 1908. (Courtesy of the Westchester Township History Museum.)

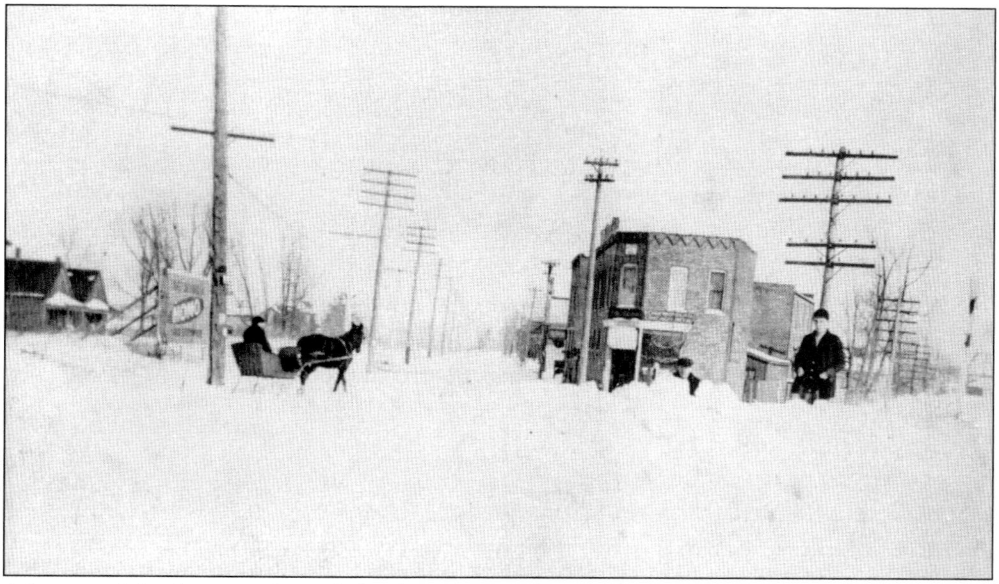

A horse and sleigh moves through the deep snow in front of the Arvidson Building, also known as "The Point" because of its distinctive triangular shape. Even when the sun wasn't shining, Miller residents and visitors made sure to have a good time. Miller resident Mr. Olson owned a hauling business and used teams of horses to haul sand and timber for the construction of buildings in Gary and Chicago. He also rented sleighs and buggies to Miller residents and out-of-towners. (Courtesy of Len PrGyweller.)

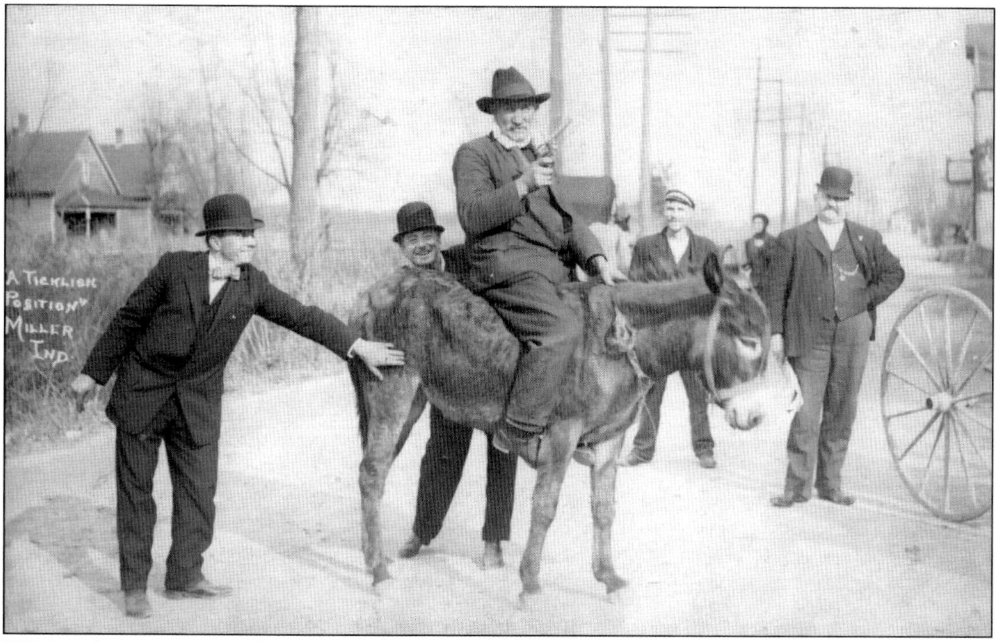

While joking around with horses was always fun, there were several ways to stay amused in Miller. In the early part of the 1900s, the beach was also a place for movies to be filmed. One such film, the silent movie *Lost in the Desert*, filmed in 1910, told the story of a young British officer who, after escaping the Bedouins, wandered the Sudan until he was rescued by the cavalry. (Courtesy of Marilyn Leech and Holly Rodino Breese.)

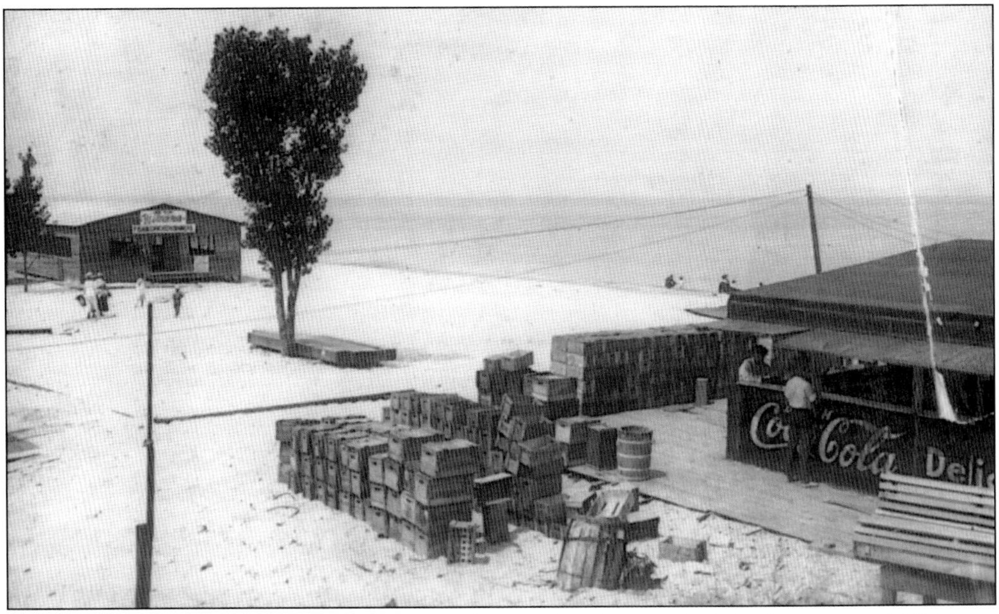

When sun-seekers first started flocking to the beaches lining the lakeshore east of Chicago, amenities were lacking. "If someone would only put up sheds for horses, and a house for shelter for people at the beach, and serve something to eat, and provide some kind of amusement for the crowds, there would be money in it," read an article on the popularity of the beaches in a 1904 edition of the *Chesterton Tribune*. Very quickly, concessionaires began appearing on the beach. (Courtesy of Joyce Davis, Lake Street Gallery.)

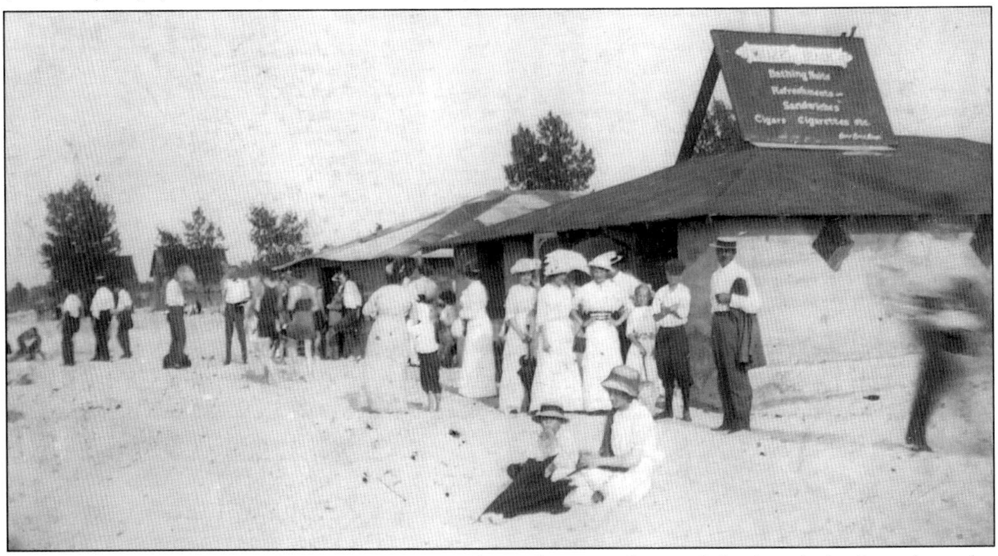

Before the crowds came, when squatters were the only ones who used the beach, birds such as the trumpeter swan, the white pelican, and the bald eagle, as well as owls, whippoorwills, mocking birds, and blue herons nested in the dunes. Deer, badgers, porcupines, possum, beavers, minks, raccoons, and red foxes lived here too. But there were more dangerous residents as well, including copperheads, rattlesnakes, blue racers, black bears, timber wolves, and wildcats. But by the time people like these women in their long white dresses and white hats put a day at the beach on their agenda, the wild animals had mostly disappeared. (Courtesy of the Calumet Regional Archives, IU Northwest.)

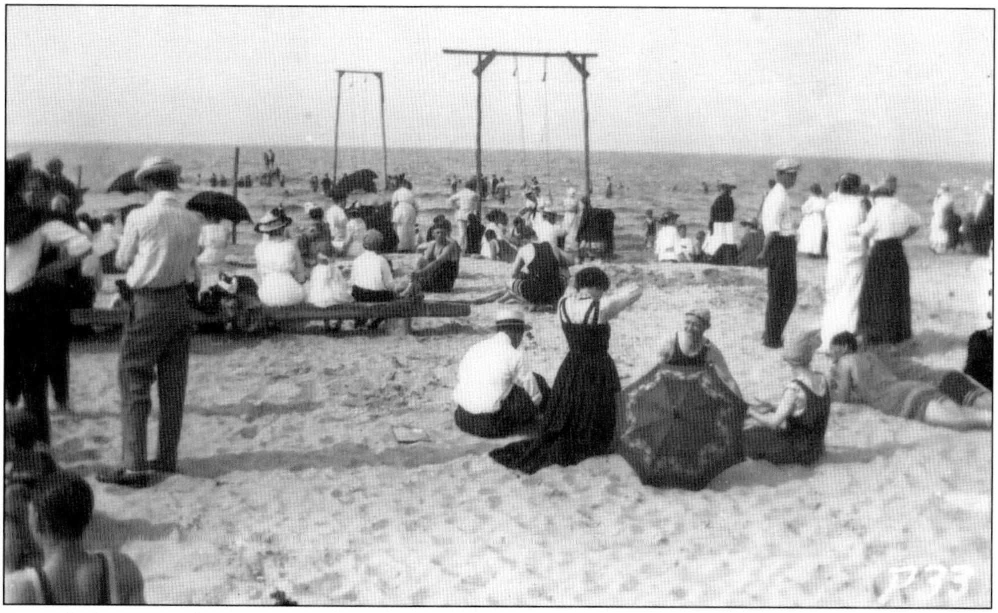

By 1917, Carr's Beach had grown with the addition of a boardwalk, dancehall, roller rink, and shooting gallery, as well as 100 cottages, which rented for $100 each a year. Drusilla Carr also charged people $100 for the right to build a cottage on her beach property. Even into the 1920s, tents, summer cottages, rooms in private homes, and cabin rentals were typical for duneland vacationers. Long white dresses and big white bonnets as beachwear gave way to clothing somewhat more revealing and capable of getting wet. (Courtesy of the Calumet Regional Archives, IU Northwest.)

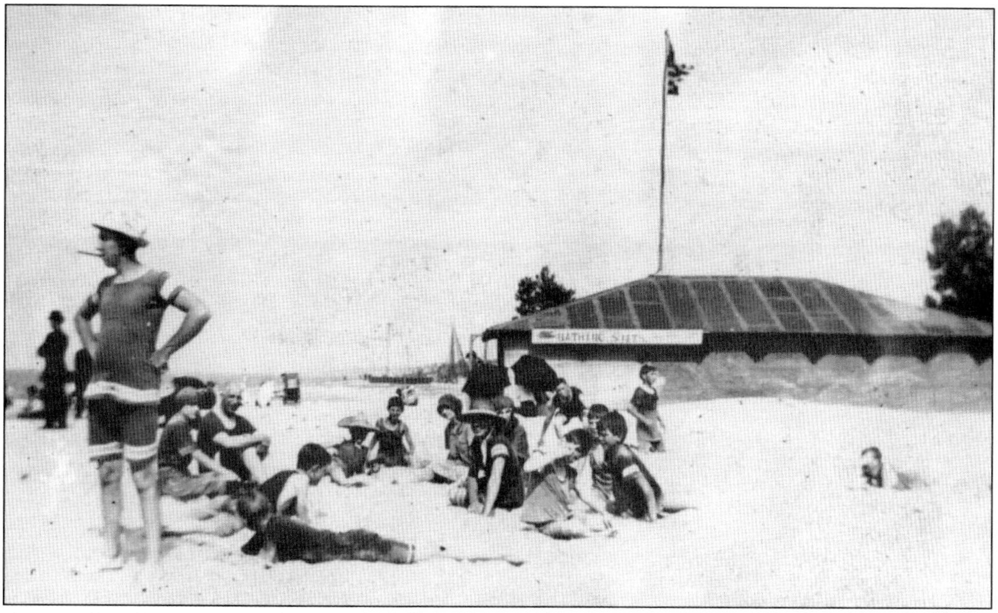

As more beachgoers arrived, creative Millerites started renting out rooms in their homes so visitors had a place to stay overnight. They also made money taking in workers who arrived in droves in 1906 during the beginning of the construction of Gary. During the 1910s and 1920s, many drawn to the area for swimming, fishing, horseback riding, and boating camped on the beach in tents or shacks. (Courtesy of the Calumet Regional Archives, IU Northwest.)

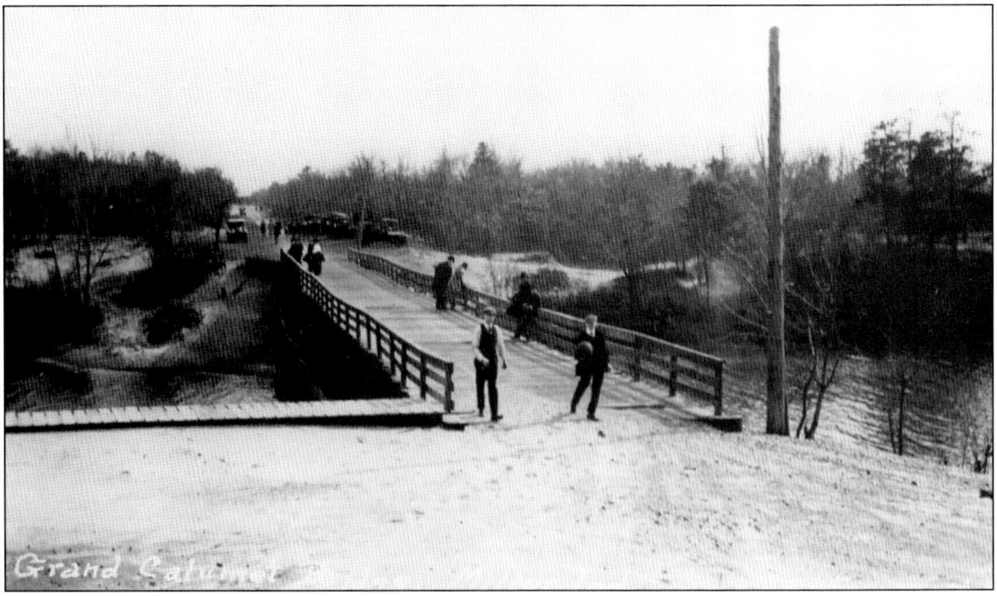

The Dunes Highway linking Michigan City to Gary was built in 1922–1923. "As soon as this highway was finished, traffic was very heavy on Sundays," Esther Pearson recalled. "The cars were bumper to bumper as far as you could see." The bumpers stopped at the old wood bridge crossing the Grand Calumet River and leading to the beach. People left their cars here to hike across the sands to the water. (Courtesy of the Calumet Regional Archives, IU Northwest.)

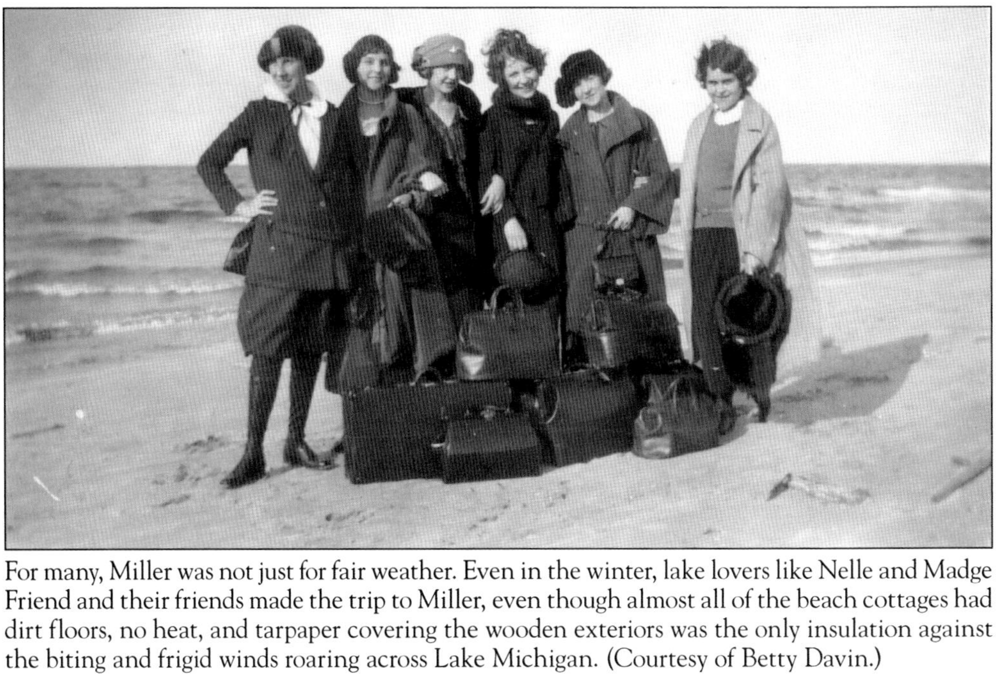

For many, Miller was not just for fair weather. Even in the winter, lake lovers like Nelle and Madge Friend and their friends made the trip to Miller, even though almost all of the beach cottages had dirt floors, no heat, and tarpaper covering the wooden exteriors was the only insulation against the biting and frigid winds roaring across Lake Michigan. (Courtesy of Betty Davin.)

Beginning in the 19th century, beach-going in America became a way for the working class to cast off the tensions of their lives in the big city. The beach lifestyle also began to change the way women dressed. Long gowns and big bonnets were worn in the late 1800s, but by the 1910s, bathing costumes, as they were called, started to show some ankle and leg as well as bare arms. Scandalous but comfortable, the bathing suit kept getting smaller, eventually leading to the bikinis of today. (Courtesy of the Calumet Regional Archives, IU Northwest.)

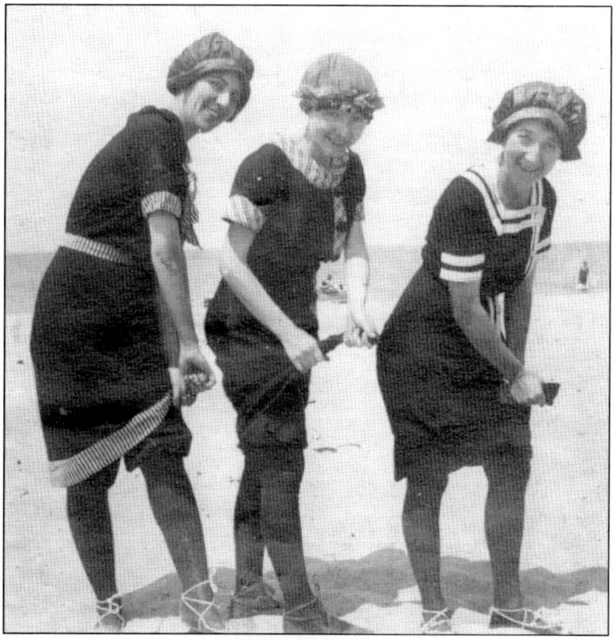

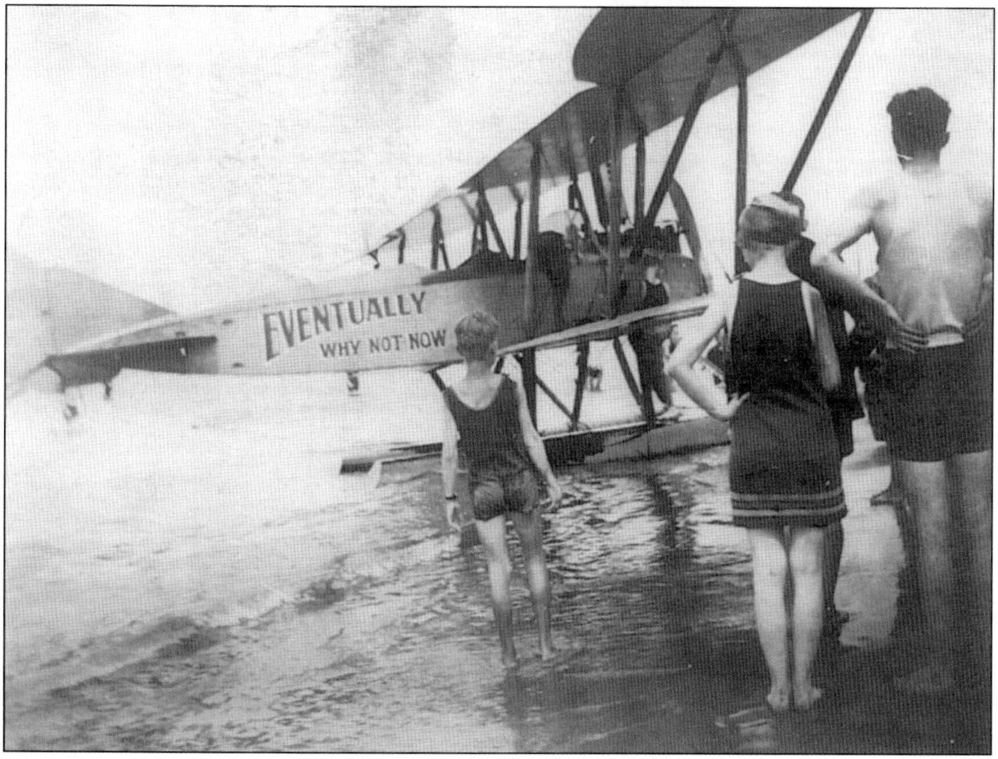

Though it was Octave Chanute who created history by launching the first flight over the dunes, in the early days it was not uncommon for small planes—the only kind at the time—to land on the beach. Laura Jones recalls her father coming home and telling them there was a plane on the beach. They walked down to see this pontoon plane and her father took this photograph. (Courtesy of Laura Valentine Jones.)

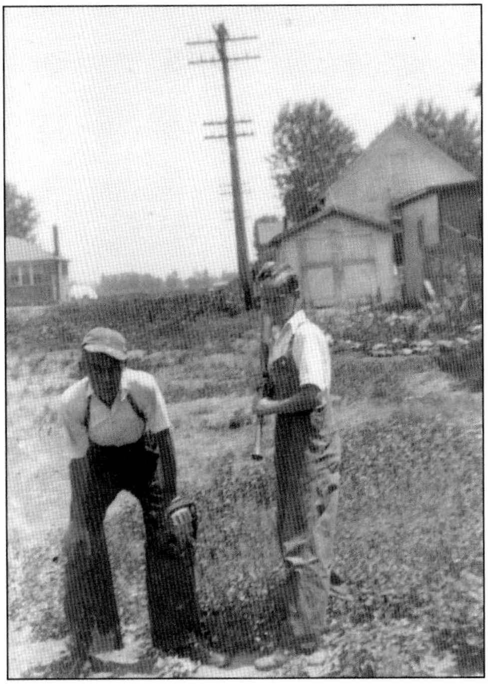

This photograph is labeled "Sabinske" on the back. The Sabinske family were early settlers in Miller and made their living fishing and cutting ice in the winter to store and sell in the summer. Augie Sabinske would net fresh perch for teenagers having beach parties and let children come into his icehouse on hot days to take a few chips of ice. Having grown up when the dunes held nature's bounty for fishing, flora, and wildlife, Augie lamented the changes that took place toward the end of his life. (Courtesy of Marilyn Leech and Holly Rodino Breese.)

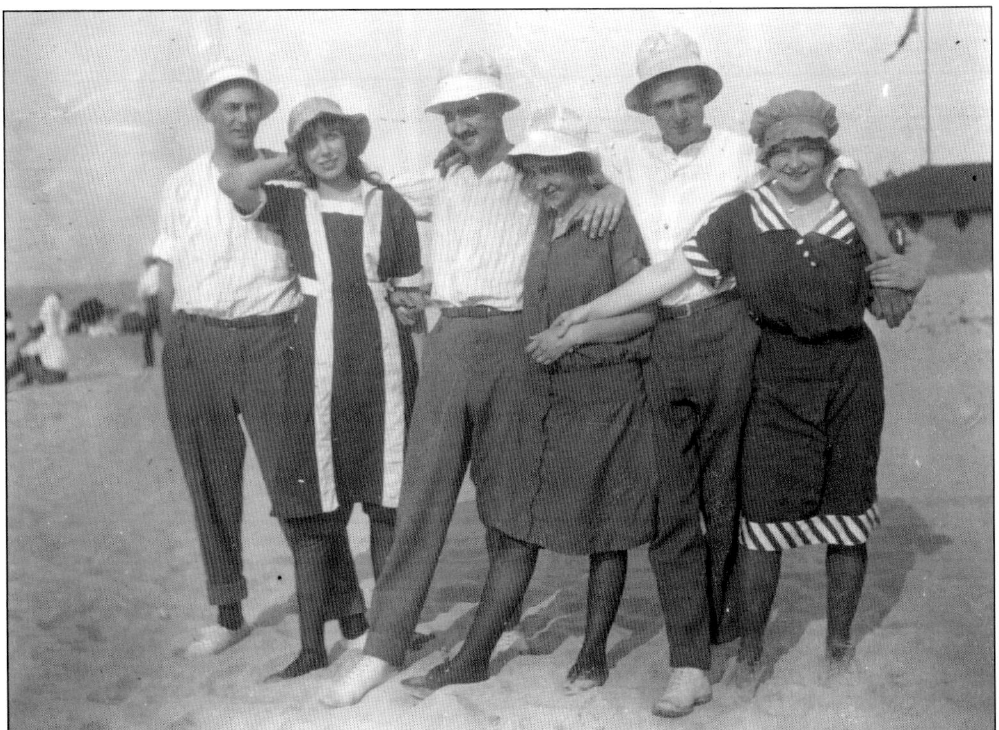

Until the late 1800s, swimming was considered a male sport. But once women began swimming, they needed bathing suits, such as the popular 1880 "princess suit" consisting of a one-piece blouse and trouser. These ladies wear the beach attire typical of the late 1800s and early 1900s. (Courtesy of the Calumet Regional Archives, IU Northwest.)

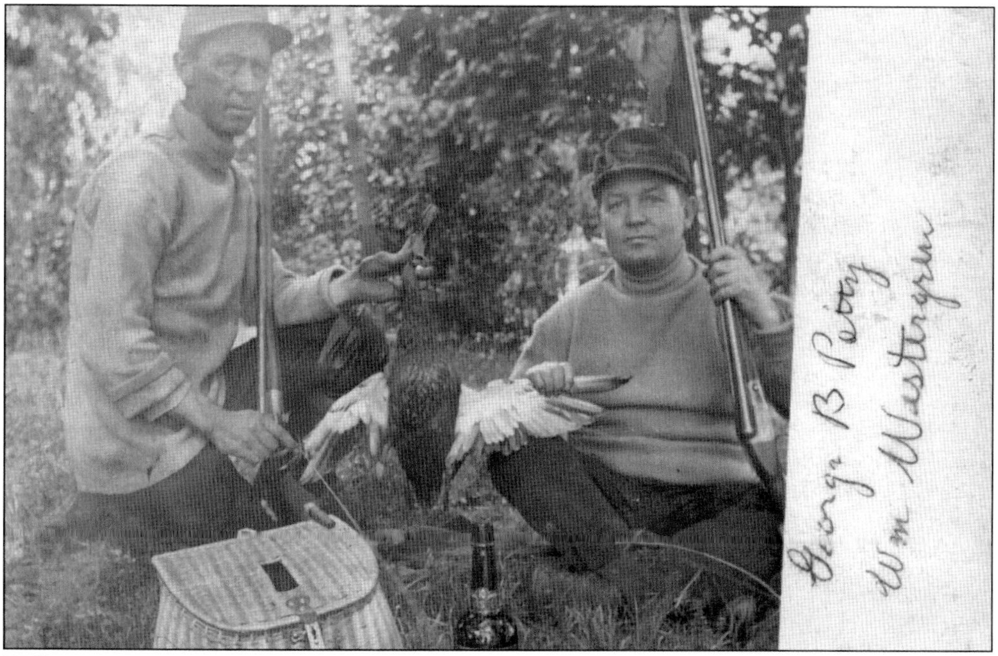

William Westergren was a longtime resident of Miller. He and his friend George Petty are seen here on a bird hunt. In the late 1800s, some area hunters still used muzzleloaders to shoot mallards, which, in the 1870s and 1880s, sold for between 90¢ and $1.15 per dozen in Chicago. Drusilla Carr once recalled that her husband was on his way to the store when she heard gunshots, only to find that he had shot 57 ducks in a very short period. (Courtesy of the Calumet Regional Archives, IU Northwest.)

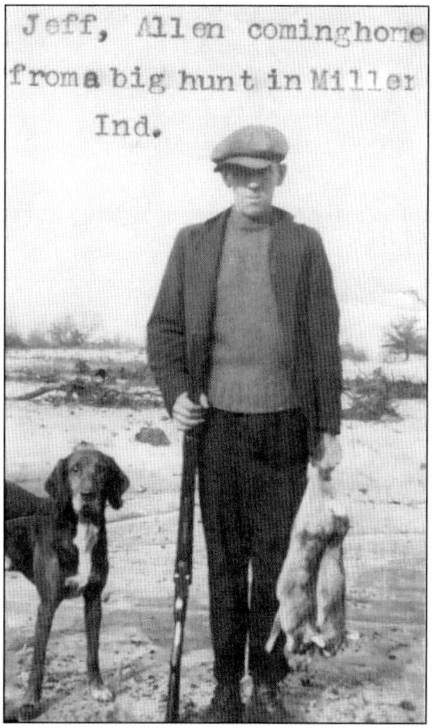

Old-time Miller residents, who often hunted for necessity, were enraged when gun clubs for elite urbanites opened and they were barred from land where their families had hunted for generations. There were often fights between members of the hunting clubs and locals. Guards were said to have beaten poachers. The animosity boiled over in 1893 when a local, Albert Looker, shot and killed two gamekeepers, James Conroy and John Cleary. A local jury found him not guilty on the grounds of self-defense. This family photograph of an early hunter is from the Lillian Westergren Weiger collection. (Courtesy of the Calumet Regional Archives, IU Northwest.)

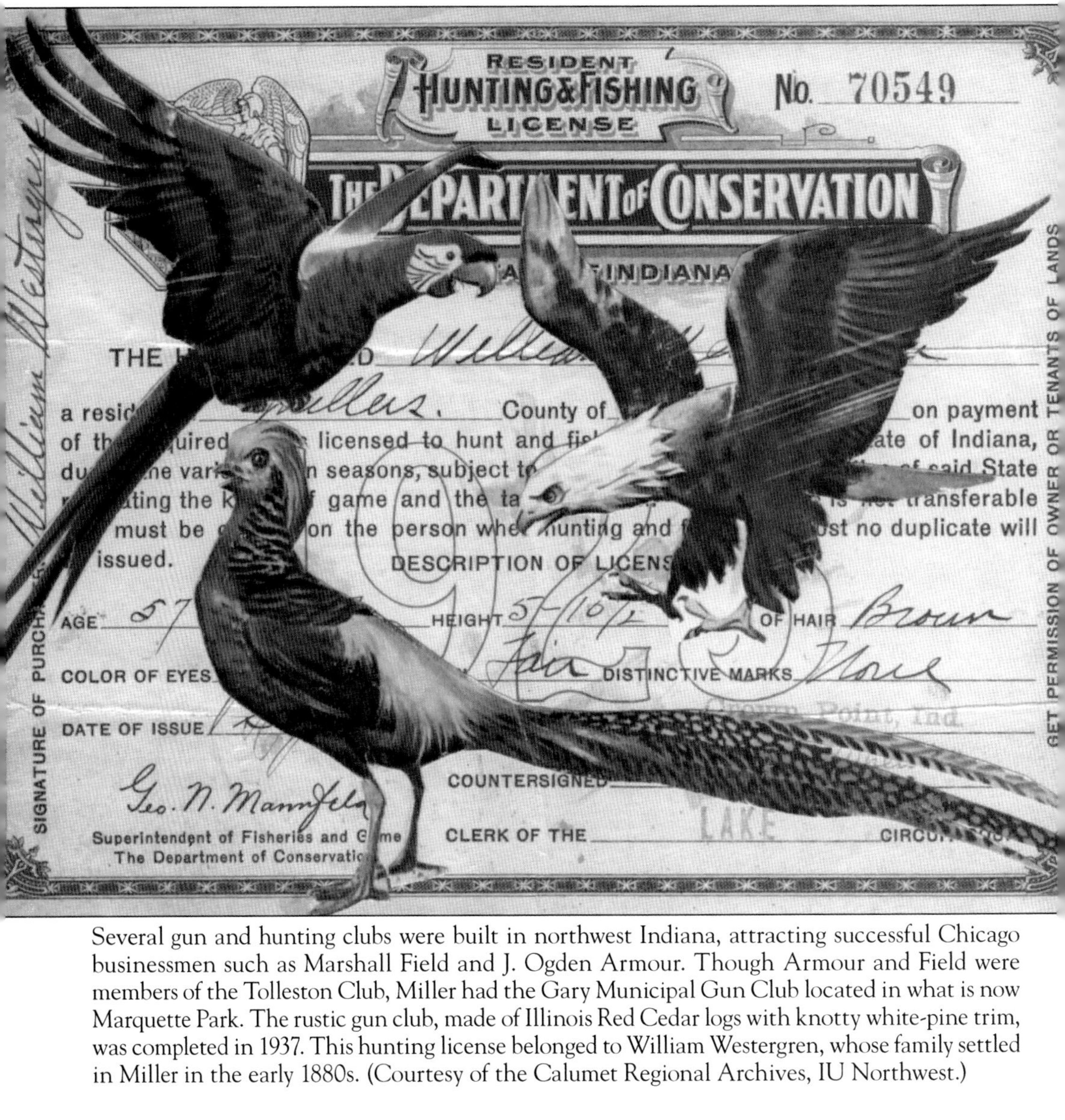

Several gun and hunting clubs were built in northwest Indiana, attracting successful Chicago businessmen such as Marshall Field and J. Ogden Armour. Though Armour and Field were members of the Tolleston Club, Miller had the Gary Municipal Gun Club located in what is now Marquette Park. The rustic gun club, made of Illinois Red Cedar logs with knotty white-pine trim, was completed in 1937. This hunting license belonged to William Westergren, whose family settled in Miller in the early 1880s. (Courtesy of the Calumet Regional Archives, IU Northwest.)

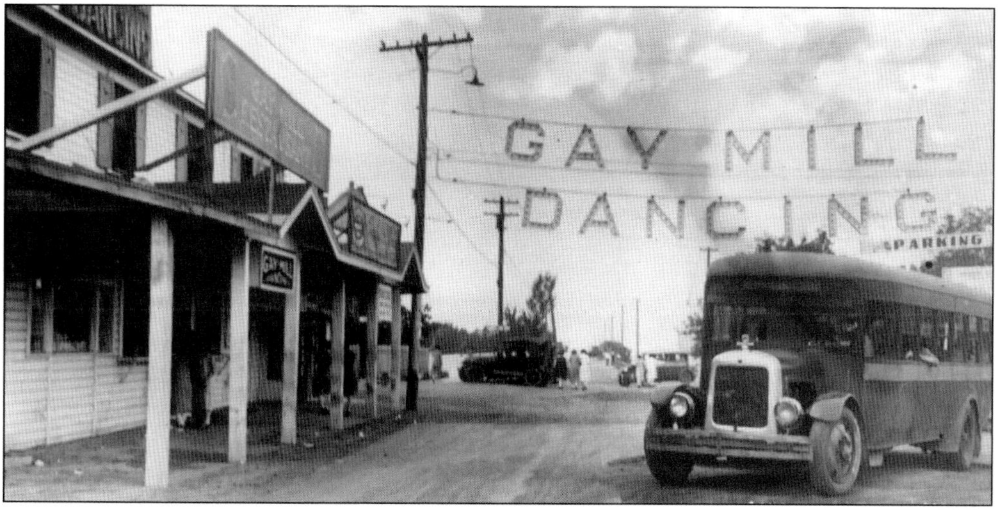

In the 1920s, Chicago attorney Thomas Johnson and his wife, Frances Kennedy, a vaudeville performer, opened Gay Mill, a dance and recreation hall on Lake Street just south of the Grand Calumet River. Big-name bands from all over the country including Jack Benny, Paul Whiteman, Ted Weems, and Wayne King performed there. Laura Jones remembers going on double dates there to roller skate and describes the dance floor as being made of glass panels with lights underneath. Gay Mill was not the only fun spot in Miller—the Dunes White House, a roadhouse, restaurant, and dancehall, was located on the Dunes Highway, and Rahutas Gardens was nearby—but neither figured in residents' memories as Gay Mill did. In 1927, Gay Mill received a license to operate Gary's first radio station, WJKS, which was affectionately known as "Where Joy Kills Sorrow." (Courtesy of the Calumet Regional Archives, IU Northwest.)

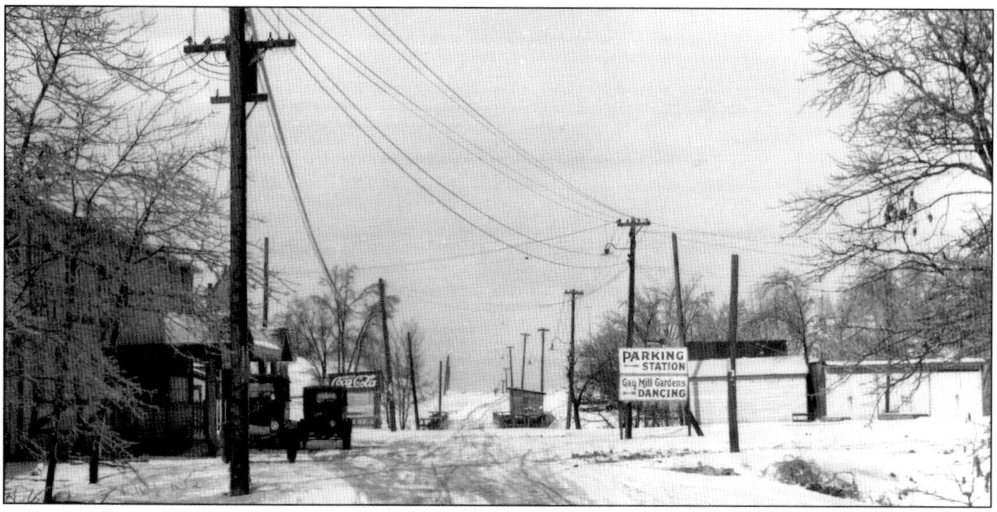

Lillian Westergren Weiger remembers dressing in a white satin dress and white felt tams as one of six hostesses at Gay Mill, whose job was to take dance tickets. Her boss acted as a bouncer and made sure that couples did not dance too closely and that no one performed a dance called "the shimmy." "I suppose it did look a little immoral," Weiger recalled. "But it sure was fun to get there and really wriggle." For 25¢, a jitney took people from Fifth Avenue and Broadway in Gary to Gay Mills. Though the dance floor was immensely popular for a time, the early days of the Depression forced Gay Mills to close and the building burned down in 1930. (Courtesy of the Calumet Regional Archives, IU Northwest.)

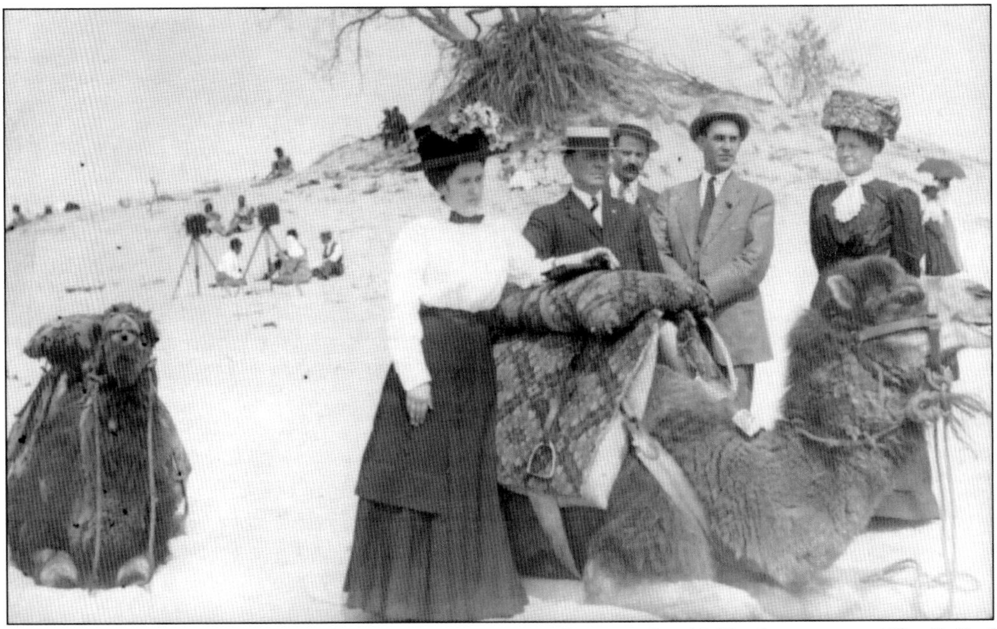

Miller Beach had a starring role as a Mexican coastline in the 1912 silent movie *The Fall of Montezuma* produced by Selig Polyscope Company of Chicago and starring, as Hernando Cortez, actor Francis X. Bushman, whose long list of credits ended only with his death in 1966. In the same year, it was also a substitute for a Mexican beach in the Chicago-based Essanay Film Manufacturing Company's three-reeler *The Plum Tree*, also starring Francis X. Bushman, along with Wallace Beery and the Chicago-born Lester Cuneo. (Courtesy of the Westchester Township History Museum and Porter County Museum of History.)

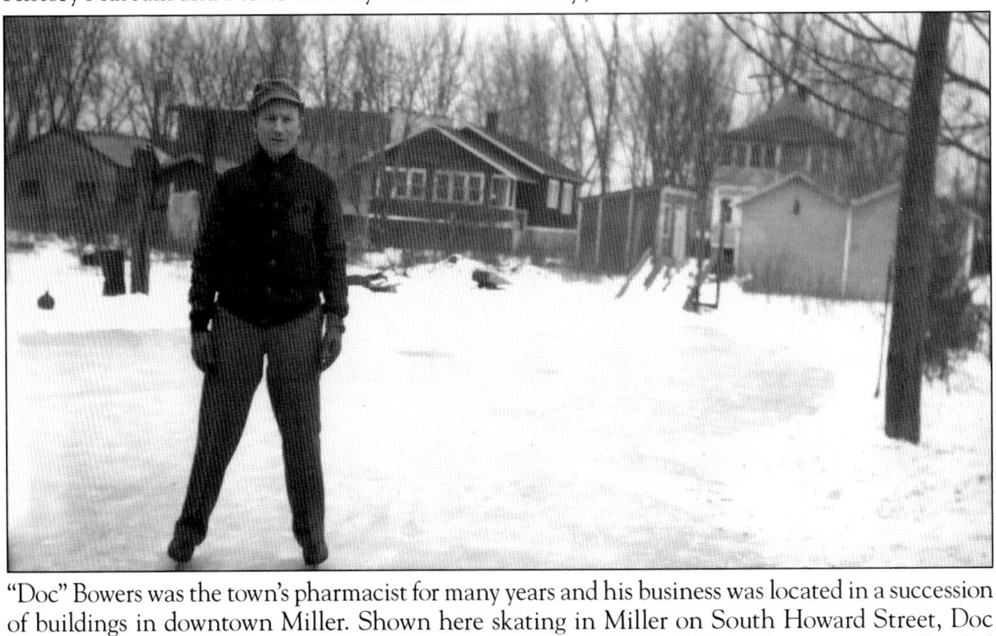

"Doc" Bowers was the town's pharmacist for many years and his business was located in a succession of buildings in downtown Miller. Shown here skating in Miller on South Howard Street, Doc Bowers was known for his sage advice. Ice skating was popular in Miller and some parents flooded their backyards so kids could skate. Other times, they would skate on the river once it had frozen solid. (Courtesy of the Calumet Regional Archives, IU Northwest.)

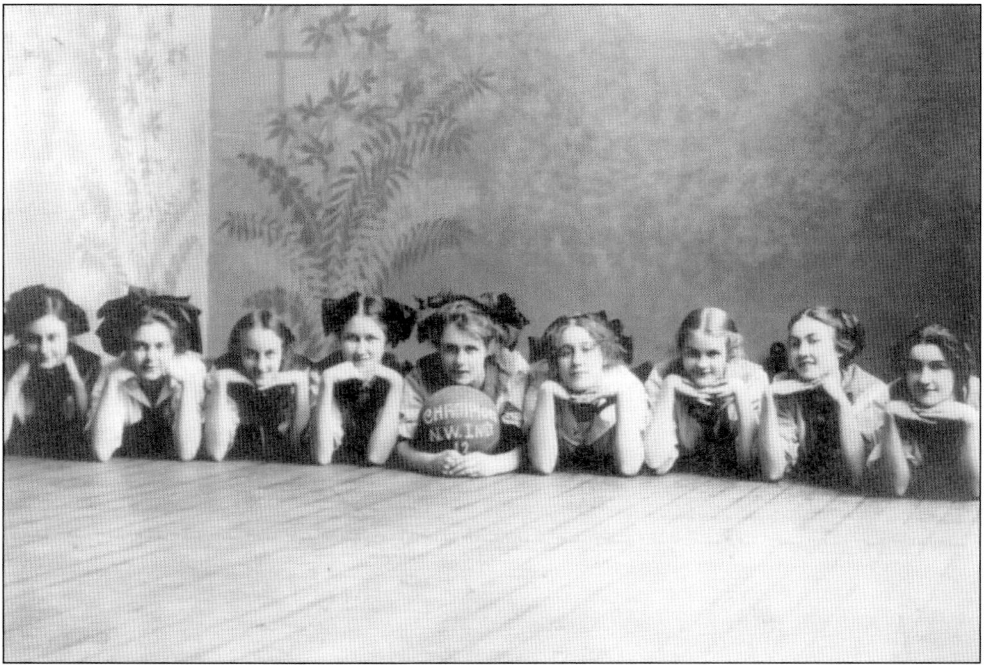

The 1913 Miller women's basketball team, featuring these ladies, won the Northwest Indiana championship. (Courtesy of Joyce Davis, Lake Street Gallery)

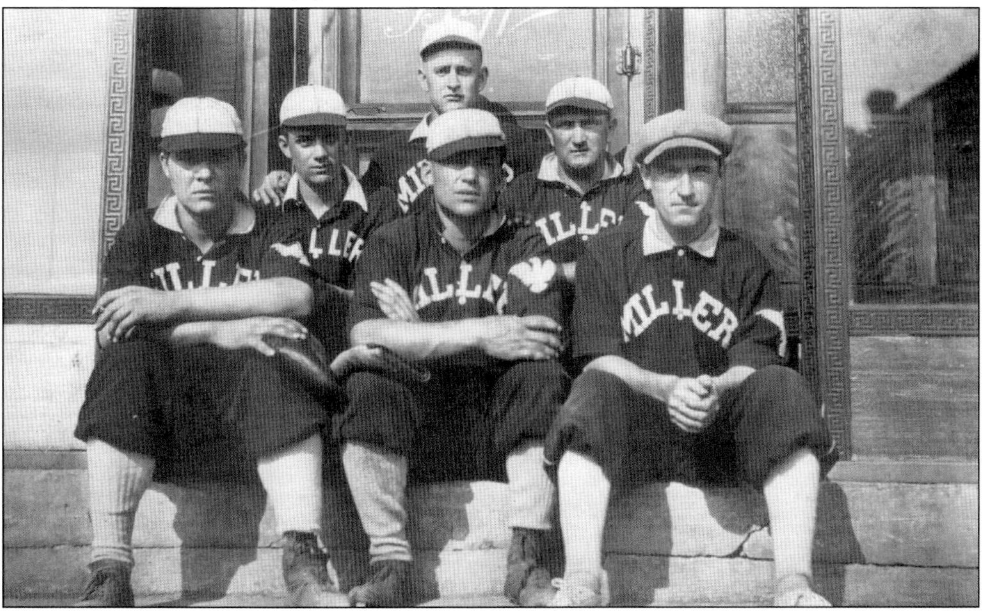

This 1910s Miller baseball team was sponsored by Isaac Leech (first row, right), the owner of Leech's Tavern on Lake Street. Baseball was very popular in Miller for more than a half-century, and even up to the late 1930s and early 1940s, Miller had a softball diamond and a six-team league with teams such as Club Miller, Vanderburg Sluggers, the Beach Combers, and Stillson's Butchers. Many of the players had interesting nicknames like "Foots" Leech, "Nothing Ball" Swede Lindstrom, and "Ducky" Ahlgren. Often, hundreds of fans would show up to watch the games. (Courtesy of Marilyn Leech and Holly Rodino Breese.)

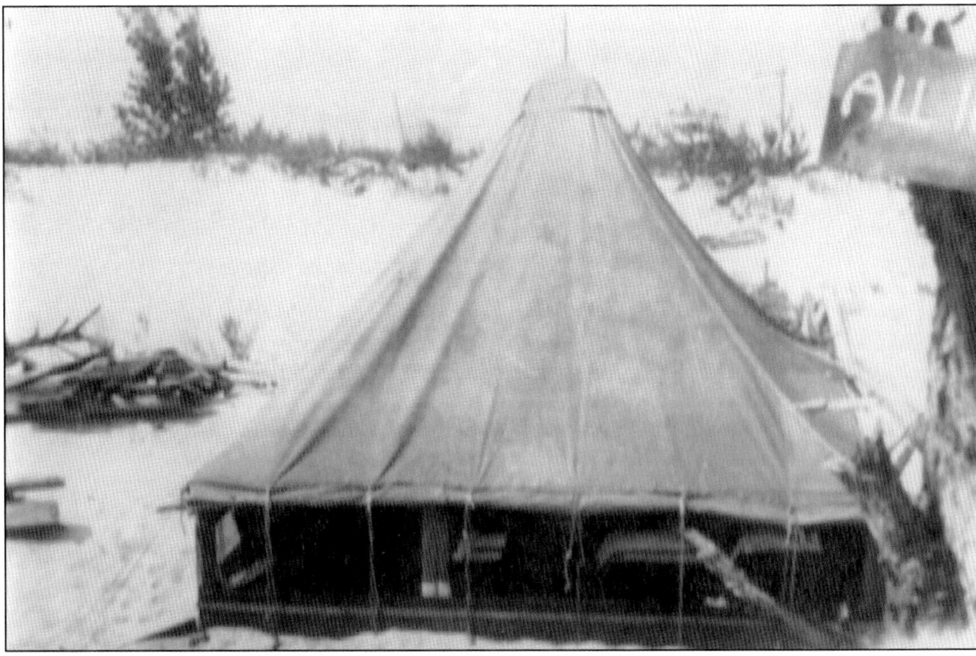

Pitching a tent and camping on the beach was very popular in the 1910s and 1920s and earned people the nickname "dune bugs." But real estate developers touted Miller Beach as more than just a place to scamper around and more substantial lodging was eventually built. Pictured is one of the tents used by the Hough family in the early 1920s before their cottage was built. (Courtesy of Alice Pickford.)

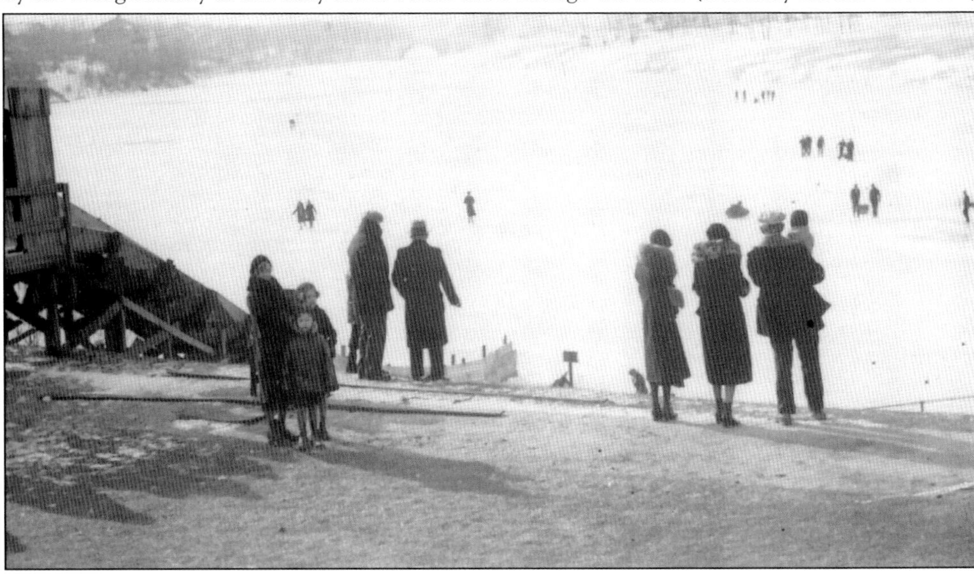

At one time, the eastern lagoon, part of the Grand Calumet River, flowed south past the bathhouse and into Lake Michigan. But the landscape was altered more than a century ago, when a horse-drawn wagon burdened with Christmas trees tried to ford the river entrance from the lake and got stuck. To lighten the load, the trees were pushed off and the wind eventually buried them in the sand. According to some accounts, this manmade barrier severed the connection between the lake and the river. The lagoon is still remembered, however, as a great skating spot. (Courtesy of the Calumet Regional Archives, IU Northwest.)

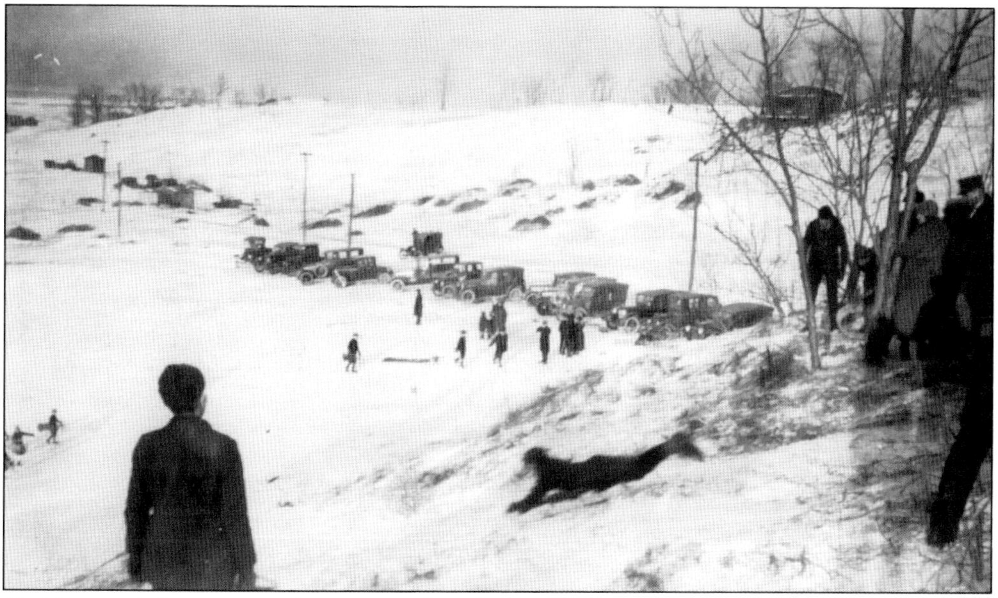

Sledding and skiing were also promoted to draw people to the dunes. South Shore Railroad posters from the 1920s featured drawings of young women sledding and skiing down the dunes to encourage people to ride the train no matter what the weather was like. Fathers made skis out of barrel staves and groups of kids headed to the dunes. (Courtesy of the Calumet Regional Archives, IU Northwest.)

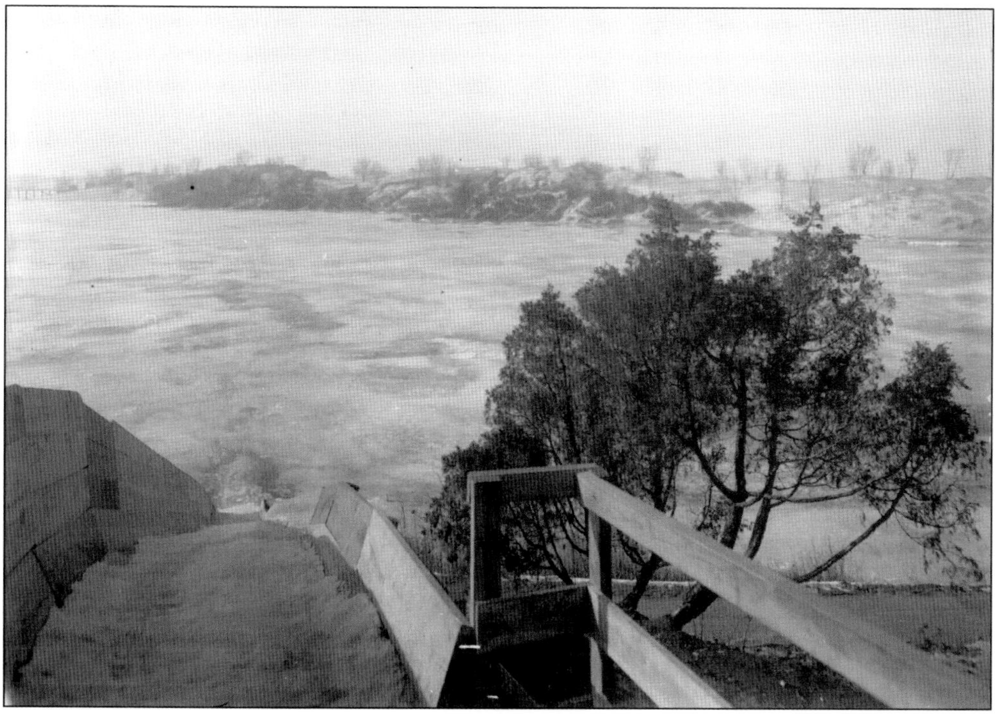

On icy winter days, those brave enough pulled their sleds or toboggans to the top of the hill on the south side of the pavilion's outdoor dance floor and slid down toward the Marquette Park lagoon. (Courtesy of the Calumet Regional Archives, IU Northwest.)

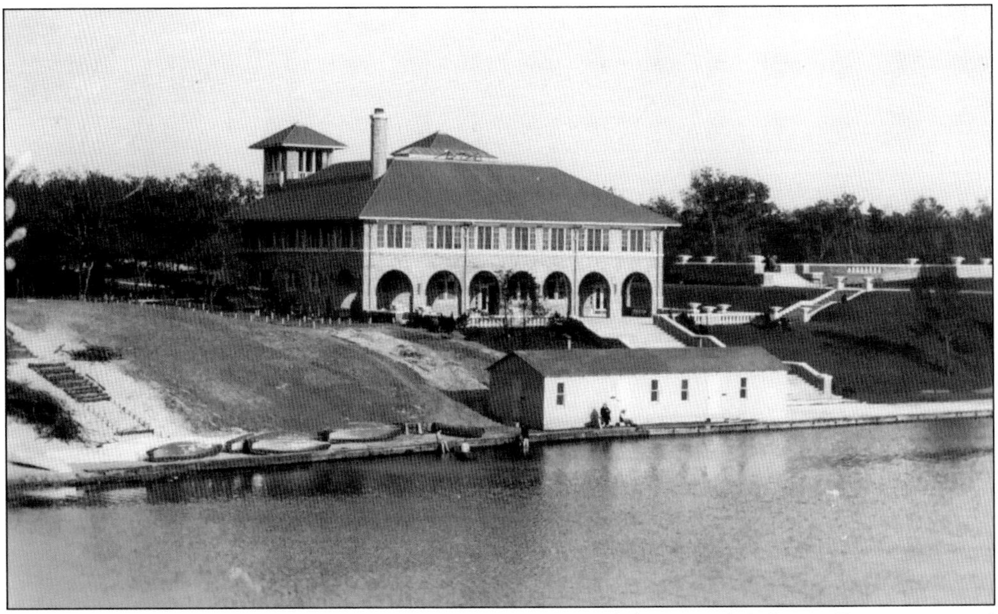

Used year-round, the Marquette Park lagoon, once a part of the Grand Calumet River, attracted boaters, kayakers, and fishermen. In the winter, once the water froze solid, ice skaters headed there. Rising majestically above the lagoon, the Marquette Park Pavilion, with its twin towers, its grand two-story entryway, and its brick façade, has long been a focal point of the community. Through the decades, families have celebrated parties, weddings, graduations, family reunions, and other community events there. (Courtesy of the Calumet Regional Archives, IU Northwest.)

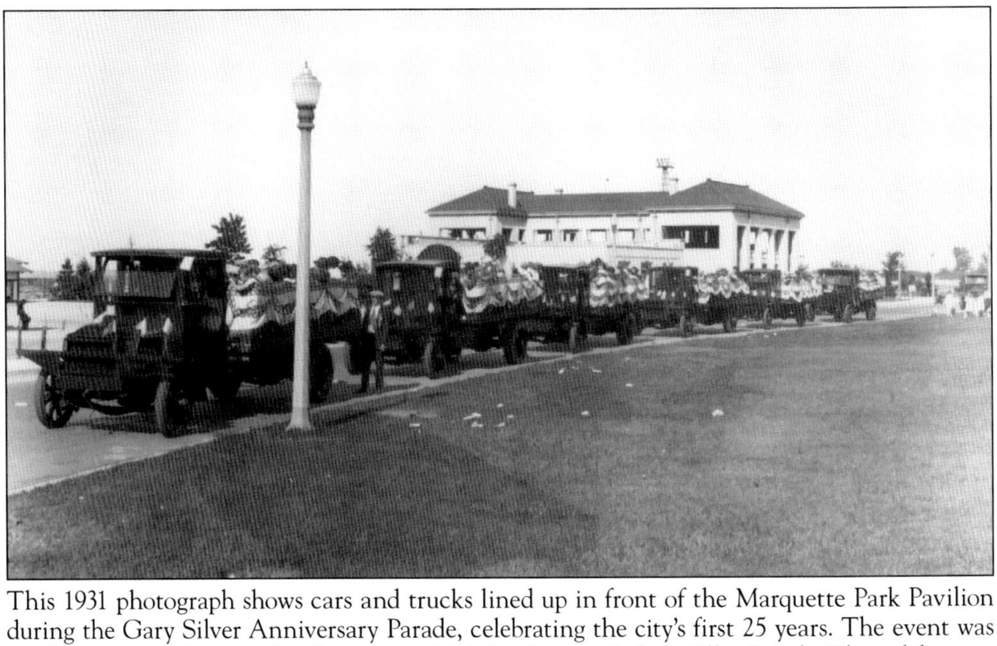

This 1931 photograph shows cars and trucks lined up in front of the Marquette Park Pavilion during the Gary Silver Anniversary Parade, celebrating the city's first 25 years. The event was a celebration of the growth of the city, which by then included Miller Beach. The celebration involved gala displays erected along the lagoon, including a billboard replica of the Gary steel mill's main area. Other displays included a birthday cake, which floated along topped with 25 candles. (Courtesy of the Calumet Regional Archives, IU Northwest.)

Eight

Beach Living

Settling the Dunes

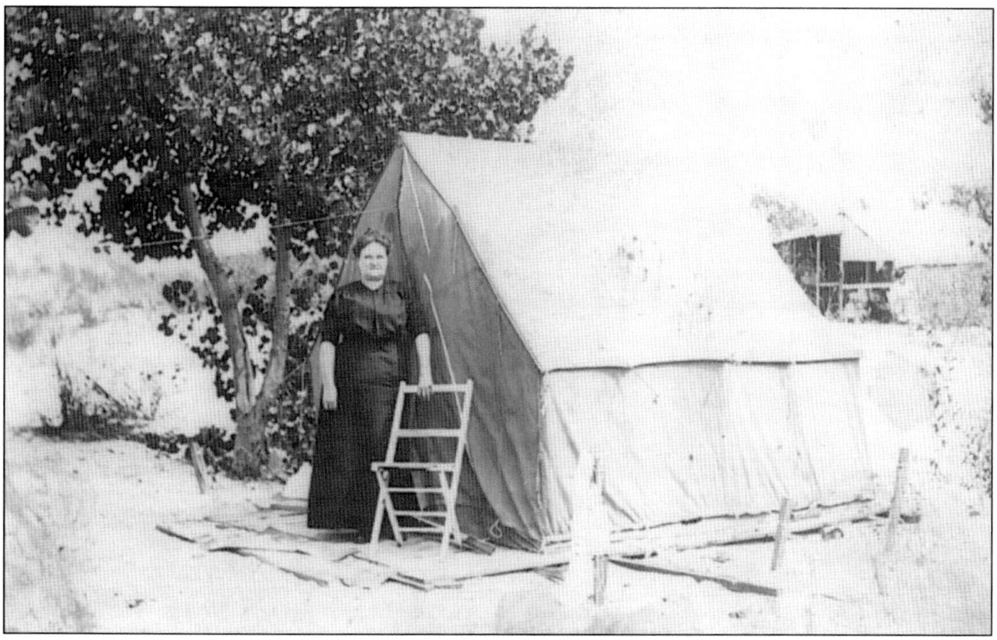

"In the 1920s, despite Miller's growth and annexation to Gary, the beachfront was still an exciting, primitive place to live," writes James Lane in his book *City of the Century*. "Mrs. A.C. Fonville recollected that on one occasion huge pieces of driftwood almost knocked over her rented home." Another time, Mrs. Fonville's porch was taken apart by beachcombers for firewood. It wasn't unusual for people to live in a tent while building their home. (Courtesy of Joyce Davis, Lake Street Gallery.)

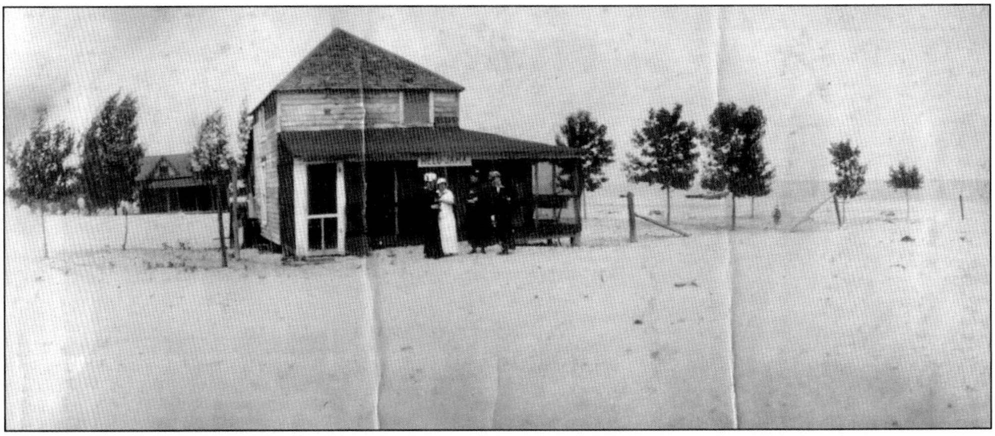

Going to the beach in the late 1800s and early 1900s still seemed like a formal affair. Women wore long dresses and hats and men donned hats too and put on suits. (Courtesy of the Calumet Regional Archives, IU Northwest.)

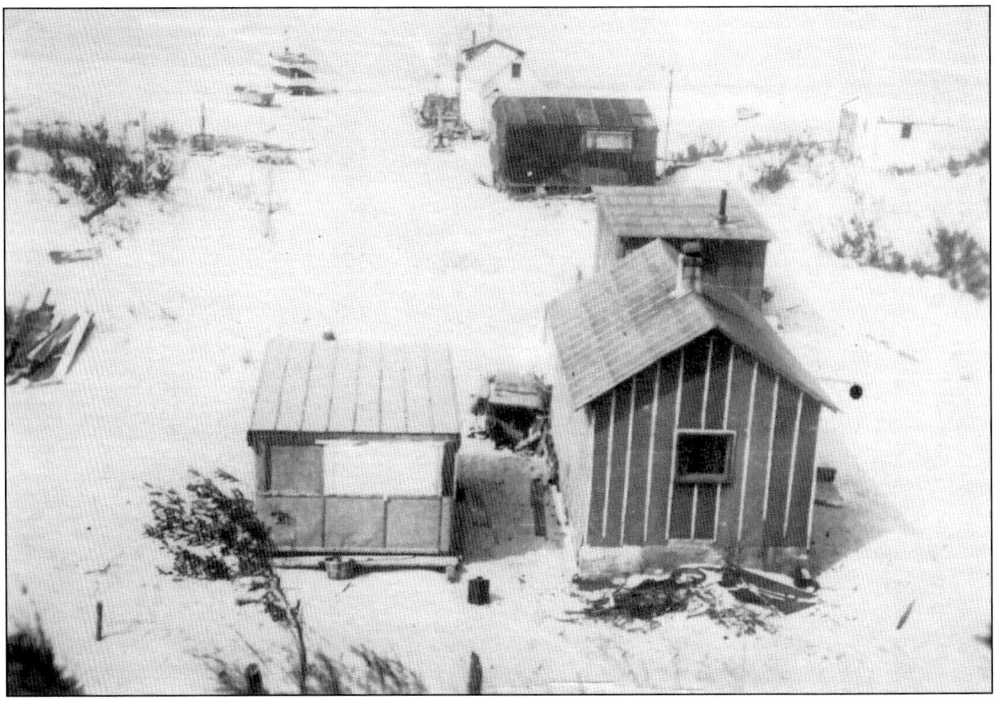

Early Miller Beach homes were primitive, often with dirt floors and outhouses. The area was primitive as well; Drusilla Carr recalled how an eagle once tried to snatch her young son. She fought the eagle, taking swipes at it with her bonnet. Luckily, her husband, who was out on the lake, heard her calls and made it back to the beach, where he drove the eagle away with his paddle. The eagle wasn't done, however. He later attacked another man and was shot at the dam about a mile east. (Courtesy of Alice Pickford.)

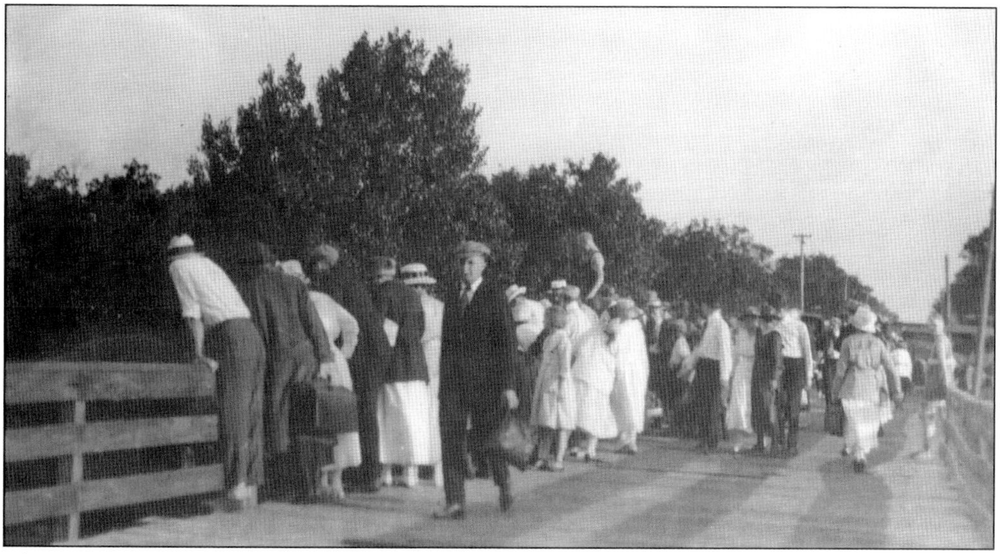

The Doyne family, long a part of Miller Beach, lived in Gary and rode the trolley car out to Lake Street to the Grand Calumet Bridge. Because the bridge could not hold the weight of cars, everyone had to walk it. The Doynes were met there by the Carr family, whose model T with balloon tires took their belongings to their cottage, with the family following on foot. (Courtesy of the Calumet Regional Archives, IU Northwest.)

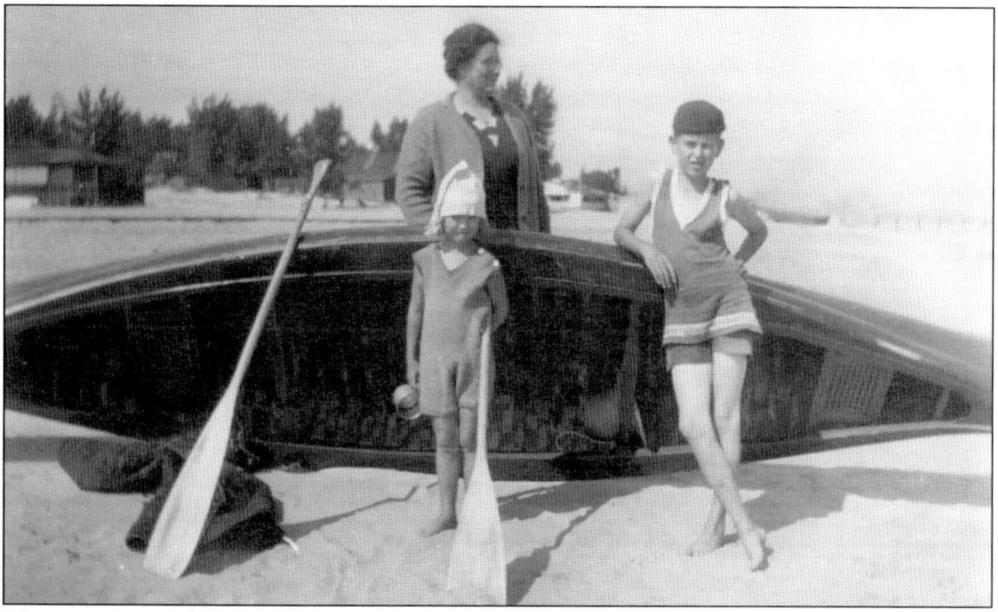

The caption on the back of this photograph reads: "Alice Anchors Clark with Bertha Maude Clark and James Cather Jr. at Miller Beach—Gary, IN." The blueberries and sand started to disappear as tourism increased in the 1920s. But the loss of the cranberries had already occurred. Magnus Anderson, who moved to Miller's Station with his wife Anna in 1864, gathered the white moss growing in the marsh to sell. The moss, used for wrapping trees, was loaded into crates of 175 pounds each and shipped to other states, for which Anderson was paid $3. The moss had protected the cranberries from cold weather and the summer sun, and once it disappeared, so did they. (Courtesy of the Calumet Regional Archives, IU Northwest.)

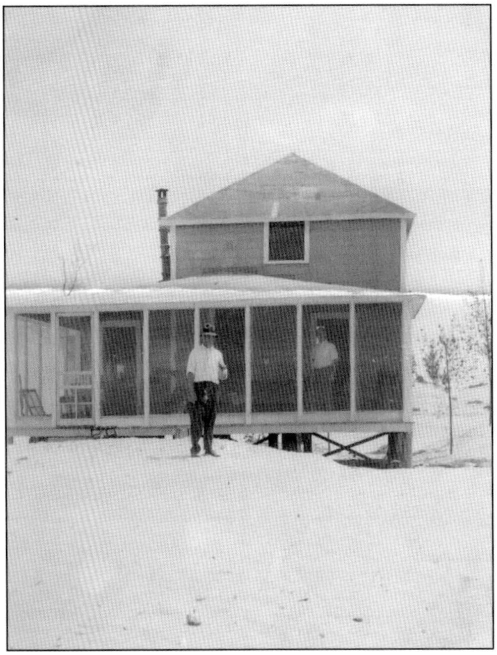

In May 1907, Albert Lee Anchors, seen here in front of his cottage, was passing through Chicago when he saw a sign advertising train fare to Gary for 35¢. The 33-year-old Anchors decided to take a look and ended up staying, starting several successful businesses. Women were scarce in Gary and so the enterprising Anchors befriended new schoolteachers and held parties for them at his beach cottage in Miller. In 1921, he married one of those teachers, Nellie Cary, a teacher at Emerson School. (Courtesy of the Calumet Regional Archives, IU Northwest.)

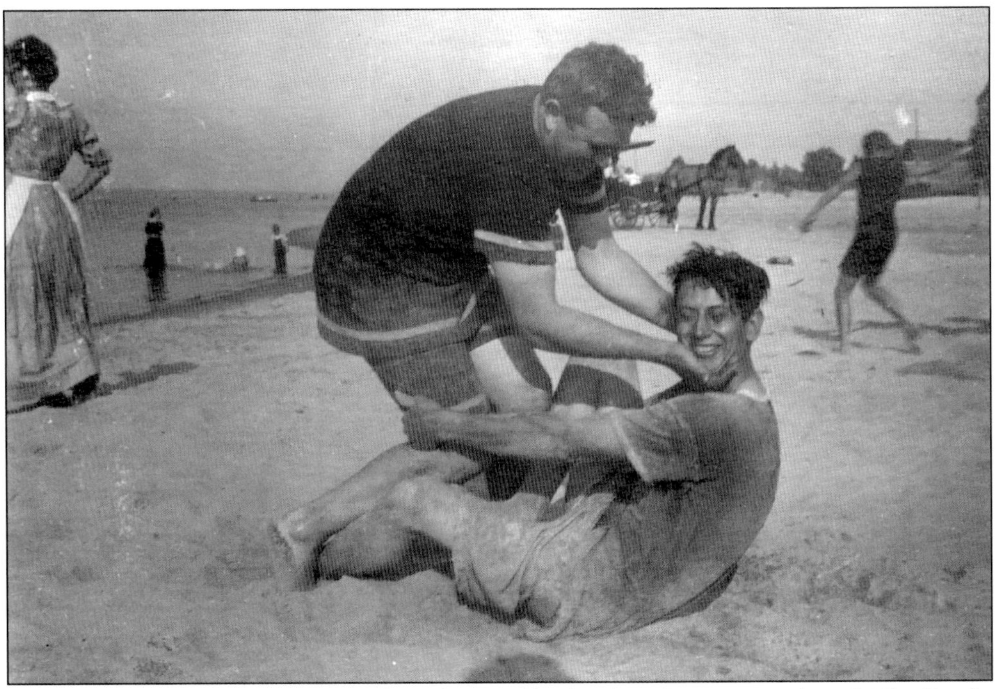

In this postcard from around 1910, Al Anchors and his brother, George, wrestle on Miller Beach. Anchors was one of Gary's pioneer residents and built apartments on the West Side and also formed Gary Transportation and Storage Company as well as several other enterprises. When Anchors arrived in the very new city of Gary, he knew immediately it was his type of place. "What I could see looked like a brand new gold mining camp," he recalled. "I knew how to handle myself in a mining camp and I knew what to do here." (Courtesy of the Calumet Regional Archives, IU Northwest.)

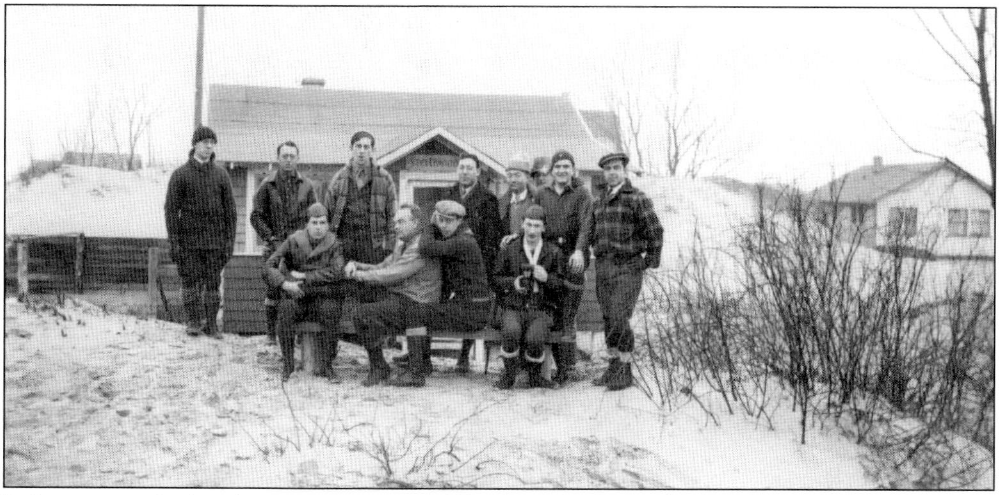

Isolation vanished with easier access to Miller from large population centers like Chicago and Gary, and more cottages began to be built. Unfortunately, as progress advanced, the abundance of native plants and animals began to disappear. After the marshes were drained, many of the plants disappeared, never to grow back. (Courtesy of the Calumet Regional Archives, IU Northwest.)

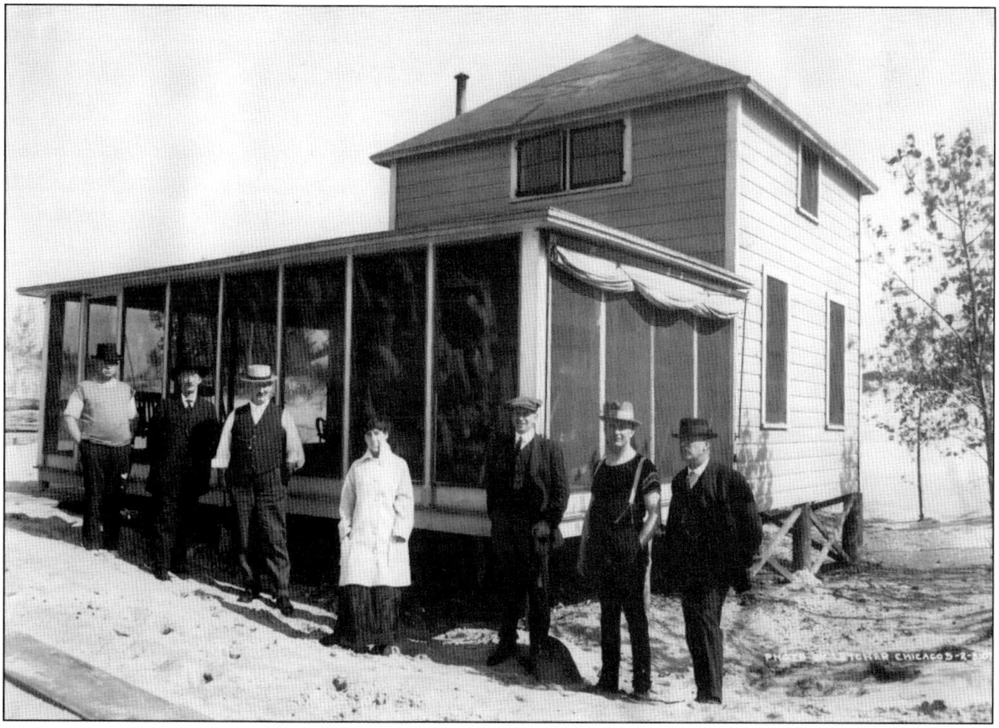

This photograph from the Lillian Westergren Weiger collection shows a lakefront cottage around 1910. There were not many cottages there at that time, but development increased in the years to follow. With the new development, the old ways of fishing, hunting, and gathering started to disappear. "The fish are gone, the gull are gone. The nuts have ruined everything," August Sabinske, a fisherman whose family had lived in Miller since the mid-1800s, said in 1964, referring to the development of the beach, including the steel mills. (Courtesy of the Calumet Regional Archives, IU Northwest.)

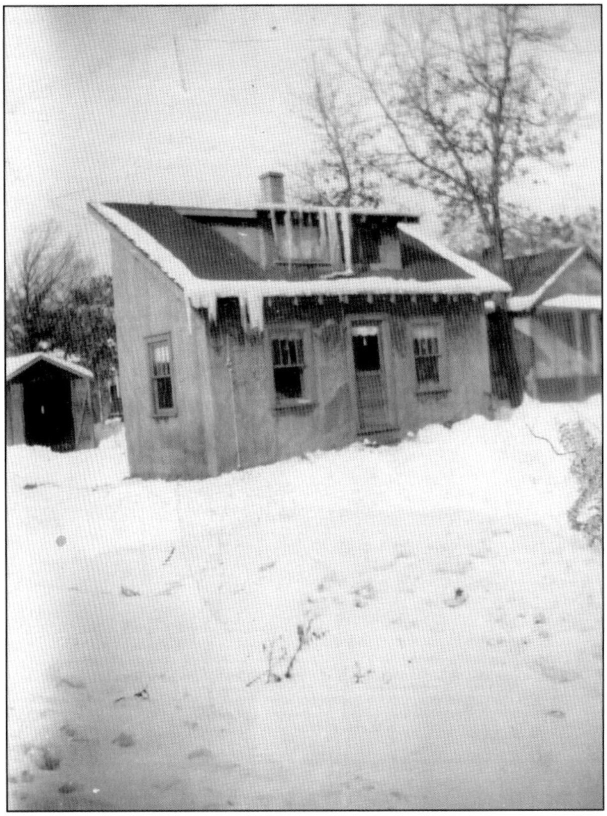

According to Laura Jones, people often built half of their house, like the one shown here, and then moved in. This resourcefulness gave them a place to stay while finishing the other half and saved the cost of having to pay rent. Often, there were open slats between the two halves of the house after they were finished and Laura, who was born in 1917, remembers helping fish out items that had fallen into the narrow cracks. (Courtesy of Laura Valentine Jones.)

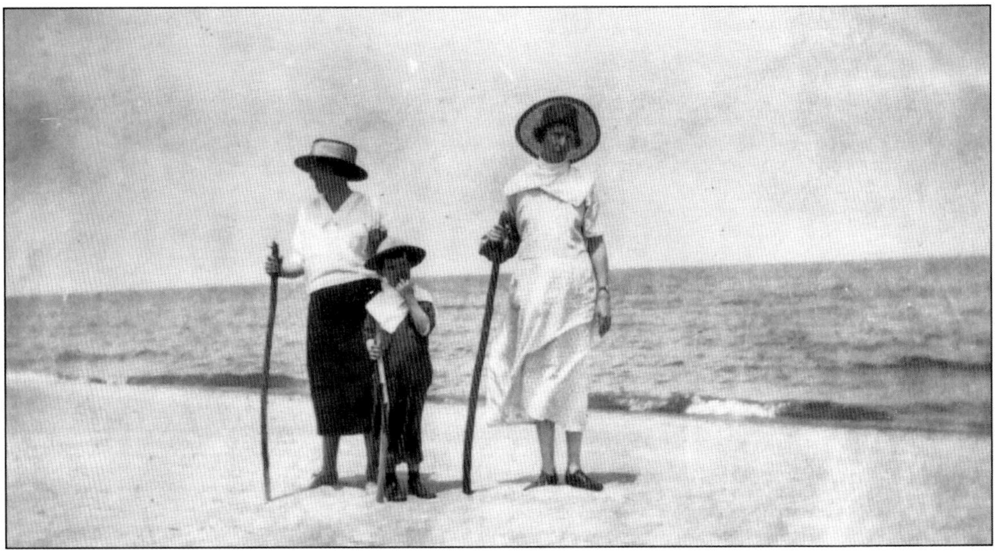

Young William Davin walks the beach with his mother in this 1920s photograph. In 1922, William's aunts, Nelle and Madge Friend, built their own cottage from materials transported down the beach by a horse hauling a raft through shallow water. Writing in a 1998 issue of *Steel Shavings*, a magazine published by Indiana University Northwest, William's sister, Betty Davin, recalled: "When I was a little girl, we'd stay at the cottage all summer. And take the train back to Chicago on weekends to meet my father who was a traveling salesman." (Courtesy of Betty Davin.)

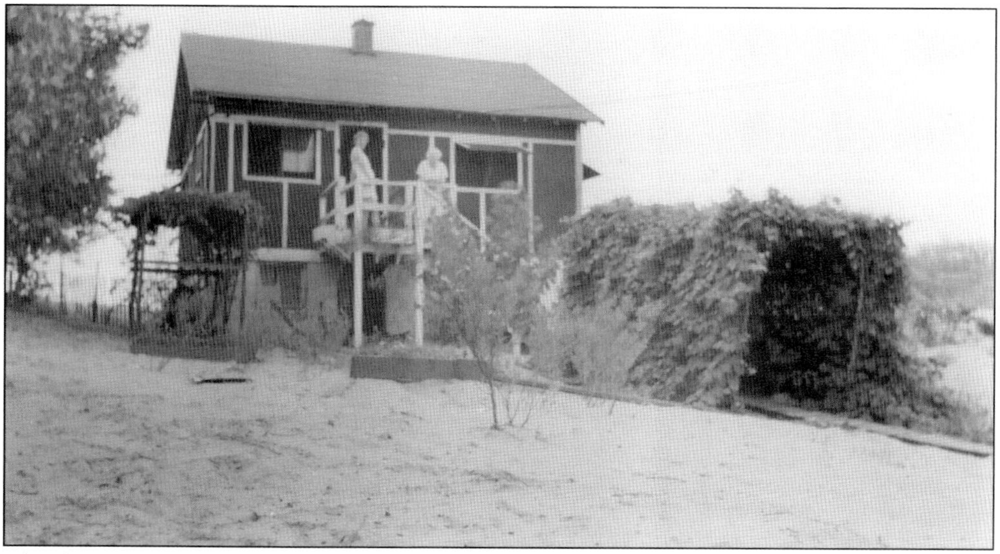

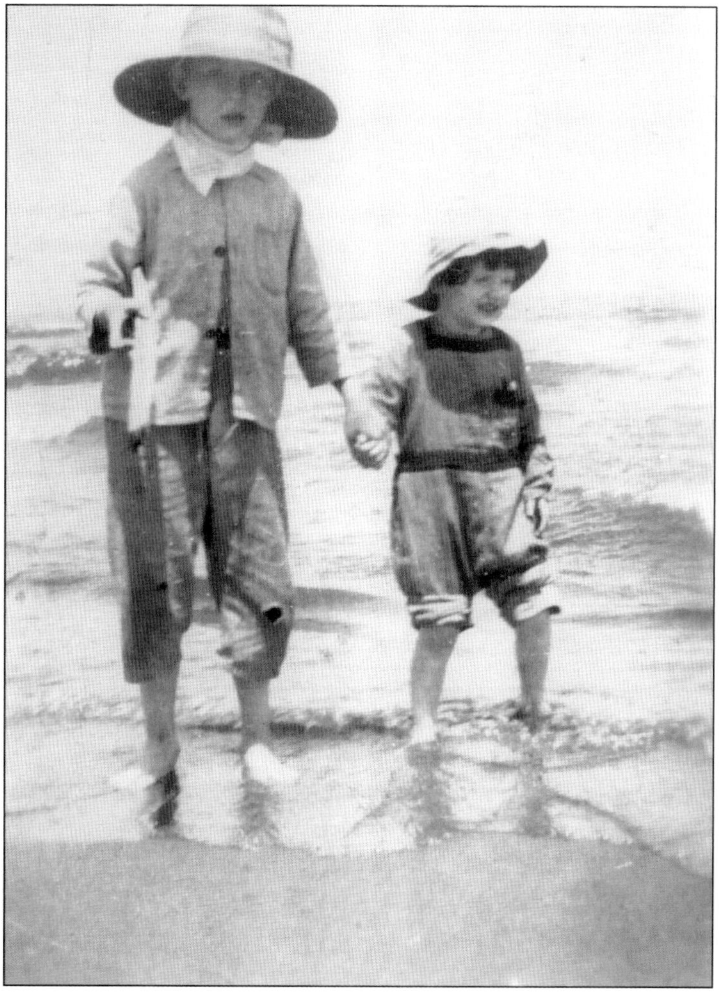

The above image shows the cottage where Betty Davin stayed with her aunts, Nelle and Madge Friend. The cottage, initially built on stilts in 1922, had a dirt floor and ropes to pull up the shutters. Bushes of wild sand cherries grow in the front of the cottage. The family made wonderful jelly from the sand cherries. Nelle and Madge's cottage was later raised and renovated and a concrete basement was added, along with insulation. Betty, shown at right with her brother, remembers the cottage having the grape arbor pictured above. These wild grapes were used to make the best jelly she remembers ever eating. (Courtesy of Betty Davin.)

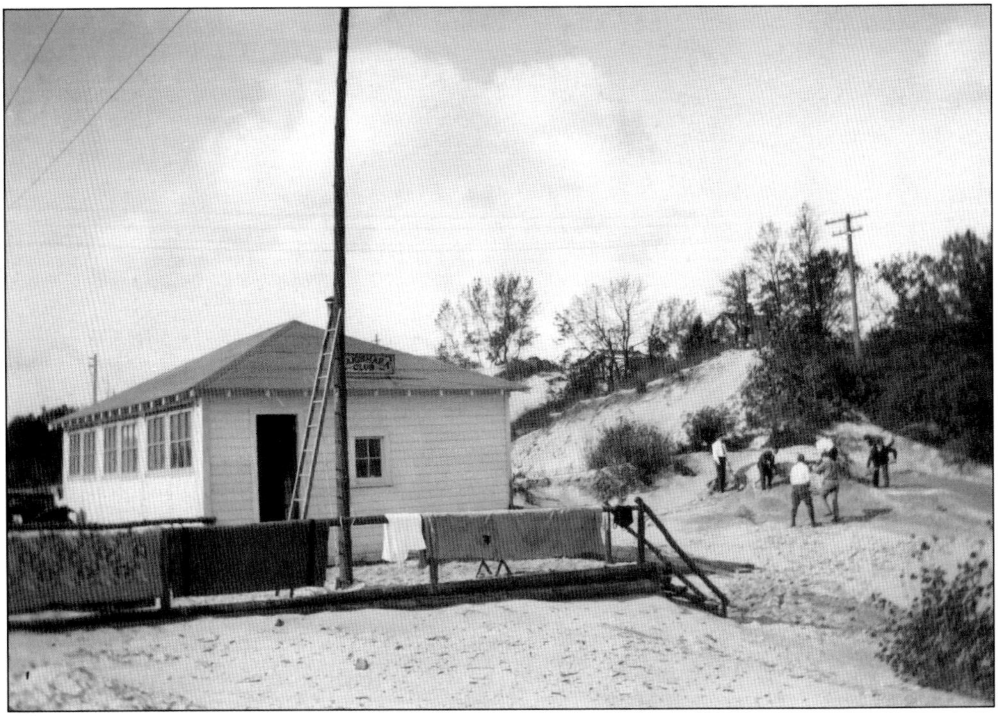

Miller resident Ed Newell established the Wakashaka Club in 1929 to promote hiking in the dunes. The name of the club was taken from the Pottawatomie and meant "Ones Who Never Tire." The group had a clubhouse on the corner of Oak Avenue and Warren Street. (Courtesy of the Calumet Regional Archives, IU Northwest.)

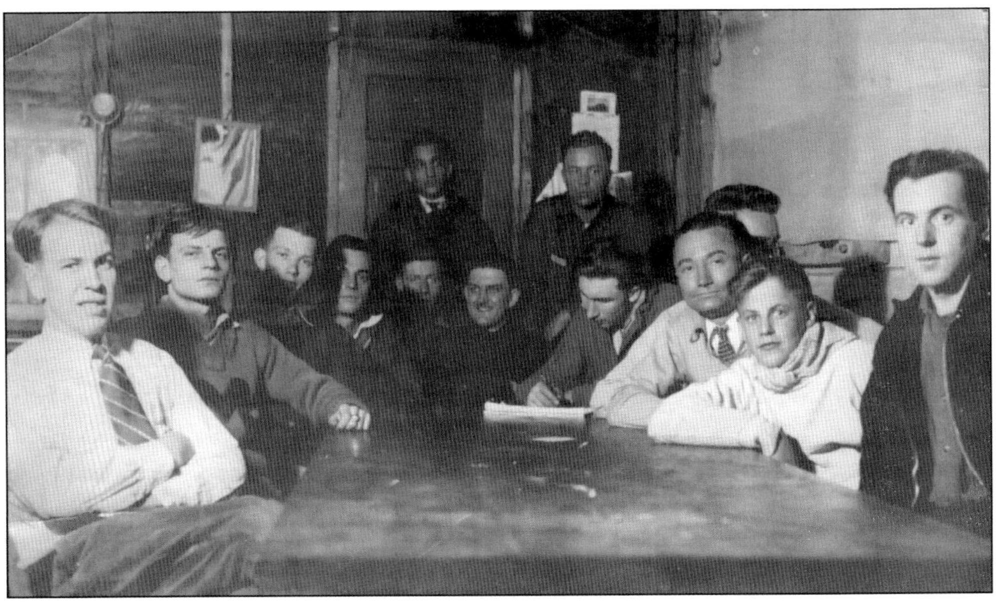

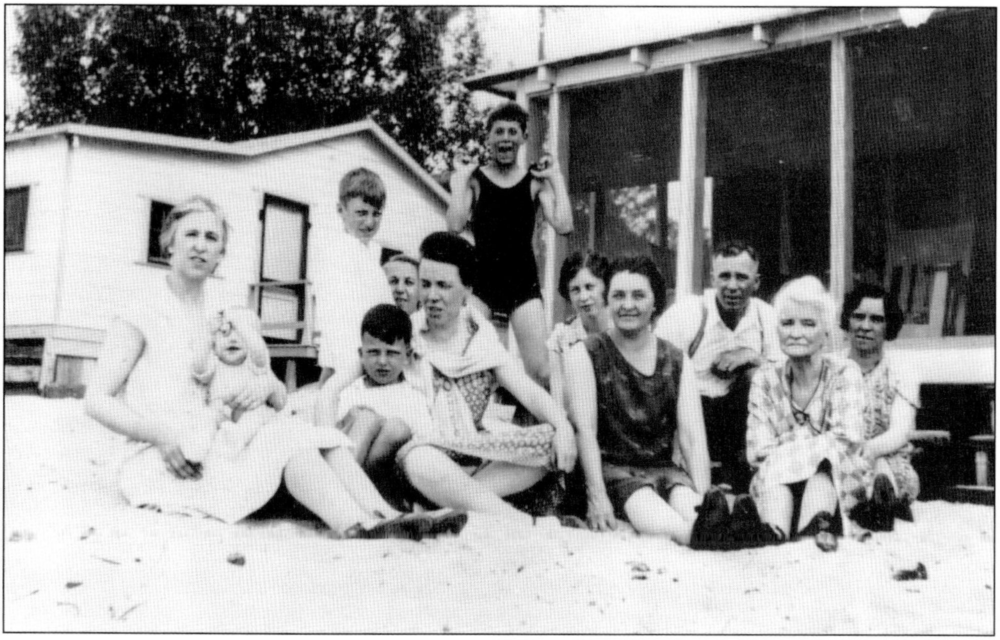

The Doyne family sits on the steps of the cottage they rented from the Carr family for $50 a season in the 1930s. Many generations of Doynes enjoyed Miller Beach, starting with Edward Thomas Doyne and his wife, Mary, and their daughters Katherine "Kittie" and Harriet, and son, Edward Jr., and his wife, Martha. A horse-drawn excavator removed sand from around the cottages every spring. (Courtesy of the Doyne family.)

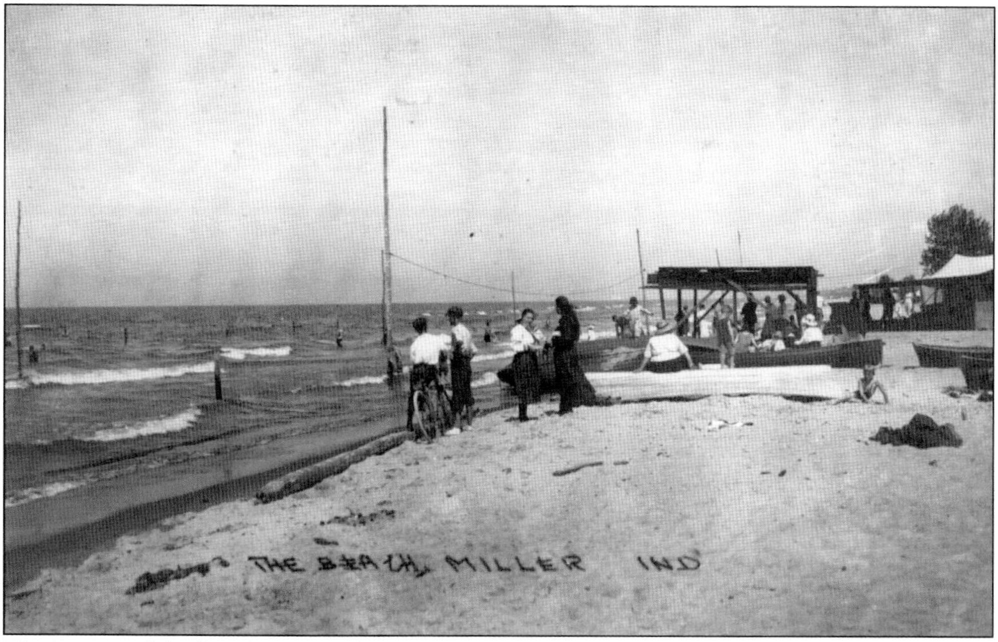

The beauty of the beach attracted more and more people to Miller. And as beachgoing became more popular, bathing suits changed—going from almost dress-like to more practical beachwear for swimming and sunning. (Courtesy of the Calumet Regional Archives, IU Northwest.)

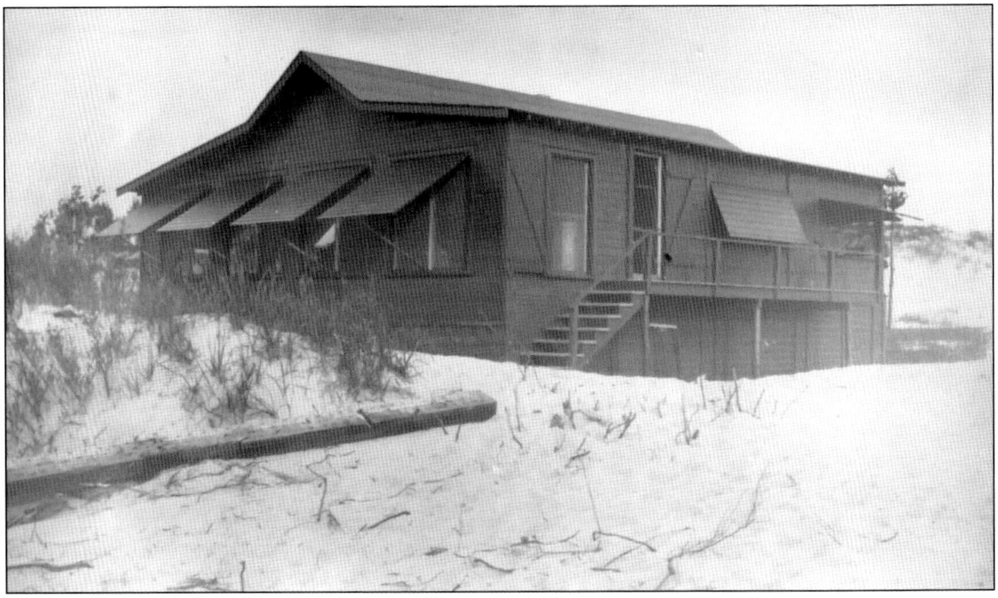

When he first came to Miller in the 1910s, Frank Hough, like many beach visitors, camped on the beach while building his beach house (above). Hough lived in Chicago, where he owned a shoe store called Stetson's. The house was built with old doors and gates from his store. Below, Hough helps an unidentified person on a horse in front of the house. Frank's daughter, Grace Hough, is in the background. Note the electric pole in the image; electricity came to Miller in the early 1900s. (Courtesy of Alice Pickford.)

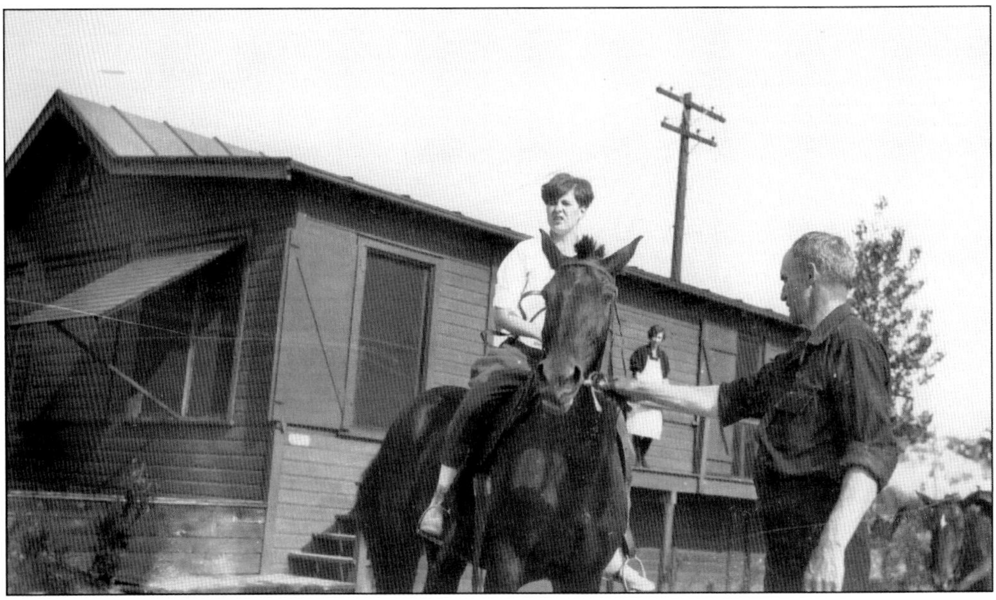

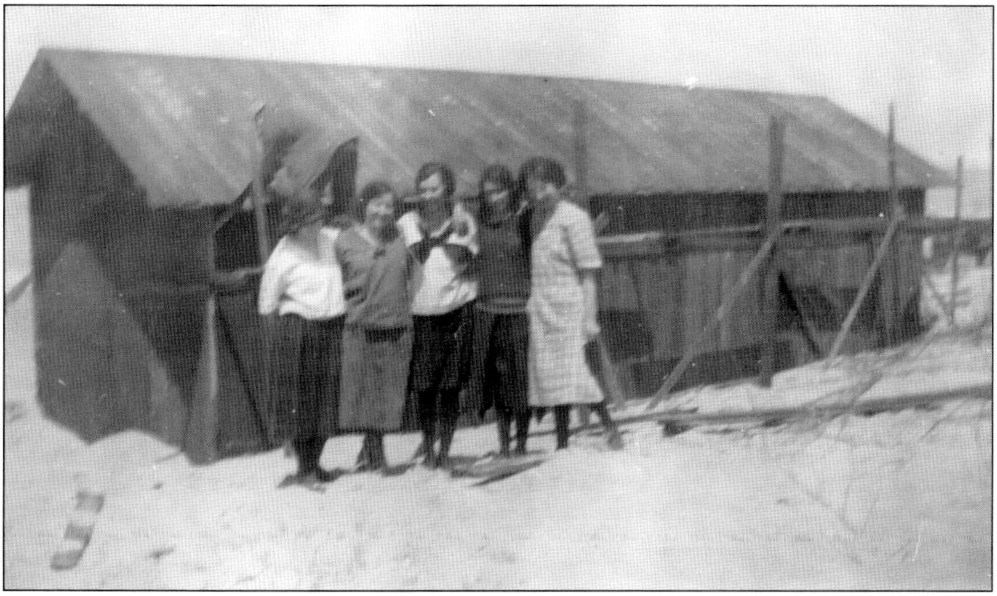

These women appear to be standing in front of a stable, perhaps the one that Frank Hough owned. Hough, who kept horses on the beach, maintained a stable in the hollow of a dune near his house on Vermillion Street. Though the family returned to Chicago, the horses remained at the stable. In the winter, they were taken care of by the Carr family, who fed and watered them. When the Hough family returned to Miller in warm weather, the Carrs met them at the station with the horses. (Courtesy of Alice Pickford.)

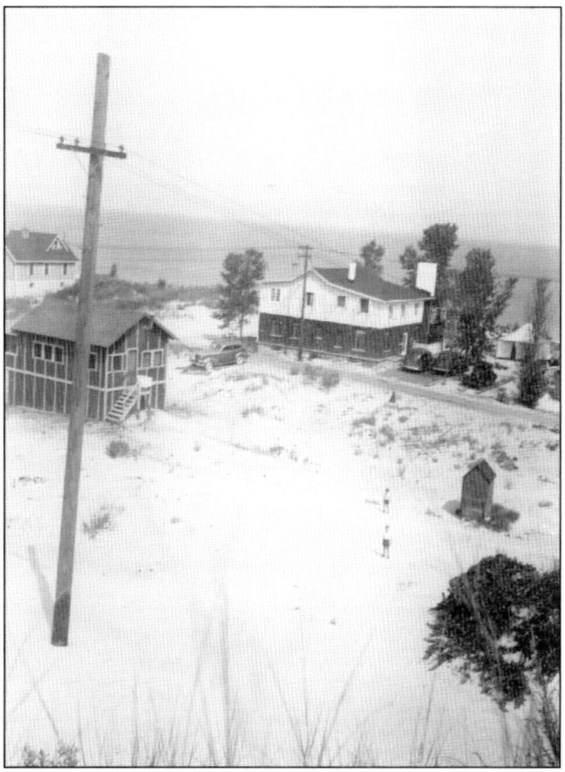

Frank Hough's house was eventually raised up for an additional floor and a basement was added. The hole for the new basement was dug by a mule-driven excavator. The house still remains in the family. (Courtesy of Alice Pickford.)

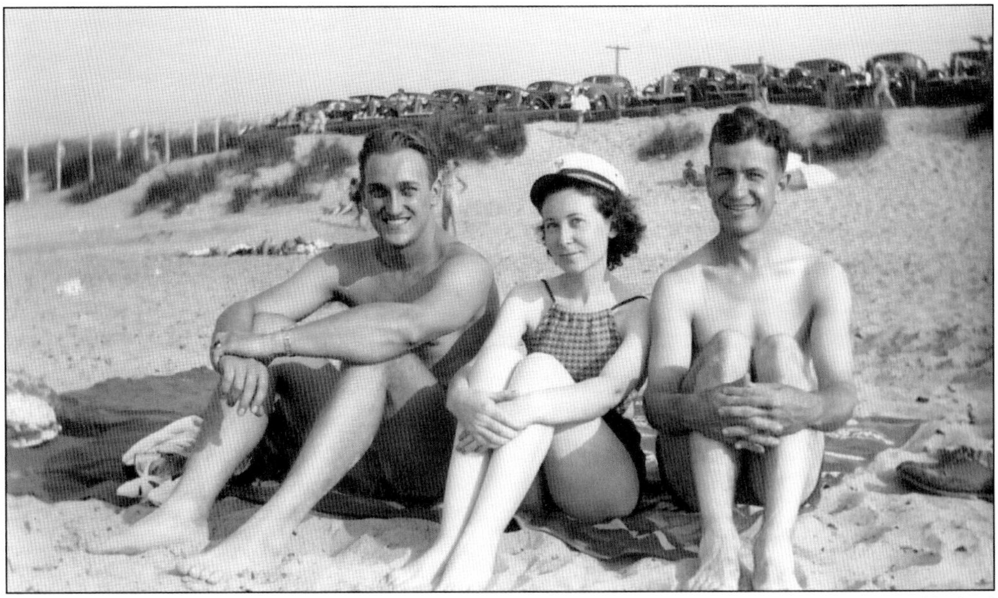

Frank Hough was in the second wave of settlers or perhaps even the third, but he established a legacy that still exists. Miller has the only unspoiled beachfront in the city of Gary, and its beaches, including Marquette Park, Lake Street Beach, and Wells Street Beach, comprise 241 acres. Hough bought the lakefront acreage that is Wells Street Beach and it remains in his family. It has a concession stand, a parking lot, and a beautiful shoreline. This postcard shows visitors to Wells Street Beach in August 1938. (Courtesy of Alice Pickford.)

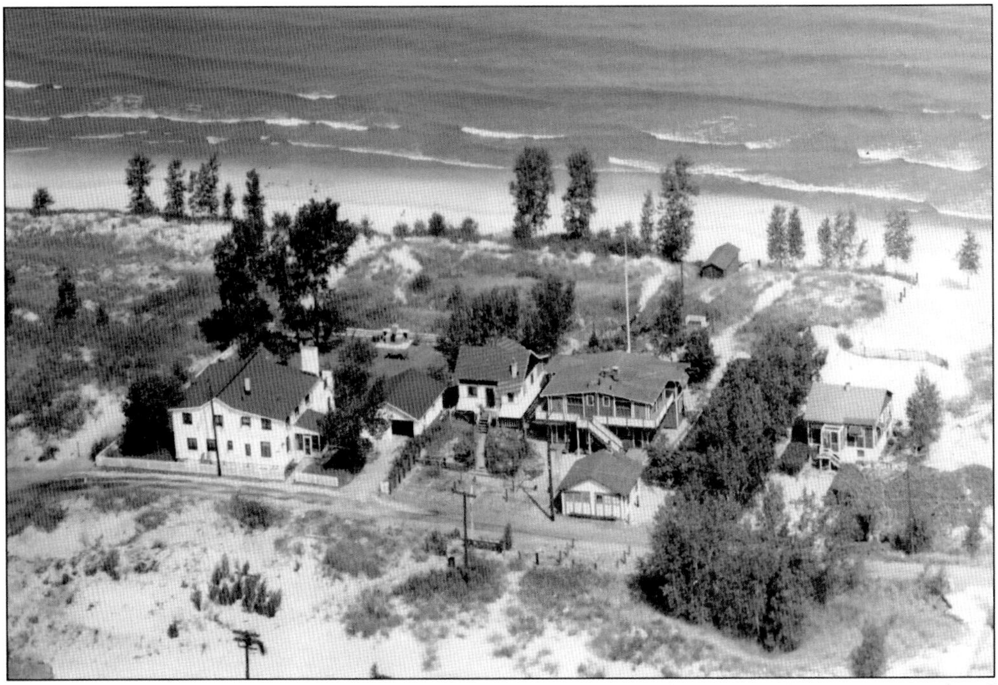

This aerial photograph shows, from left to right, the Hough family cottage after it was raised and winterized, Oscar Anderson's house, including rental cottages, and at far right, the Friend sisters' cottage. (Courtesy of Alice Pickford.)

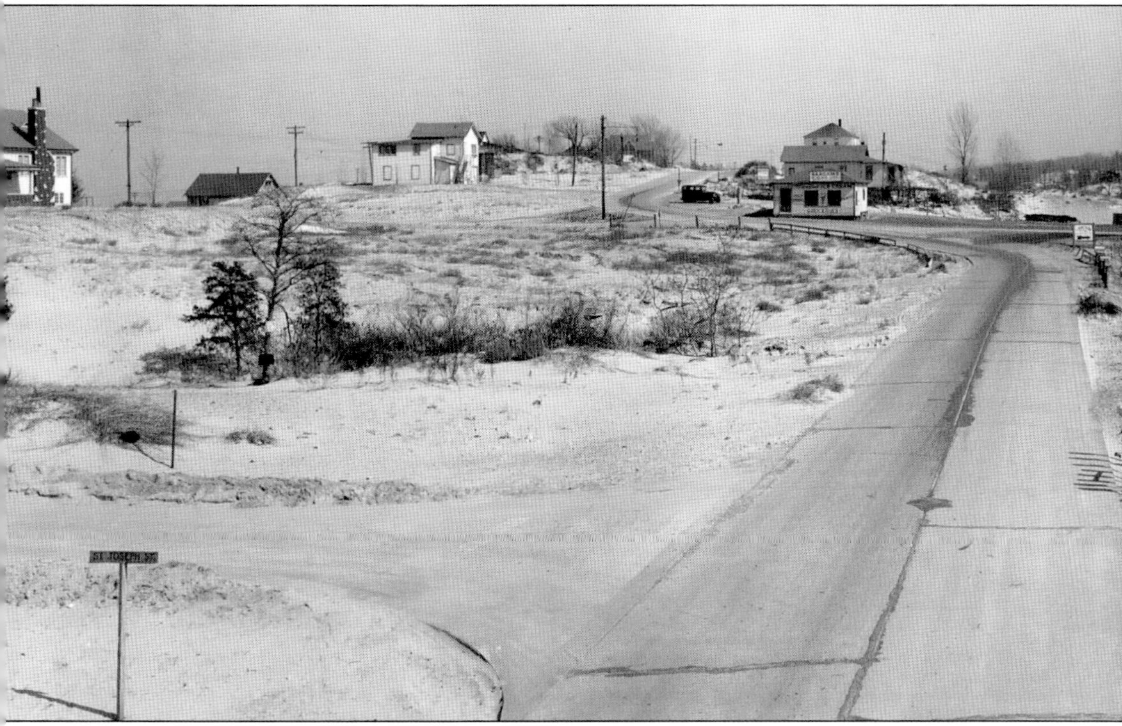

This 1931 photograph shows Oak Avenue where it meets Shelby Street at a small business district located in the main residential area of Miller. The concession on the corner offers groceries, cold drinks, and Cloverleaf ice cream. (Courtesy of Calumet Regional Archives, IU Northwest.)

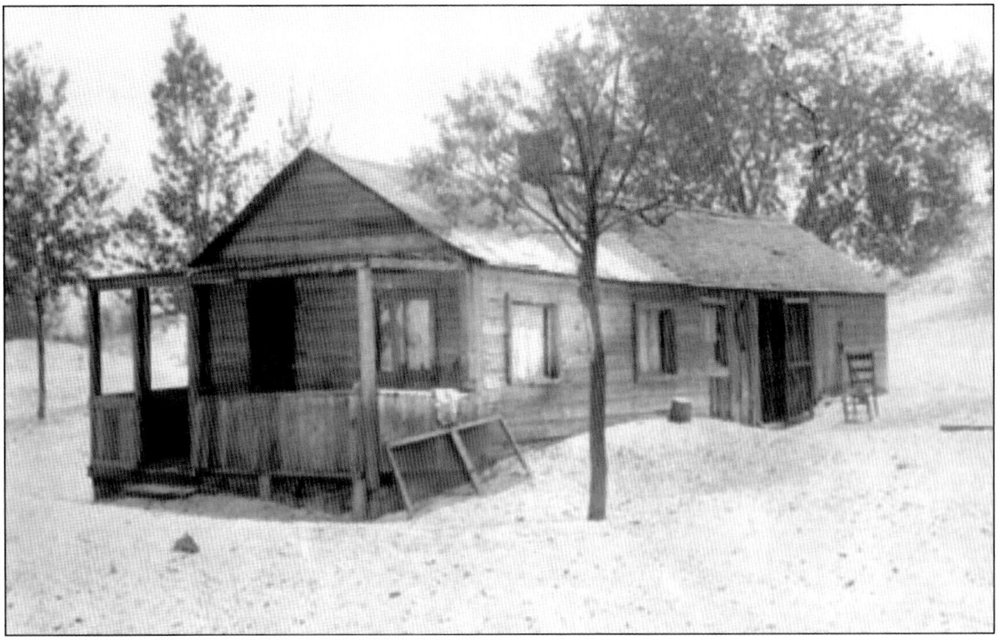

The beach looked very different in the winter than in the busy summers. Above, the Carr cottage sits alone in the empty dunes, and below, Carr's Beach is full of swimmers in 1917. A decade later, a big storm caused havoc on the beach. "All night long, waves knocking and knocking, hitting the house then going back out," recalled one Miller Beach resident. "They came up as high as the rear wall—even over the roof once." The house started tilting and the roar of wind and waves was so loud that two people in a small room could not hear each other. By dawn, it had died, but shoes, canned goods, splintered wood, and even the insides of squashed beach houses lined the shore. A six-foot wave swept the oak plank floor of the dancehall away, never to be seen again. (Courtesy of the Calumet Regional Archives, IU Northwest.)

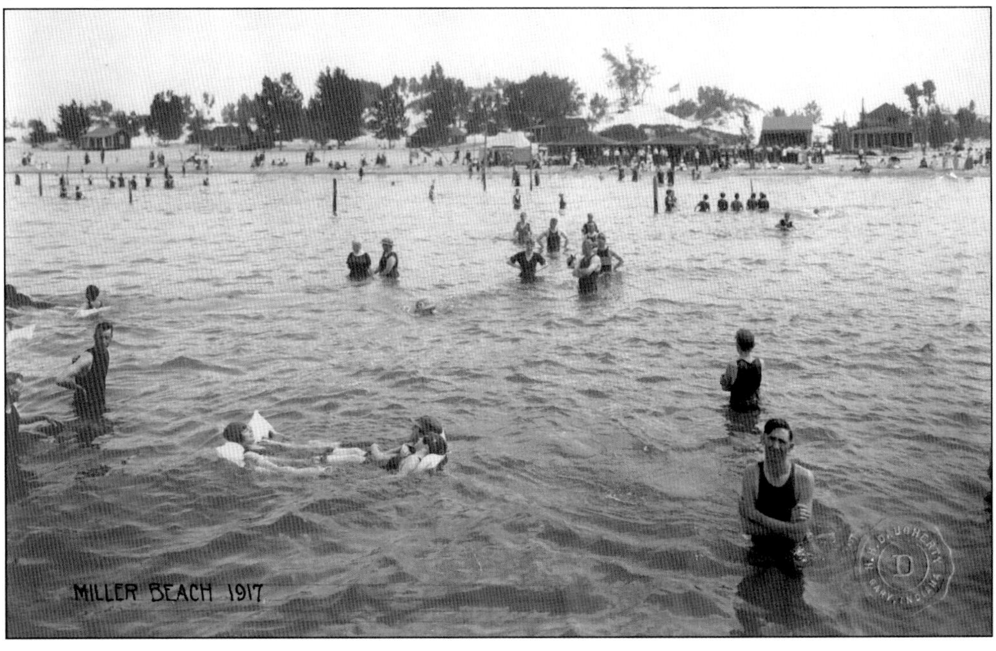

Nine

BUSINESS DISTRICT

LIFE ON MAIN STREET

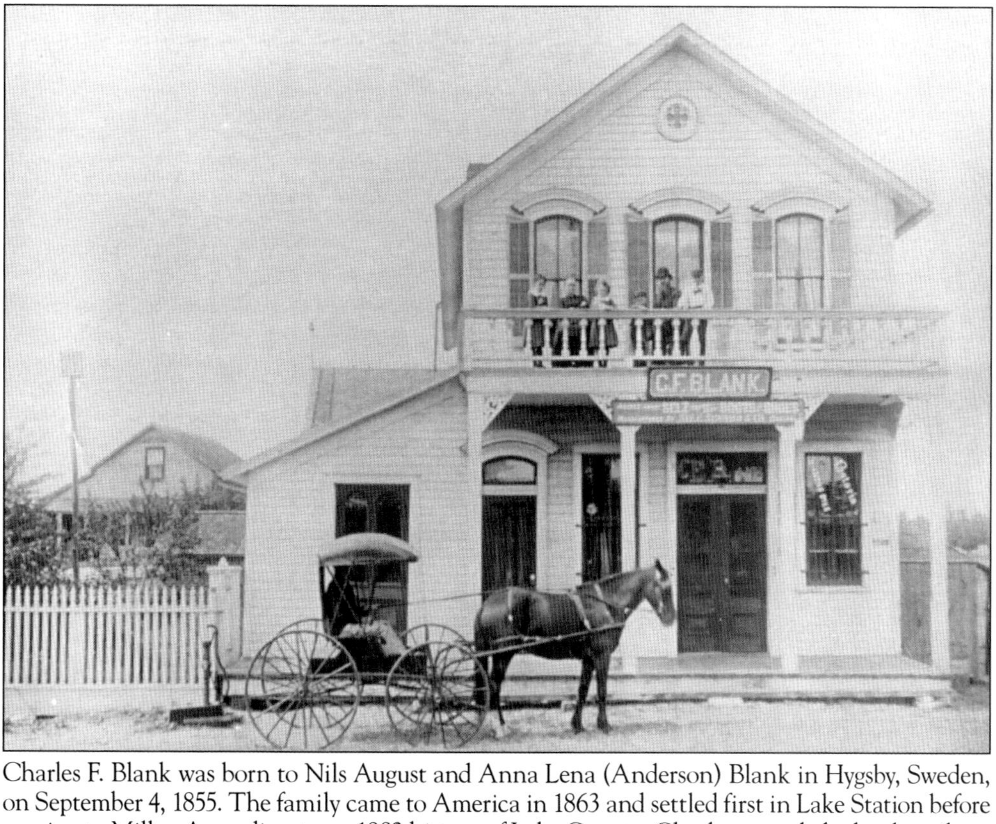

Charles F. Blank was born to Nils August and Anna Lena (Anderson) Blank in Hygsby, Sweden, on September 4, 1855. The family came to America in 1863 and settled first in Lake Station before moving to Miller. According to an 1882 history of Lake County, Charles attended school until age 13 and then worked in a general store in Lake Station before studying watchmaking in Chicago. After working in the same general store for four more years, he moved to Miller's Station in 1874 and opened a small store. A year later, he married Johanna Erlandson and within six years, the couple had six children. Business was very good and in the fall of 1882, Charles built a two-story house and a large store fronting the railroad tracks selling general merchandise, staple and fancy groceries, dry goods, notions, drugs, hardware and tin ware, watches, clocks, jewelry, musical instruments, sewing machines, pistols, and revolvers. (Courtesy of the Calumet Regional Archives, IU Northwest.)

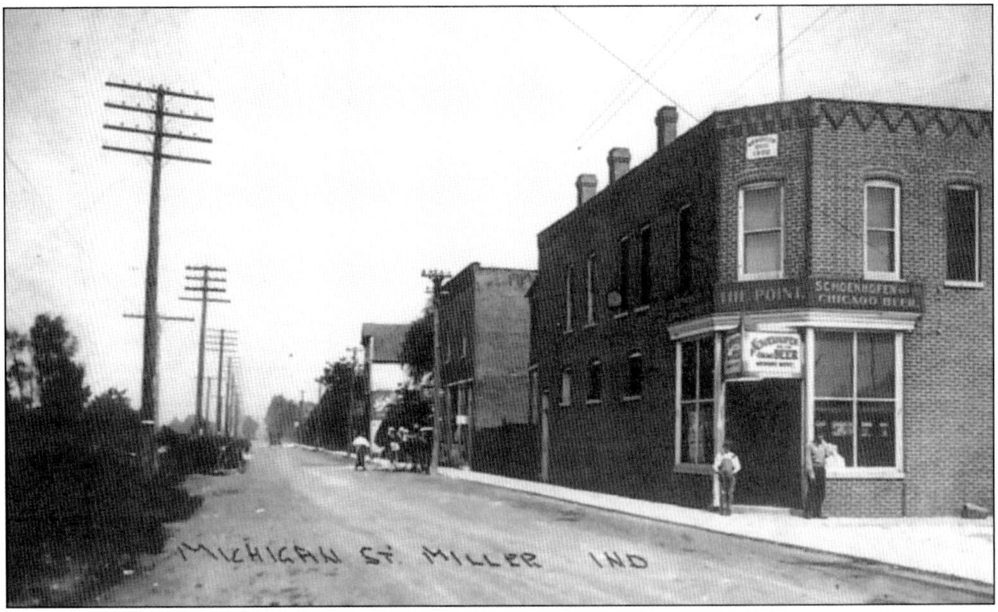

Looking east down Miller Avenue from Lake Street, one sees the distinctive triangular-shaped Arvidson Building that still stands in Miller's downtown today. According to Miller resident Laura Jones, whose mother had one of the first telephones in town, Miller's newly established phone company was on the second floor of the two-story building next door to the Arvidson Building for a time. Around the time this photograph was taken, the town of Miller boasted a general store, a cigar factory owned by the Zelibor brothers, Olson's Livery Stable, Kerleen's Glove Factory, two churches, two saloons, and two schools—a small frame building for the primary grades and a two-story brick building for the upper grades. (Courtesy of Joyce Davis, Lake Street Gallery.)

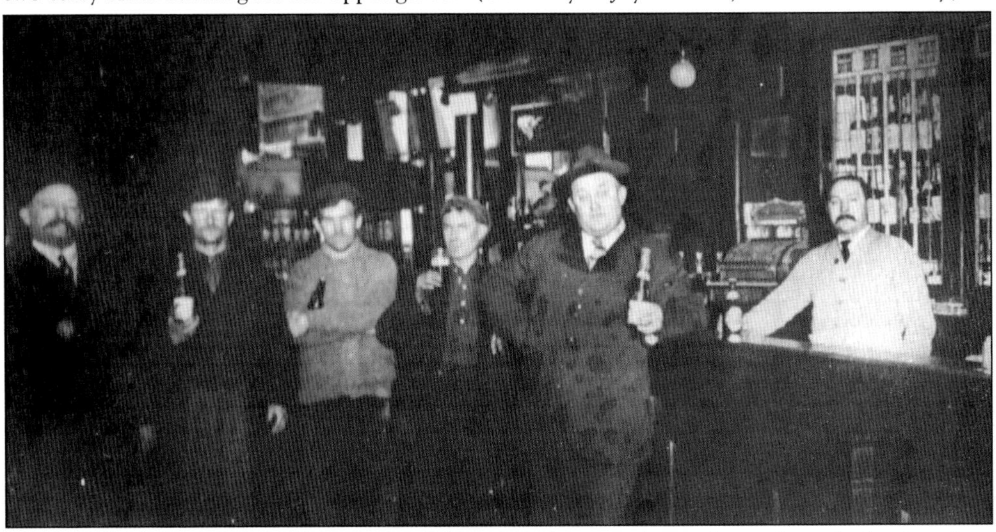

The Point Bar, being enjoyed by patrons in this 1903 photograph, was located inside the Arvidson Building built by the Arvidson Brothers. It was called the point because of the building's triangular shape, constructed that way to accommodate the railroad tracks. It must have been a noisy place when the trains came roaring into town, as it was just a few steps from the tracks. According to Len Pryweller, a longtime Miller resident whose realty business later occupied the building, the interior boasted an oak bar. (Courtesy of Len Pryweller.)

The sign above the Bee Hive Saloon, on Lake Street south of the railroad tracks and opposite the Point Bar, advertised "Schlitz: The Beer that Made Milwaukee Famous." Both the Point Bar and the Bee Hive were probably built close to the tracks and the depot to give passengers a chance to disembark from a hot and dusty ride for a sip or two of refreshment. The Bee Hive building would later house Bowers Drugs. (Right, courtesy of Joyce Davis, Lake Street Gallery; below, courtesy of Marilyn Leech and Holly Rodino Breese.)

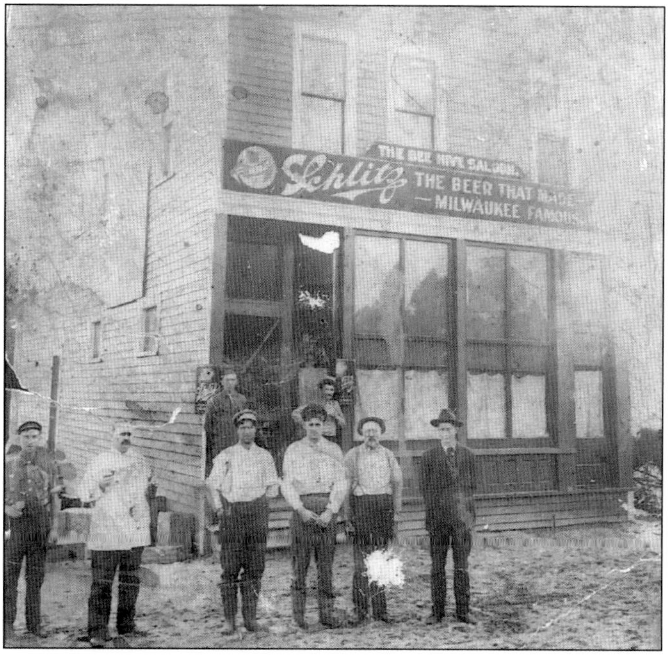

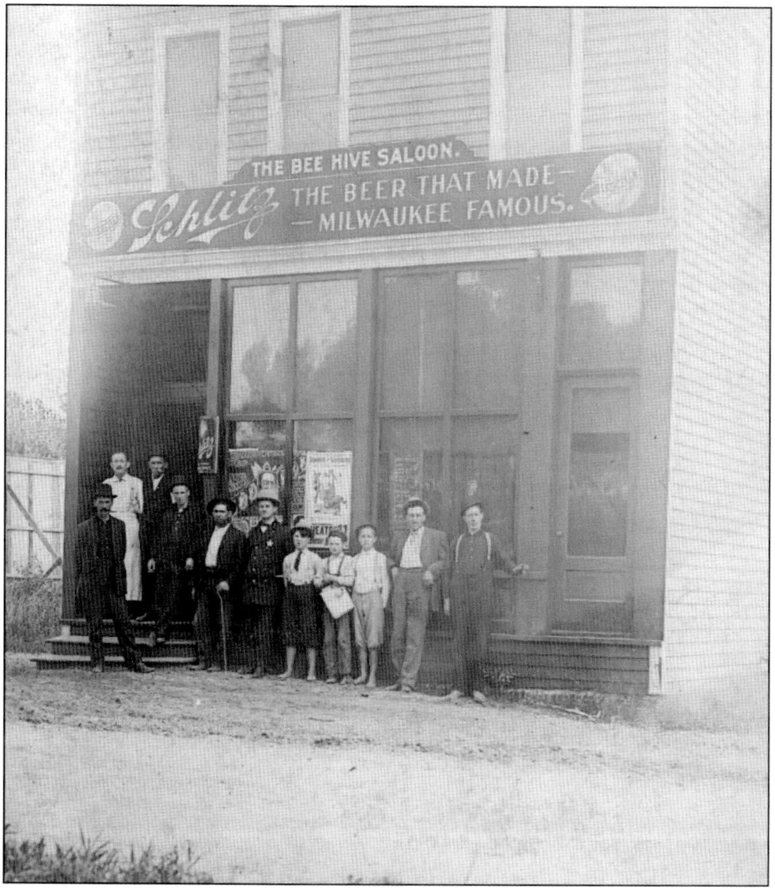

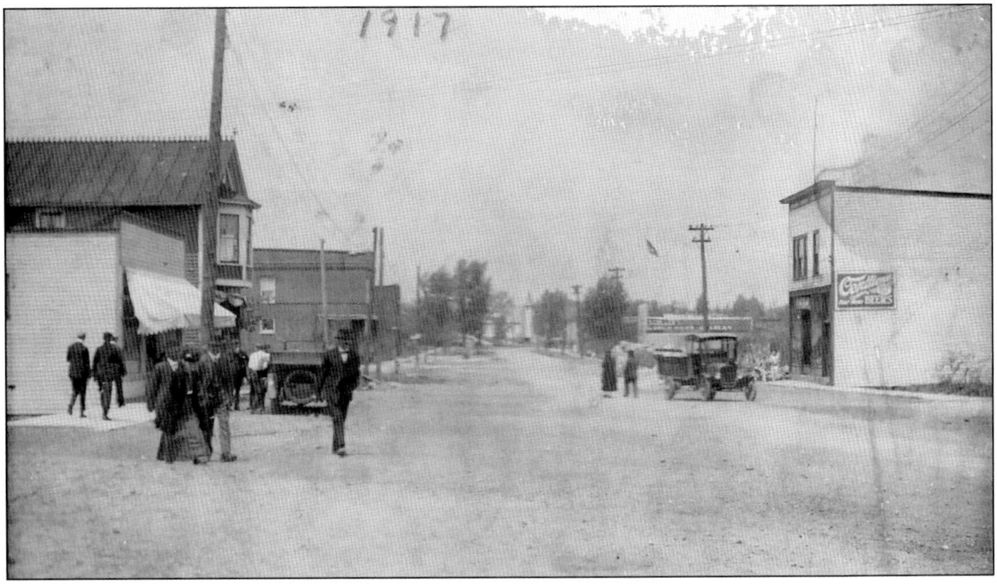

Looking north on Lake Street in 1917, the above image shows Leech's Tavern—the white two-story building on the right—whose sign advertises that they served the popular Centlivre's Beer. Below, downtown Miller is seen a few years later. Leech's Tavern moved one building down and its previous building now housed Stillson's grocery store. Inside it, Gertrude Stillson, postmistress, ran the Miller post office. The building on the left with the white awning has the name Gantz painted on the side in the later image. Note the signboard pointing the way to Michigan City, St. Joe, and South Bend and the one posted on the telephone pole at left with the top arrow pointing toward Gary and Chicago. The bottom arrow points the way to what was then called the Gary Municipal Beach. (Courtesy of the Calumet Regional Archives, IU Northwest.)

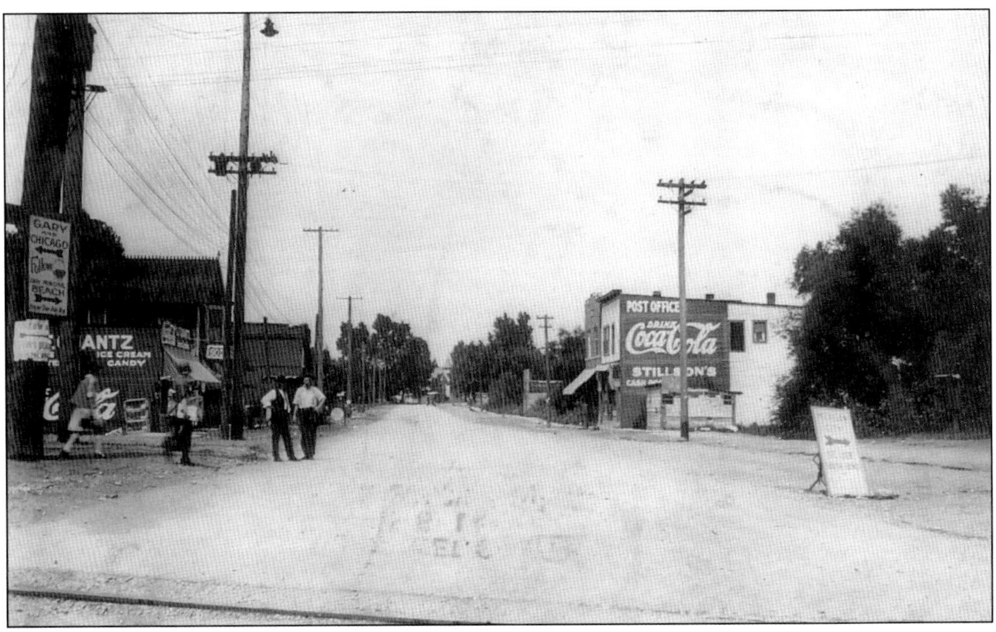

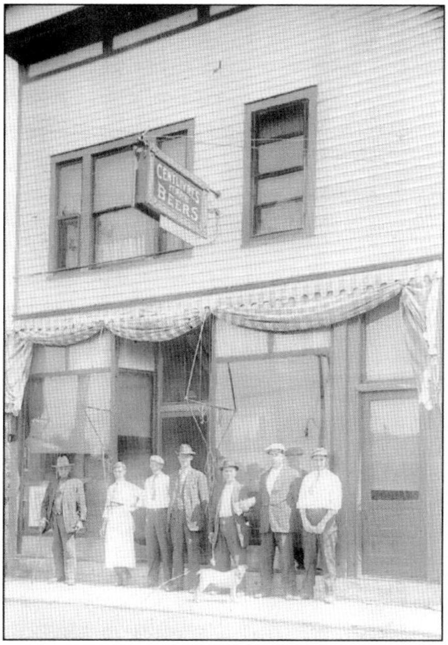

The Leech family, who moved to Miller from Gary, built two buildings downtown on Lake Street. This wooden two-story building was their first, with a sign above the door and another on the side advertising Centlivre's Fort Wayne Beers. C.L. Centlivre, described in a newspaper article as an enterprising Alsatian, first opened his French brewery on the banks of the St. Joseph River about a mile from downtown Fort Wayne, Indiana, in 1862. When the brewery burned down in 1895, he and his sons rebuilt it. The brewery stayed open until 1918, when it was closed during Prohibition and then reopened again in 1933 before closing for good in 1961. In 1897, Kaiser Beck Company, a brewery in Bremen, Germany, sued Centlivre's for naming one of their beers Kaiser. During Prohibition, the business facility changed its name to Centlivre Ice and Cold Production Storage Company, though they continued, for two years, to make a near-beer named "That's It." (Courtesy of Joyce Davis, Lake Street Gallery.)

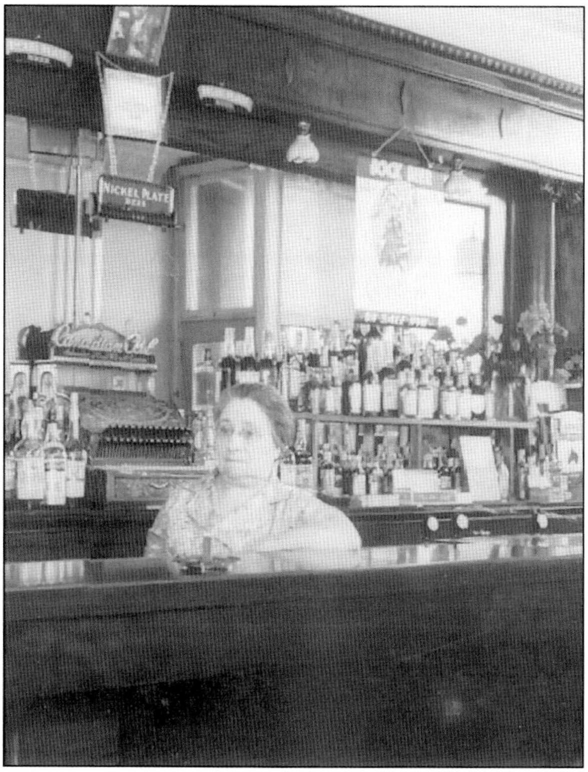

Mamie Zimmerman Leech stands behind the bar at Leech's Tavern on Lake Street. This is one of two buildings the Leech family—sometimes spelled Leach—built on Lake Street. Isaac Leech is listed in the 1910 census as a glass blower but by 1920, his profession was listed as a retail merchant selling soft drinks. During Prohibition, the tavern became a confectionery store. (Courtesy of Joyce Davis, Lake Street Gallery.)

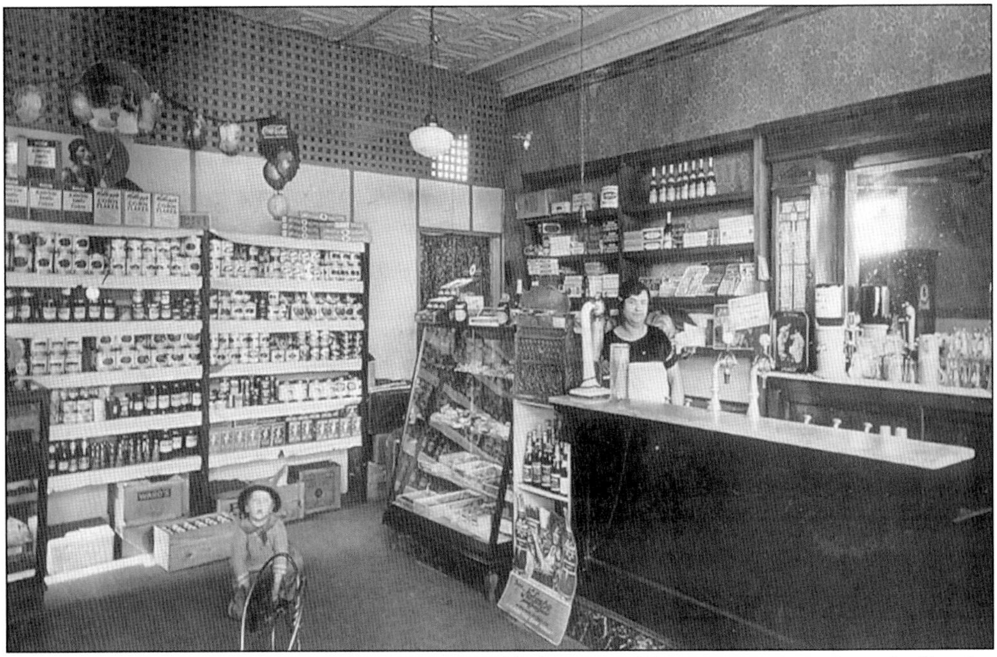

Small-town stores like this 1917 downtown establishment sold a variety of goods and offered a variety of services. Note the tin ceiling, the drop-down lights, the elaborate crown molding, and the glass-fronted display case filled with what looks like candy and pastries. The fancy cash register is also an eye-catcher. Other general stores in Miller around this time, such as Blank's, offered a diverse collection of goods, including pianos that were made in nearby Chesterton. (Courtesy of Joyce Davis, Lake Street Gallery.)

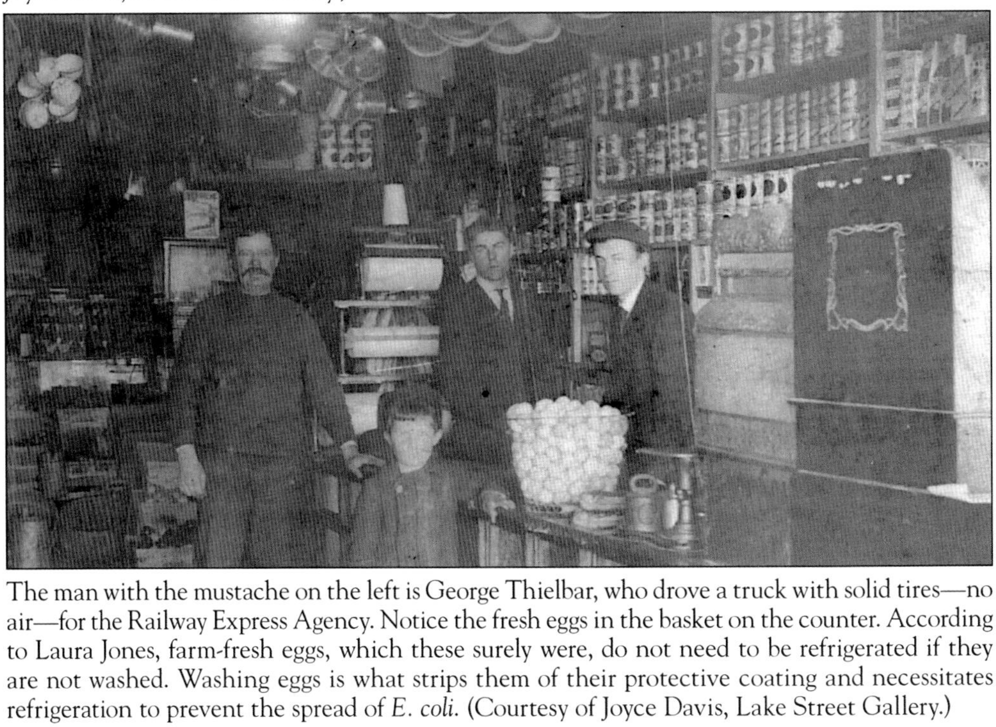

The man with the mustache on the left is George Thielbar, who drove a truck with solid tires—no air—for the Railway Express Agency. Notice the fresh eggs in the basket on the counter. According to Laura Jones, farm-fresh eggs, which these surely were, do not need to be refrigerated if they are not washed. Washing eggs is what strips them of their protective coating and necessitates refrigeration to prevent the spread of *E. coli*. (Courtesy of Joyce Davis, Lake Street Gallery.)

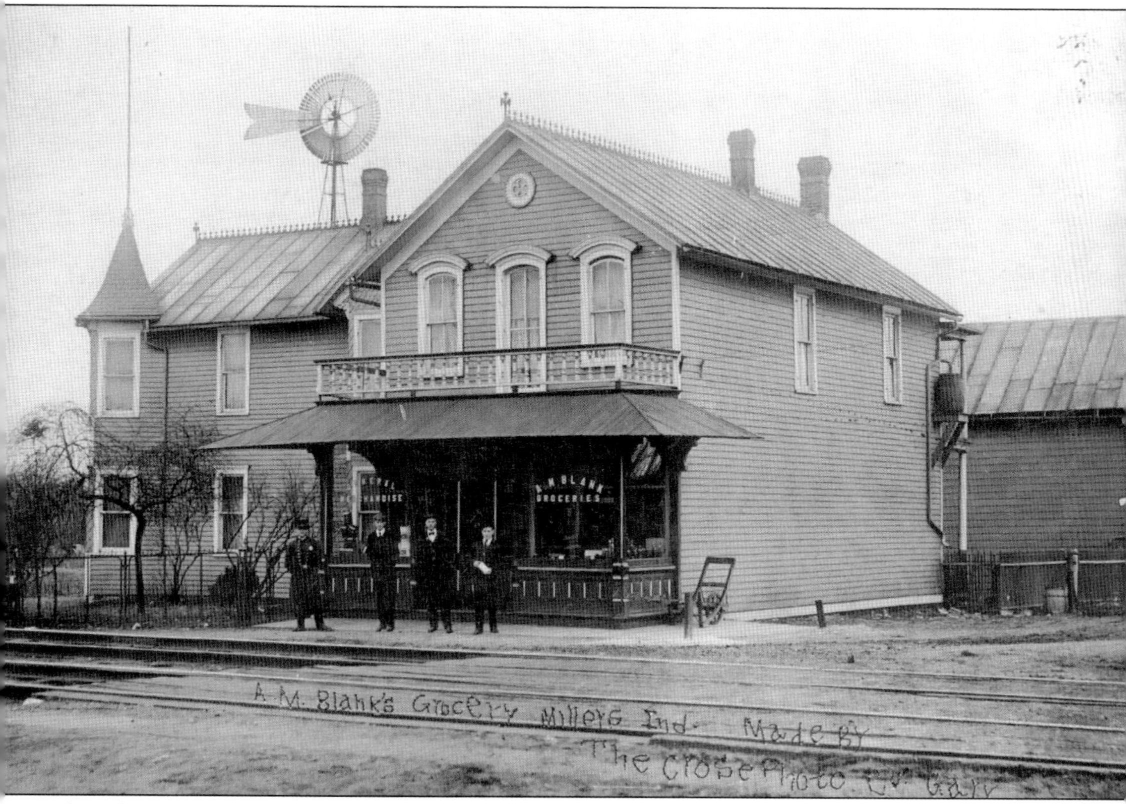

This photograph shows A.M. Blank's in the late 1900s or early 1910s. Arthur M. Blank, the seventh child of Charles F. and Johanna (Erlandson) Blank, took over the family store from his dad, the store's original founder, in 1906, operating it until 1927. He later founded A.M. Blank Company, a Gary insurance agency, and also helped organize the Miller State Bank. As a young boy, Arthur and his older brother, Charles A., worked at their father's store and made grocery deliveries throughout the area. According to a family story, Octave Chanute stopped in the store on his visit to Miller in 1896 and bought supplies, including food and four blankets to be used for camping at the beach. Charles F. Blank had his son Arthur carry the blankets down to Chanute's campsite before nightfall. (Courtesy of Laura Valentine Jones.)

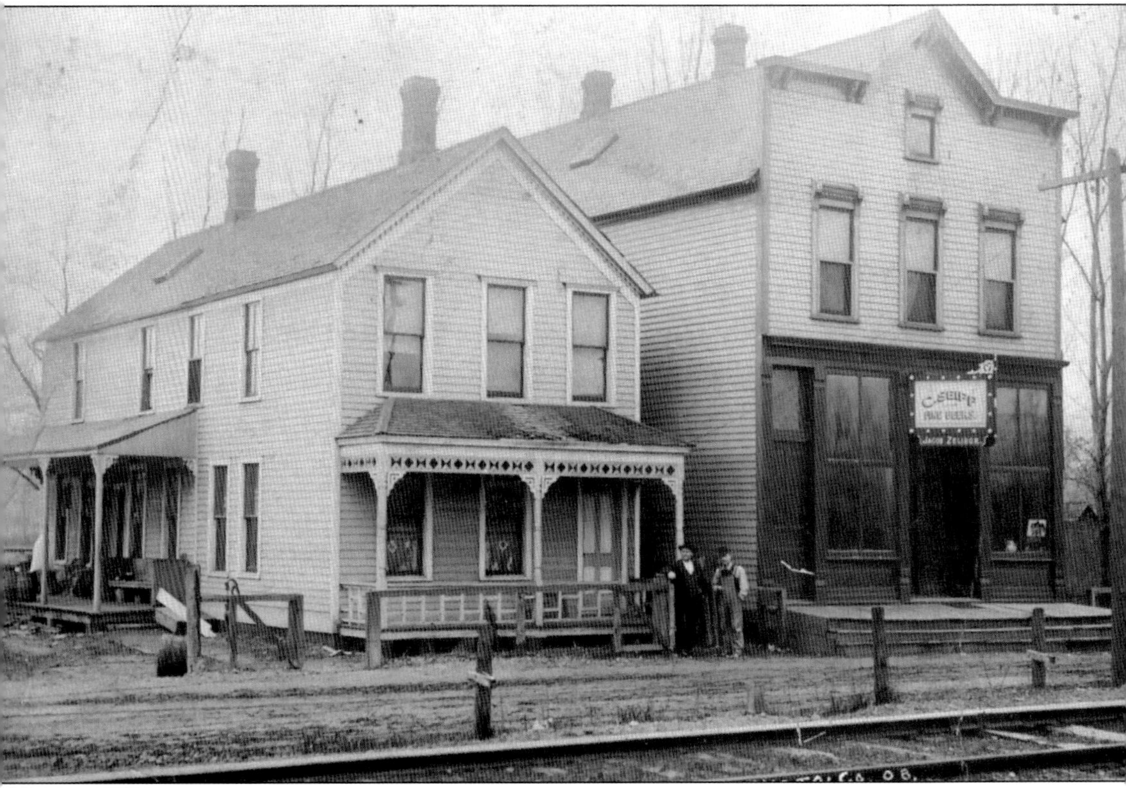

This 1908 image shows two buildings on Miller Avenue near Lake Street. The building on the right mentions Jacob Zelibor, who, along with his son, Michael, had a cigar manufacturing business in Miller. The 1910 census lists three other Zelibor sons as also working here, two as cigar salesmen and one as a tobacco stripper, stripping stems from tobacco leaves. The Zelibor family was among the early settlers in Miller. (Courtesy of the Calumet Regional Archives, IU Northwest.)

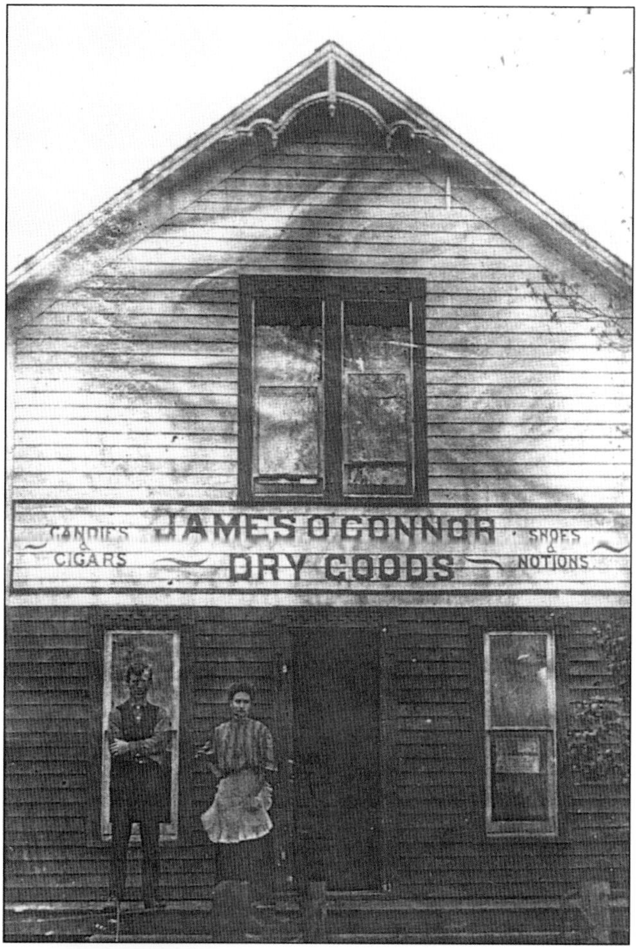

Not much is known about James O'Connor Dry Goods, but it sold items typical of the time including cigars, candies, notions, gents' furnishings, and shoes. The store itself looks to be from the late 19th century, as does the clothing of the people standing out front in the image at right. Seen again below, the store was located at 430 S. Lake Street near the original Bethel Lutheran Church. (Courtesy of the Calumet Regional Archives, IU Northwest.)

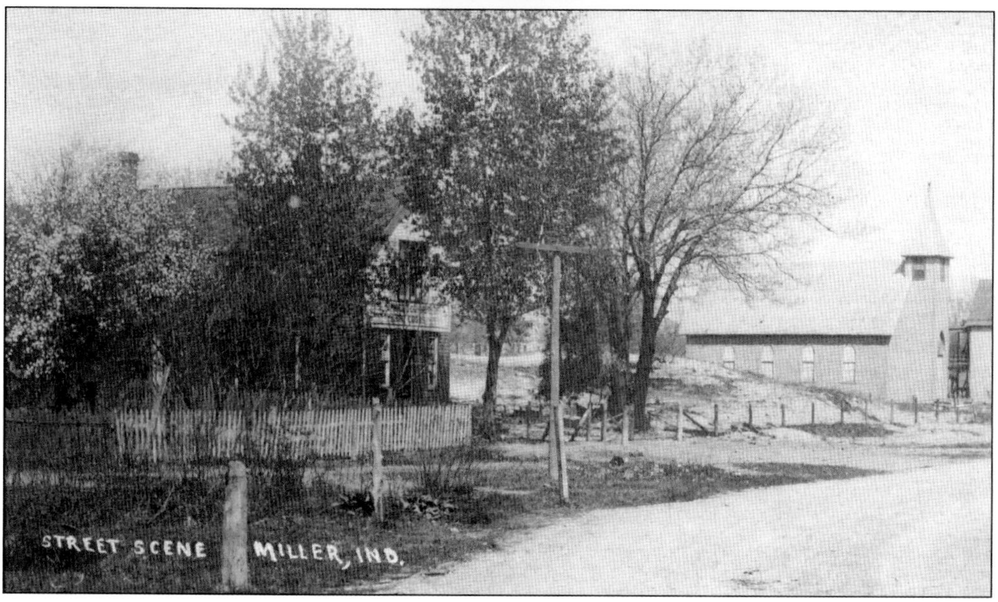

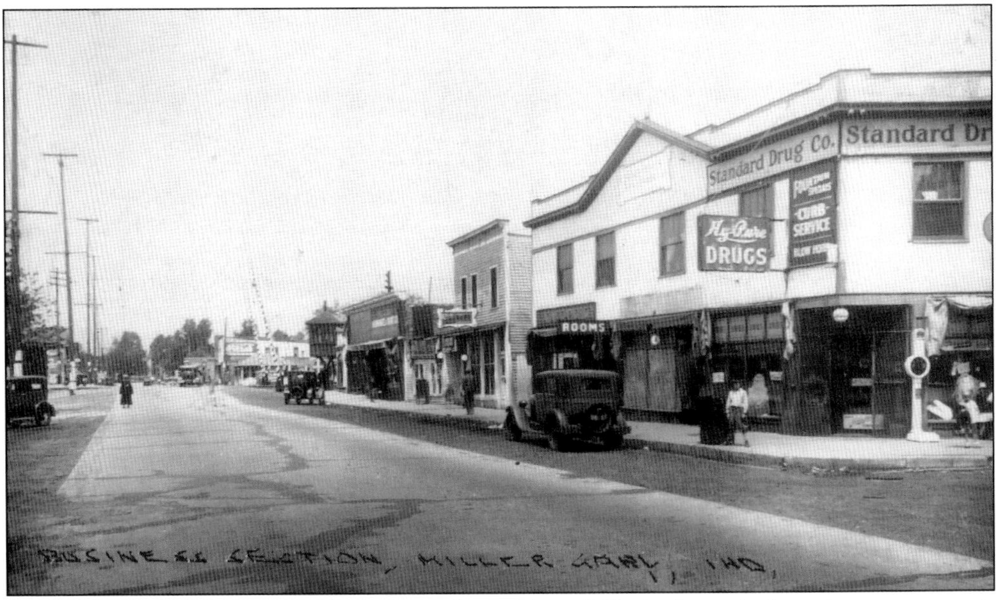

These two Lake Street scenes from the early and late 1920s look north from downtown south of Miller Avenue. There are little changes here, like the scale for weighing oneself in front of the Standard Drug Company—where Chase Bank now stands—in the first image. Curb service is available in both and rooms are available as well, though the traffic seems much more dense in the more recent photograph. The Standard Drug Company predates Bowers Drugs. Locally made Henderson's Ice Cream is advertised. Mrs. Todd's Confectionery housed the post office at the time, but it would later move next door into what was, at the time these photographs were taken, a hardware store. In the more recent photograph, there is a billiard parlor near the water tower, and in the drugstore building, Pal's Lunch advertises hot coffee. The railroad gates were manned by Hazel Gray's father. Across the tracks, Stillson's grocery's big Coca-Cola sign is plainly seen. A sign for Bungalow Barbecue can be seen on the left. (Courtesy of the Calumet Regional Archives, IU Northwest.)

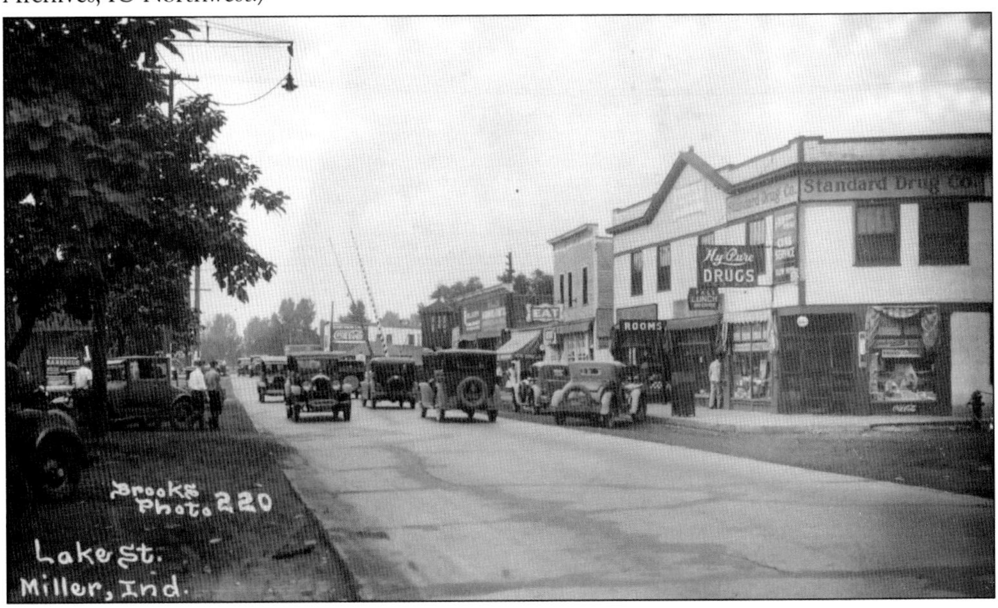

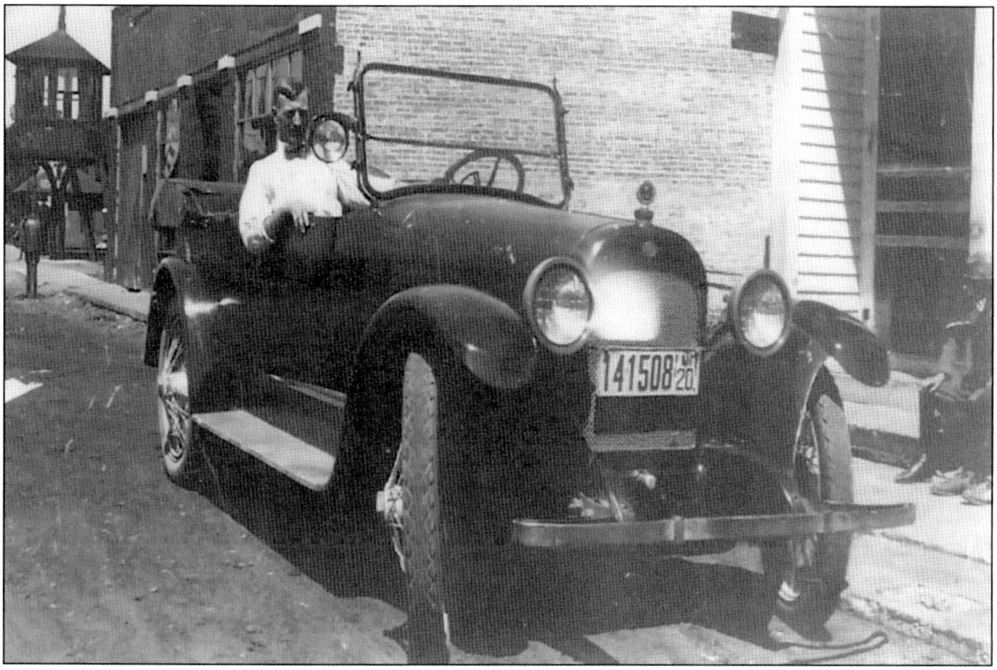

This sporting car traveled down Lake Street in 1920. The roads were still unpaved and it looks like that odd contraption on the right near the sidewalk is an old gasoline pump. In the background is the watchtower for the railroad. (Courtesy of Joyce Davis, Lake Street Gallery.)

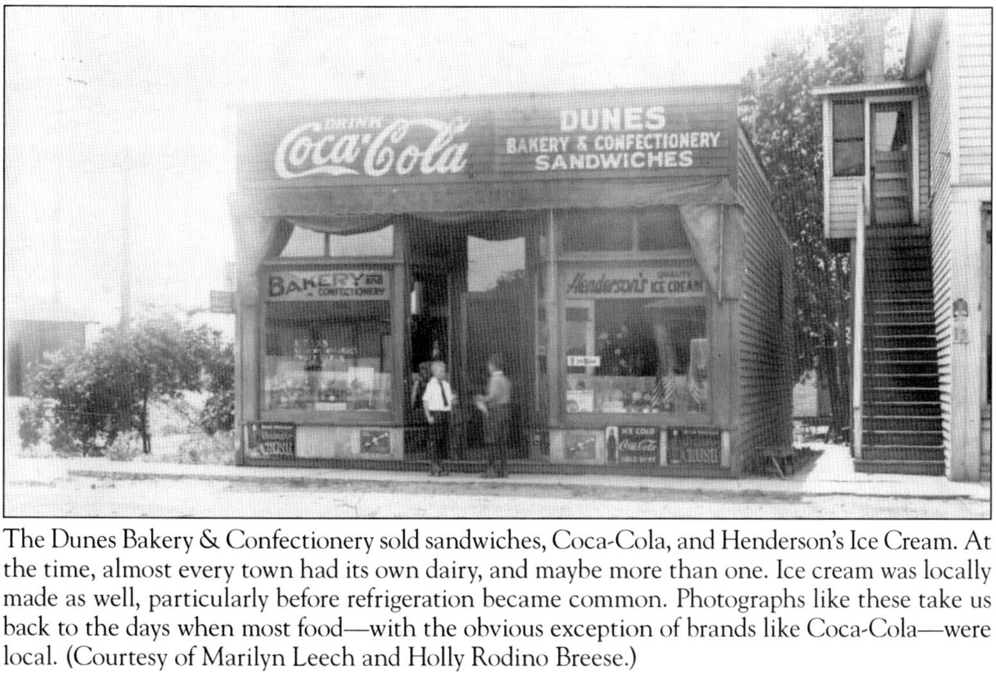

The Dunes Bakery & Confectionery sold sandwiches, Coca-Cola, and Henderson's Ice Cream. At the time, almost every town had its own dairy, and maybe more than one. Ice cream was locally made as well, particularly before refrigeration became common. Photographs like these take us back to the days when most food—with the obvious exception of brands like Coca-Cola—were local. (Courtesy of Marilyn Leech and Holly Rodino Breese.)

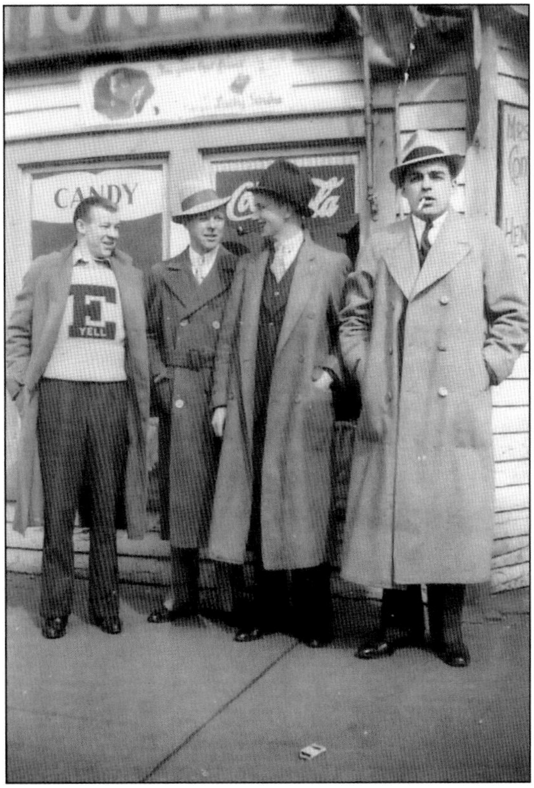

Widowed at an early age with three young children to raise, Minnie Todd opened a confectionery in downtown Miller in 1926. Over the next 30 years, the sign was moved four times as Todd changed locations but never moved off Lake Street. Known as Ma Todd, people loved to gather at her store to listen to her radio, order a Coca-Cola, read her magazines, and talk. Todd and her three children, Frank, Becky, and Junior, worked long hours, but she always made people feel happy to be there. Betty Davin remembers stopping at the post office to mail letters and then heading down the street to Ma Todd's. (Courtesy of Joyce Davis, Lake Street Gallery.)

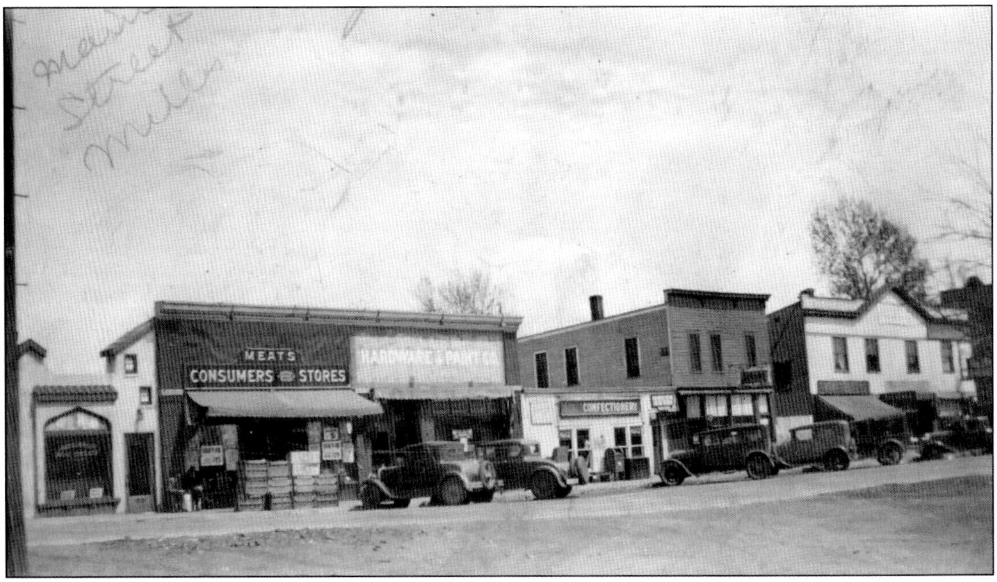

The east side of Lake Street in May of 1931 showed a small but well-established town. Odd as it may seem, in the early 1900s, the Mountain Ridge Riding Academy was located at the south end of Lake Street across from what was at the time a major sand pit. The academy offered trail rides on horseback and also stabled horses for their owners. Special riding occasions brought more horses and riders into Miller. Another riding stable was located at the old IHB Railroad track on Lake Street just before the hill leading up to Birch Avenue. (Courtesy of the Calumet Regional Archives, IU Northwest)

N. Guy Ayers opened his realty business in 1922 just as the explosion of tourists and second-home ownership was beginning in Miller Beach. His nephew Bruce Ayers moved here after the war to work with his uncle. Ayers Realtors, Inc. is still part of Miller's downtown and is now owned by Bruce's son, Gene Ayers. (Courtesy of Gene Ayers, Ayers Realtors, Inc.)

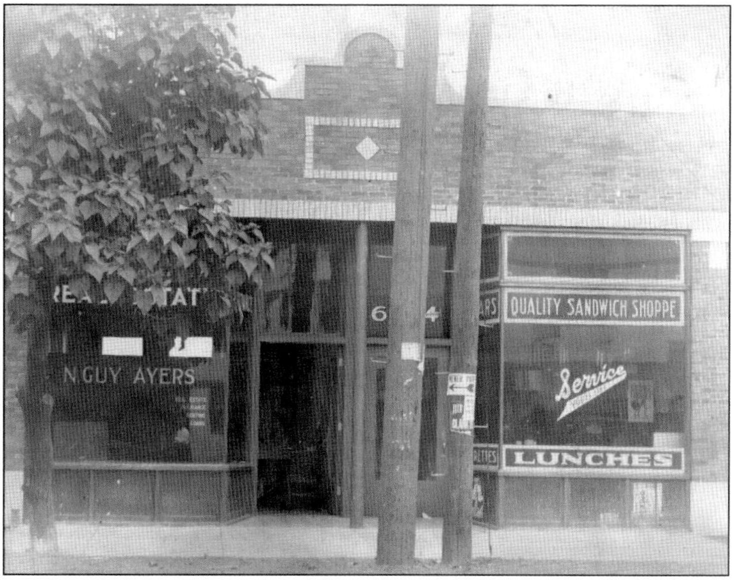

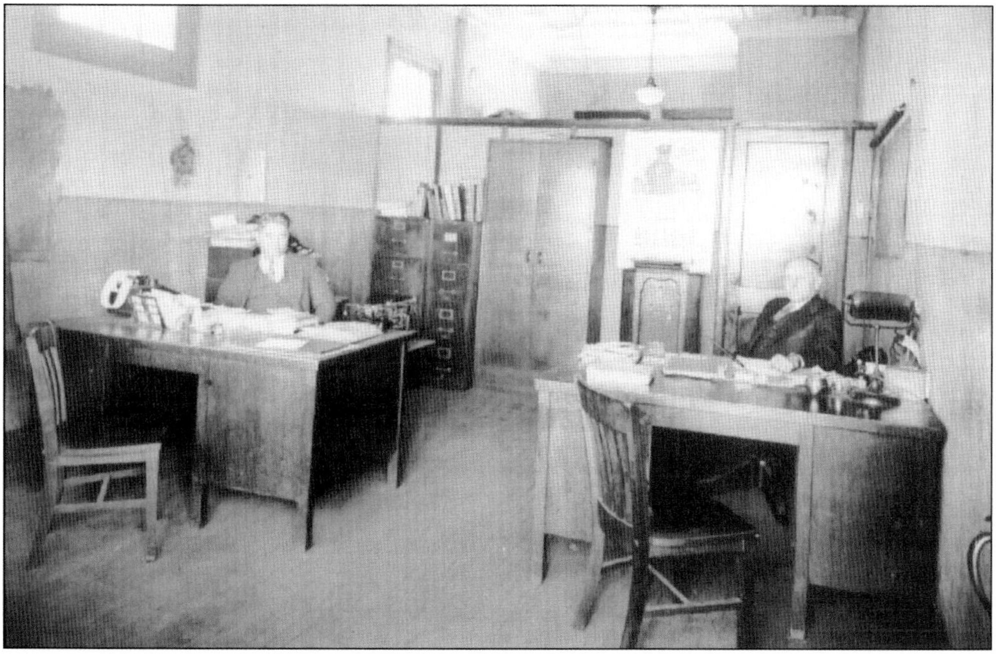

This image shows the interior of Ayers Realtors, Inc. in the 1930s, with N. Guy Ayers at right and Joseph Boo at left. Betty Davin remembers Guy Ayers selling her family a beach lot back in the 1920s. "I think they paid $1,000 for 50 feet of lakefront," she says. "It was a double lot as the lots were platted at 25 feet." (Courtesy of Gene Ayers, Ayers Realtors, Inc.)

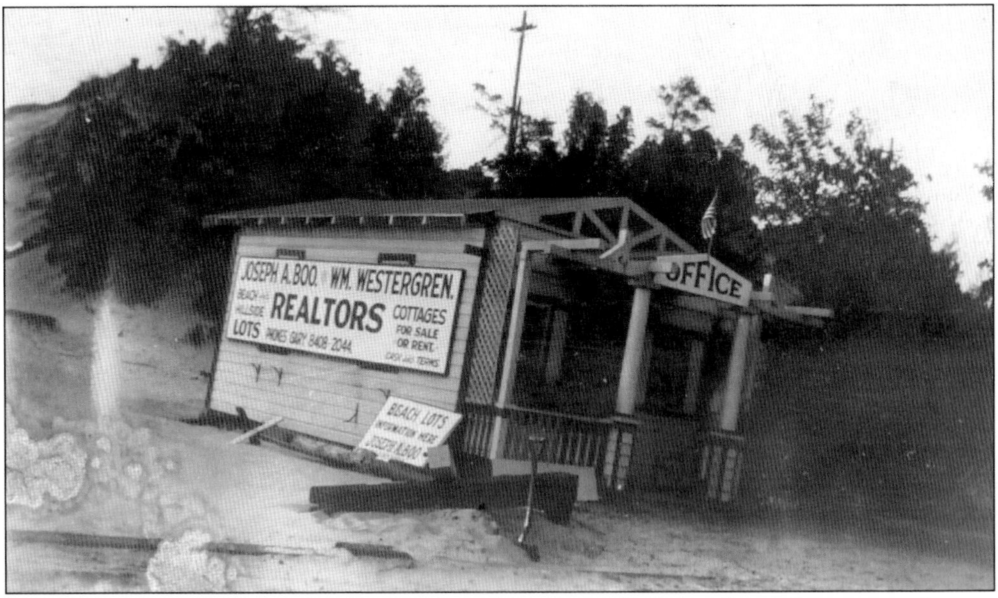

This very early photograph shows William Westergren's real estate office. Westergren, who was also a justice of the peace, a police officer, and, after retirement, a crossing guard, helped Octave Chanute with his experimental gliders in the dunes in the late 1800s. The two also became friends and fished together in Miller. (Courtesy of the Calumet Regional Archives, IU Northwest.)

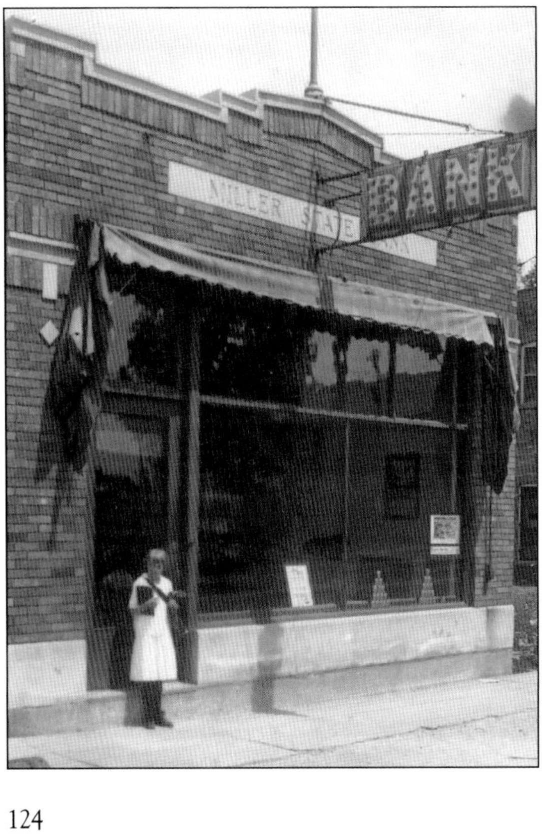

The Miller State Bank later became Jack Spratt, an ice cream parlor and a longtime Miller community favorite. Highlights for visiting out-of-towners included the Marquette Park beach pavilion, the beaches, dances at the Chapel of the Dunes, and Jack Spratt. (Courtesy of Marilyn Leech and Holly Rodino Breese.)

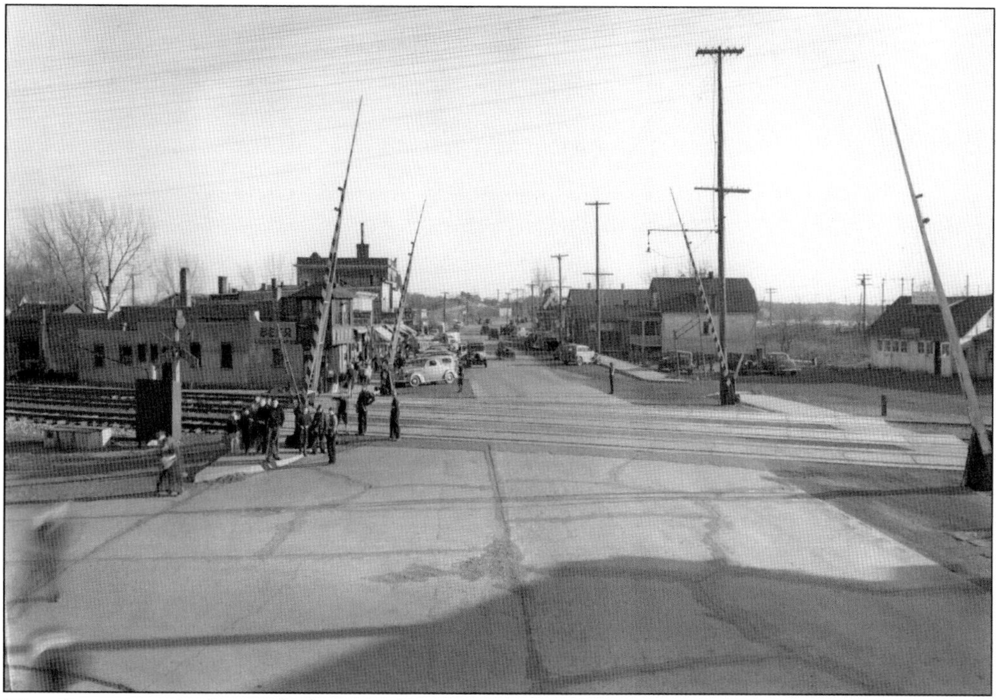

The above view looks south down Lake Street across the railroad crossing. The streetcar came from Gary down Seventh Avenue, across from the school. Miller kids would ride the streetcar to Emerson High School in Gary. The image below looks in the opposite direction and shows that the old pharmacy is now apartments and Bowers Drugs is in business. (Courtesy of the Calumet Regional Archives, IU Northwest.)

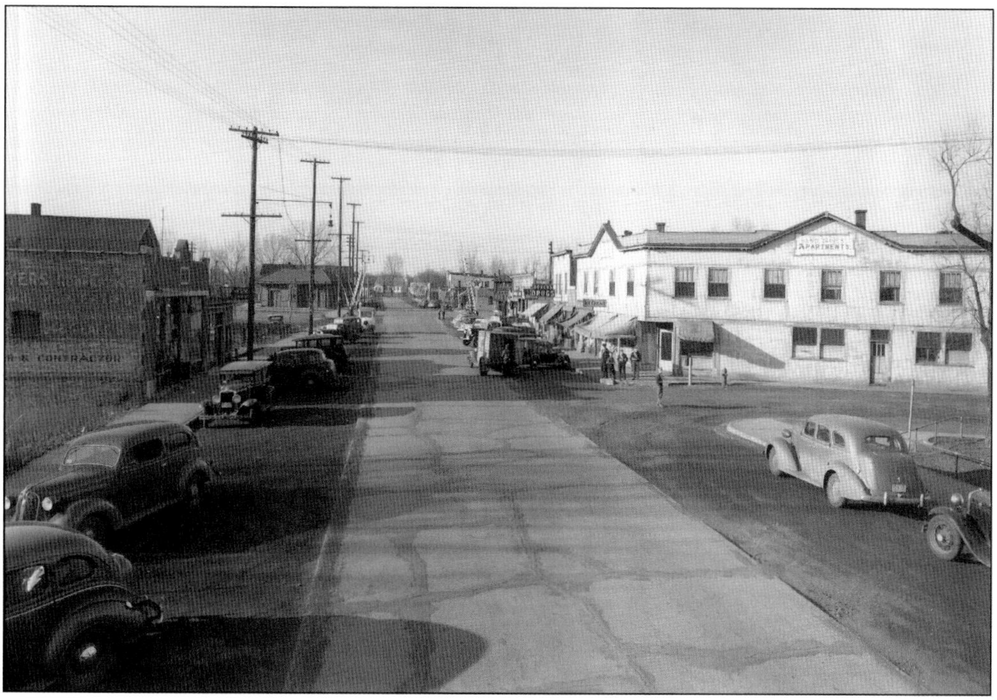

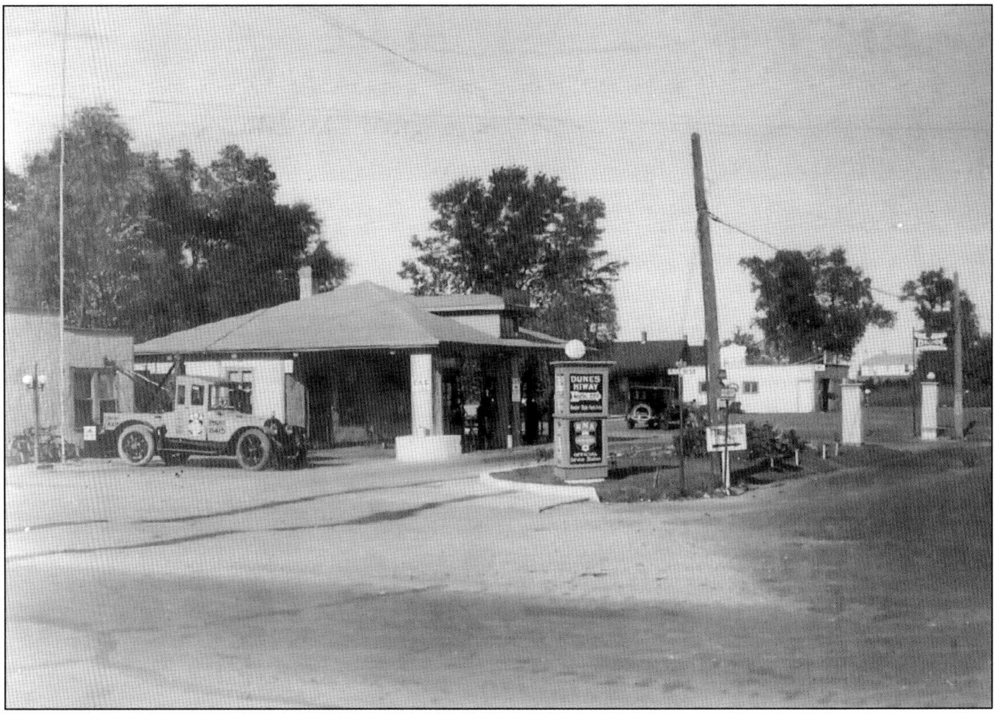

Note the old-fashioned gas pumps at this Miller service station. In front, a sign points to the Dunes Highway, which was built in the early 1920s connecting Michigan City to the east to Chicago. In some ways, despite the onslaught of visitors from Chicago, Miller remained a rural small town. Kids could not wait until spring to take their shoes off; they might not be put back on until school began in the fall. Spring also meant barefoot races through the cold sand and fishing boats being pushed back into the water. In the spring, local firemen Charley Gray and Bob Pearson readied the horseshoe pit at the Miller fire station and Charley "The Ringer" Skogseth started his daily practice. Roller skates were pulled out of closets and the marsh behind the fire station was burned off to allow for kite-flying contests. (Courtesy of Gene Ayers, Ayers Realtors, Inc.)

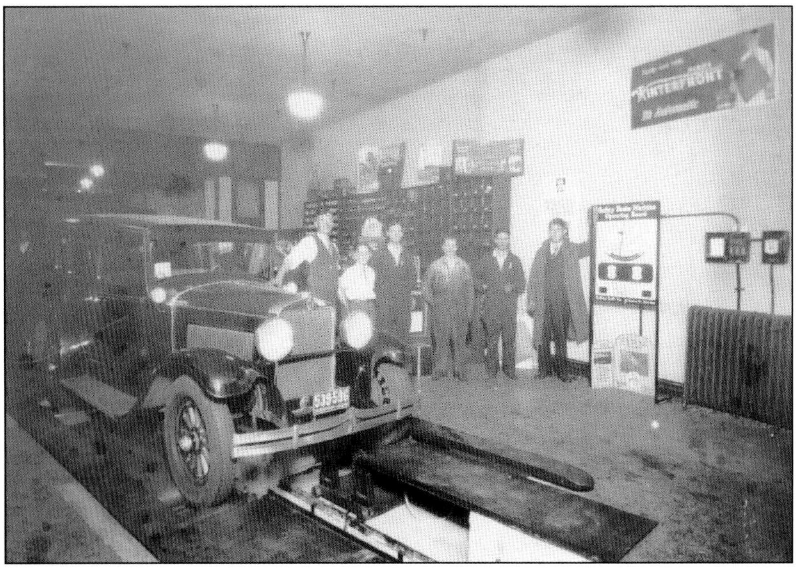

In this 1928 photograph, Herbert Leech, whose family built and ran several businesses in downtown Miller, stands inside a garage as his car gets repaired. (Courtesy of Marilyn Leech and Holly Rodino Breese.)

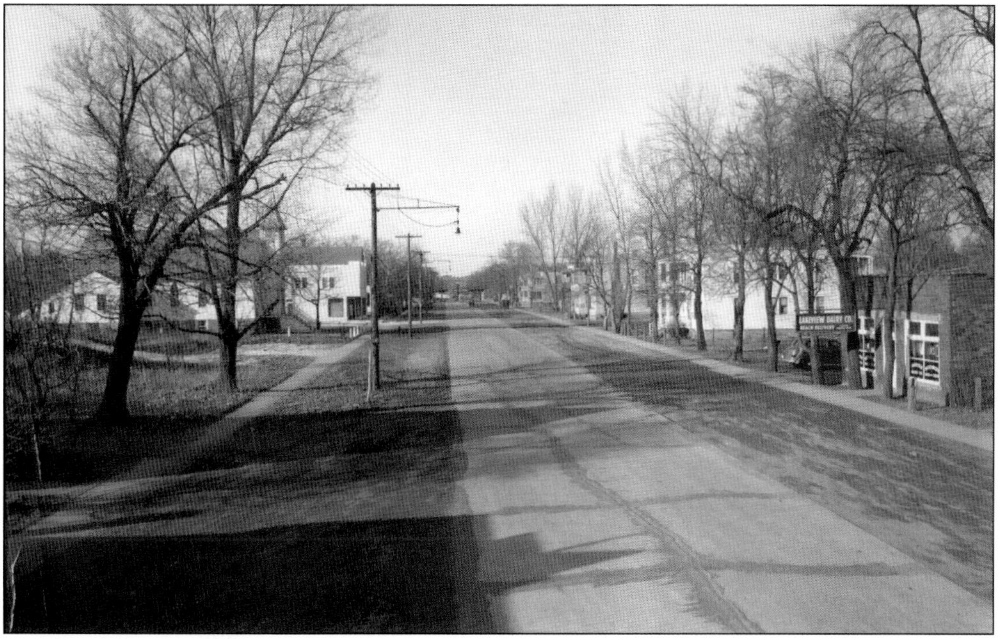

On the right of this north-looking view of Lake Street is Lakeview Dairy, owned by Arnold Erlandson and George Cook. Erlandson made the daily milk run, often accompanied by some or all of his five children, Dan, Chuck, Jean, Dick, and Dave. Erlandson would make the rounds at a dozen or so dairy farms in Lake and Porter Counties, returning by 9:00 a.m. to the dairy. The Bethel Lutheran Church is at the left, and across Fourth Avenue is the building that became Shibley's Grocery Store. If you look closely in the background, the New York Central Railway Bridge over Lake Street is visible. (Courtesy of the Calumet Regional Archives, IU Northwest.)

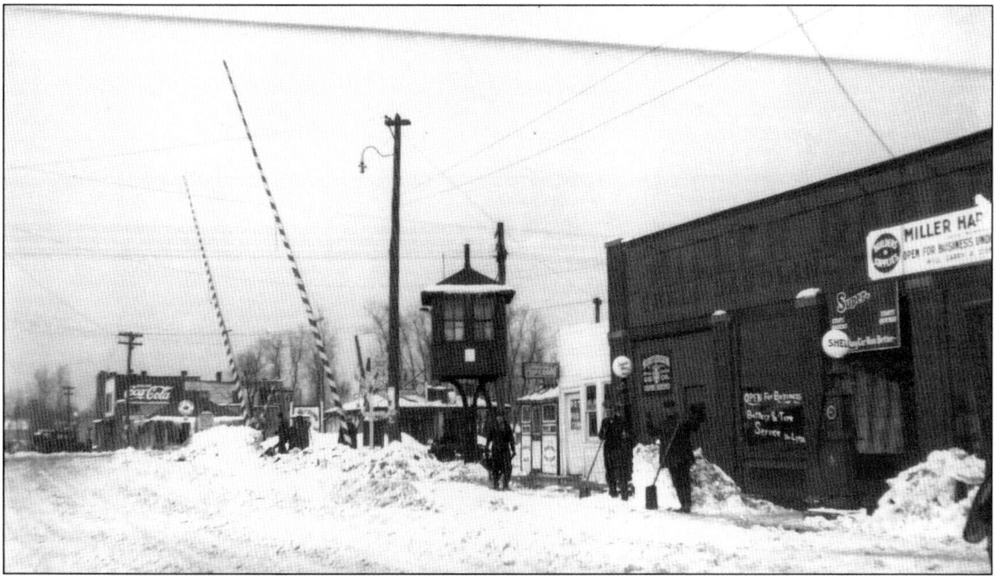

The B&O Railroad crossing is seen here after a snowfall. Snow sometimes clogged the tracks, but the most difficult weather hazard was when the cold froze the metal power lines and they snapped. Fixing frozen electric lines was a job no one relished. (Courtesy of the Calumet Regional Archives, IU Northwest.)

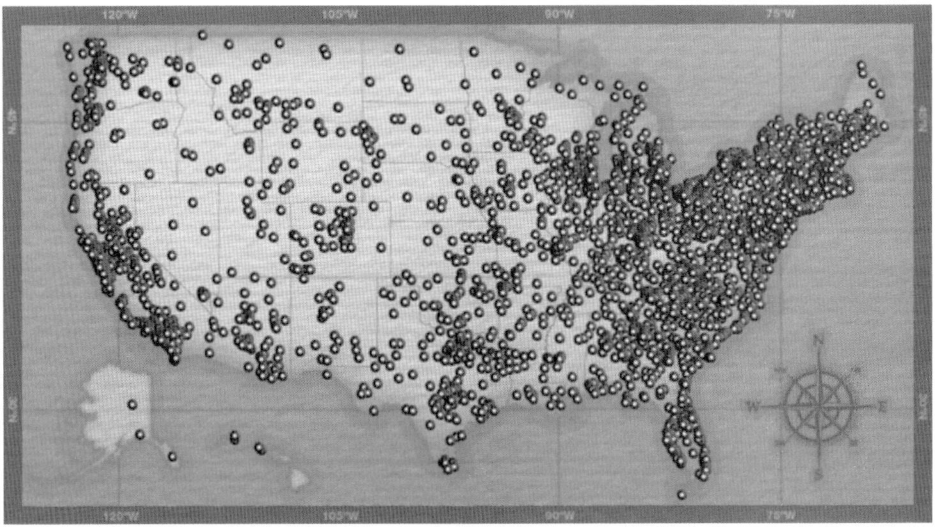